ENTANGLED IDENTITIES

Entangled Identities
Nations and Europe

Edited by

ATSUKO ICHIJO
Kingston University, UK

WILLFRIED SPOHN
Free University of Berlin, Germany

ASHGATE

Atsuko Ichijo and Willfried Spohn have asserted their right under the Copyright, Designs and Patents Act, 1988, to be identified as the editors of this work.

Published by
Ashgate Publishing Limited
Gower House
Croft Road
Aldershot
Hampshire GU11 3HR
England

Ashgate Publishing Company
Suite 420
101 Cherry Street
Burlington, VT 05401-4405
USA

Ashgate website: http://www.ashgate.com

British Library Cataloguing in Publication Data
Entangled identities : nations and Europe
1. Nationalism - European Union countries 2. European Union
countries - Politics and government 3. Europe - Economic
integration
I. Ichijo, Atsuko, 1967- II. Spohn, Willfried, 1944-   320.94 ICH
320.5'4'094

Library of Congress Cataloging-in-Publication Data
Entangled identities : nations and Europe / [edited] by Atsuko Ichijo and Willfried Spohn.
    p. cm.
    Includes bibliographical references and index.
    ISBN 0-7546-4372-7
   1. Europe--History--1492- 2. Europe--Politics and government. 3. Nationalism--Europe. 4. National characteristics, European. I. Ichijo, Atsuko, 1967- II. Spohn, Willfried, 1944-

   D210.E58 2005
   940.2--dc22

2004030678

ISBN 0 7546 4372 7

Printed and bound by Athenaeum Press, Ltd.,
Gateshead, Tyne & Wear.

Contents

List of Tables

List of Contributors

György Hunyady is Professor of Social Psychology at Eötvös Loránd University, Budapest, Hungary, and has published widely in Hungarian and English, mainly in the fields of social perception, belief systems and cognitive psychology. His book, *Stereotypes during the Decline and Fall of Communism* (1998, London: Routledge International Series in Social Psychology) summarizes his decade long stereotype research in a 'natural laboratory' of the changing Hungarian society.

Atsuko Ichijo received her Ph.D. from the University of London and is Research Fellow in European Studies at Kingston University, London, UK. Her recent publications include 'The scope of theories of nationalism: comments on Scottish and Japanese experiences', *Geopolitics*, 7(2), pp. 53-74; 'The uses of history: Anglo-British and Scottish views of Europe' *Regional and Federal Studies*, 13 (3), pp. 23-43; *Scottish Nationalism and the Idea of Europe* (2004, London: Routledge). She is Book Review Editor of *Nations and Nationalism*.

Pablo Jáuregui obtained a Ph.D. from the Department of Political and Social Sciences of the European University Institute in Florence for his thesis, entitled 'National Pride and the Meanings of "Europe": A Comparative Study of Britain and Spain', in 2001. His previous publications include 'Europeanism versus Africanism: "Europe" as a Symbol of Modernity and Democratic Renewal in Spain', in B. Strath and M. af Malmborg, *The Meaning of Europe: Variety and Contention Within and Among Nations* (2002, Oxford: Berg). He currently works as a journalist for the Spanish national newspaper *El Mundo*.

Paszkál Kiss is an Assistant Professor at the Department of Social and Developmental Psychology, Eötvös Loránd University, Budapest. He has defended his PhD thesis, *Between East and West: Hungarians Perceiving Other Nations and Europe* at the European Ph.D. on Social Representation and Communication. His major publications: *Conservativism in Psychological and Social Contexts* (1999, Alkamazott Pszichológia [Applied Psychology]); *Person and Group Perception in an International Conflict* (In Sztereotípiakutatás: Hagyományok és irányok [Stereotype Research: Traditions and Trends], 2001, Budapest: Eötvös Kiadó).

Nikos Kokosalakis is currently Research Consultant and Senior Researcher at KEKMOKOP, Panteion University, Athens. He holds degrees from Athens University and a Ph.D. in sociology from Liverpool University. He taught in Liverpool University and other universities in Britain from 1966-1995 and gave lectures and delivered papers in various institutions and conferences in Europe and the USA. He served as secretary and president of the Committee on Sociology of Religion (1980-1988) of the International Sociological Association and as a member of various academic bodies and editorial boards. He has a long and wide research experience and has written four books and over fifty articles in books, encyclopedias and international journals.

Karel Kubiš is a historian and has a Ph.D. in general history from Charles University in Prague. He has had four months attachment at Department of Economic History, Copenhagen University, Denmark, in 1983; Visiting Professor at History faculty, Tidewater Community College, Virginia Beach, U.S.A. He is a member of the seminar of Comparative Studies in the Institute of World History, Charles University, Prague. His courses and research projects are focused on modern European history, comparative studies in European economy and policy, and historical roots of the process of European integration.

Vlasta Kubišová is a historian and has a Ph.D. in general history from Charles University in Prague. She was Assistant professor of International Relations, Institute of Area Studies, Department of West European Studies at Charles University Prague in 1997-1999. Since 1992 she has been the Head of the Department of Humanities, Faculty of Transportation, Czech Technical University (CTU), Prague. Her courses and research projects are focused on International Relations and modern European history.

Michael Minkenberg is Professor of Political Science at the Europa-Universität Viadrina in Frankfurt (Oder). He received his Ph.D. in 1989 from the University of Heidelberg and has since lectured at Georgetown University, the University of Göttingen, Cornell University, the University of Heidelberg, New York University and Columbia University. Recent publications include *Die neue radikale Rechte im Vergleich. USA, Frankreich, Deutschland* (1998, Opladen: Westdeutscher Verlag) and *Politik und Religion.* PVS Special Issue 33/2002, edited with Ulrich Willems.

Iordanis Psimmenos is Lecturer in Sociology at Panteion University of Political and Social Sciences, Athens. He has undertaken research and published on aspects of work and flexibility and on the meaning of work for Albanian and Polish immigrants in Greece. His recent publications include *Globalization and Employee Participation* (1999, Aldershot: Ashgate).

Krystyna Romaniszyn is Professor of the Jagiellonian University in Kraków. She received her Ph.D. from the University of Warsaw and her Habilitation from the Jagiellonian University. She is author of three books in Polish, one on economic anthropology, and two on migration. She has written extensively, both in Polish and English, on contemporary migration and cultural pluralism resulting from international migratory flows. She has also held a number of visiting positions at universities in Europe.

Antonia M. Ruiz-Jiménez is Professor of Sociology at the *Universidad Complutense de Madrid* and researcher at the National Distance Education

University (UNED) in Spain, working on the EURONAT project funded by the European Commission. She graduated in Contemporary History from the University of Málaga in 1994, and received her Ph.D. in Political Science and Government from the Universidad Autónoma de Madrid in June 2002, when she became a Doctor Member of the Juan March Foundation. Between September 2001 and December 2002 she was a visiting researcher in the Department of Government at Harvard University.

Karolína Růžičková is a historian and sociologist graduated from Charles University in Prague in 2000.

Willfried Spohn studied and received his Ph.D. and Habilitation at the Free University of Berlin. He was an assistant professor and is now Adjunct Professor at the same institution. He has also been a visiting professor at several universities in the United States and Senior Jean Monnet Fellow at the European University Institute. He has published widely in the areas of comparative historical sociology and social history. His major publications include: *Can Europe Work? Germany and the Reconstruction of Postcommunist Societies* (edited with S Hanson, 1995, Seattle, WA: University of Washington Press); and *Modernisation, Religion and Collective Identities: Germany between Western and Eastern Europe* (forthcoming).

Anna Triandafyllidou is Senior Research Fellow at ELIAMEP and External Collaborator at the Robert Schuman Centre of Advanced Studies, European University Institute in Florence. She teaches as Visiting Professor at the College of Europe in Bruges and works occasionally as expert for the European Commission services and for the Greek state. She has held teaching and research positions at the University of Surrey, London School of Economics, CNR in Rome, New York University and European University Institute of Florence. Her recent publications include: *Immigrants and National Identity in Europe* (2001, London: Routledge), *Negotiating Nationhood in a Changing Europe: Views from the Press* (2002, Ceredigion: Edwin Mellen Press), *Europeanisation, National Identities and Migration* (2003, London: Routledge, co-editor), *Multiculturalism, Muslims and Citizenship: A European Approach* (forthcoming, London: Routledge, co-editor).

Michael Voříšek is a historian and sociologist who graduated from Charles University in Prague in 2000. Since 2003 he has been a Ph.D. student at the Department of Political and Social Sciences, the European University Institute, Florence, Italy.

Preface

This book is based on the findings from the first stage of an international research project, *Representations of Europe and the nation in current and prospective member states - political elites, media and civil society (EURONAT)*, funded by the European Commission for three years from September 2001 to September 2004 (contract no. HPSE-CT2001-00044). The research design was originally formulated by Anna Triandafyllidou and Willfried Spohn, and eight research teams (Germany and Austria are in charge of one team) who collaborated under the coordination of Anna Triandafyllidou and Bo Strath. The overall aim of EURONAT is to analyse comparatively the present national-cum-European components of collective identities in the selected countries on three levels: firstly, the historical foundations of these webs of national and European identities; secondly, the role of the political parties and media in their construction; and thirdly, the impact of public opinion and civil society on the construction of these webs of national and European identities. This book focuses on the first level.

Introduction

Atsuko Ichijo and Willfried Spohn

The end of cold war at the close of the twentieth century marked a new era. The search for a new world order which was to replace the bi-polar system began in earnest. A series of developments that took place in regard to what is often called European integration in the 1990s can be understood as Europe's response to the search for the new order. The then European Community adopted the Maastricht Treaty in 1992 and transformed itself into the European Union as if to demonstrate the will of the member states for an ever closer union. The Single Market then came into being; Europe was now the largest market in the world. Former communist countries applied for EU membership and started negotiation. Some member states started to argue for the case of a European single defence policy in the face of tragedies in the Balkans. In the early years of the twenty-first century, the single currency, the euro, came into circulation. Ten countries joined the EU in 2004. Europe seemed to be moving in towards one direction: some sort of unity supported by economic co-operation. Academic interest in the issue of a European identity and its implications were rekindled. The issue was now closely tied with democracy and citizenship, an aspect of the process of European integration the European Commission began to pay more attention (Eder and Giesen 2002).

Recently, however, the world has woken up to the fact that Europe is indeed divided. Some describe it as 'old Europe' vs. 'new Europe'; some regard it as 'Atlantists' vs. 'Europeanists'. The pretence of unity on the eve of enlargement appears to have disappeared and one can only anticipate even more fragmentation with ten new members with different social, political and economic conditions. Of course, Europe has always been divided, and even fragmented, which was somehow glossed over in the euphoria that surrounded the 1990s. The question is then: is Europe going to maintain its momentum for an ever closer union? Is an all-encompassing European identity sure to emerge? Or have the processes of European integration after all been attempts by the nation-states to rescue themselves from economic and geopolitical oblivion? (Milward 1992; 2000) And in a parallel, will primary national identities shape multiple forms of European identities?

This volume endeavours to shed light on this confusing state of affairs by examining what is behind these developments. It strives to understand the nature of differences that underpin the apparent division and the kind of similarities that an emerging European identity could be based on. The focus of our research is on the entanglement of national and European identities in different nations, which we believe would help us deepen our understanding of what is happening now. The volume assembles nine case studies: Austria, Czech Republic, Great Britain,

Greece, Germany, Hungary, Italy, Poland, and Spain. All of these have experienced different processes of state formation, nation-building and democratisation and, as a result, developed different forms of national identity. At the same time, all of them belong, in their own way, to European civilization and they have become, at different stages, members of the European Community/European Union. Each country therefore faces the issue of the entanglement of national and European identities. However, because of the historical circumstances each country's experience has been different and the way national and European identities are intertwined is unique in each of these cases. The aim of the book is to analyze the historical entanglement of national and European collective identities in the nine countries and to propose a comparative explanation for these varying developments of collective identities.

There are three aims in the introduction: (i) to explore some of theoretical approaches to the analysis of the entanglement of national and European identities; (ii) to outline the historical-comparative framework that has been employed as an analytical guideline for the current volume; and (iii) to give an overview of the nine case studies assembled here.

1. Approaches to the Entanglement of National and European Identities

The entanglement of national and European identities is hardly a new topic. At least ever since the current processes of European integration started in the 1950s, much attention has been paid to the relationship between national and European identities. Although the theories of integration, as they are often known, have had their ups and downs, the question of the future of national and European identities has never gone away and a number of approaches to it have been proposed (Kohli 2000).

The main question is whether national identities in European nation-states are going to be transformed through the on-going process of European integration, and more importantly, what will become of them. As the metaphor of the 'battlegrounds of European identity' (Kohli 2000) suggests, the relationship between national and European identities has often been seen as a competing one. One of the premises of the EURONAT project is to question this received wisdom and to investigate whether the European dimension has been incorporated in national identities rather than replacing the latter.

The evolution of a European identity in whatever form is essentially seen as a cultural process of identification with a transnational European polity that continues to develop. On the terrain of this debate, three theoretical positions can be distinguished. The first position presupposes that national identities or nationalisms tied to the nation-state are the strong core of collective identities, whereas a European identity is still weak and will continue to be so (Lepsius 1998, Smith 1996). The second position assumes that a European identity, even though relatively weak, has grown along the process of European integration and, with the further completion of the European transnational framework, will replace or at least diminish the impact of national identities (Deutsch 1979, Haas 1964). The third position is critical of the dichotomous view of placing national identities opposed to European identity and assumes the evolution of a hybrid mix of national and European identities (Citrin and Sites 2004).

These three hypotheses have been examined from different angles. Some scholars have taken what we may call constructivist approaches with an emphasis on the discursive dimension of the issue (Delanty 1995, Malmborg and Stråth 2002, Pagden 2002). These scholars argue that because Europe cannot be conceived as a fixed entity, the most meaningful way of approaching the relationship between national and European identities is looking at the idea or concept of Europe, what meaning has been attached to it and how it is used.

On the other hand, other scholars have preferred more structural approaches within the framework of International Relations or historical sociology, and we take the view that these structural approaches complement the discursive approaches, not contradict them. From the latter's angle, the debate on the existence and nature of an emerging European identity can be seen as replay of the well-known theoretical debates on the nature of the European integration process and the relation between the European nation-states and the European transnational framework (O'Neill 1996, Loth and Wessels 2001). The assumption of the continuing primacy of national identities corresponds to the confederal, intergovernmentalist and realist approaches to European integration, which presupposes the continuing salience of the nation-state. The assumption of the gradual and eventual replacement of national identities by a European identity reminds us of the federalist, functional or neo-functional approaches to European integration, insisting on the transformative effects of the establishment of transnational or supranational European structures. And the third position of a combination of national and European identities runs parallel to the growing neo-realist-intergovernmentalist consensus in the debate on the nature of the European community/EU as a transnational polity *sui generis* connecting multiple international as well as transnational regulatory levels.

The quantitative data gathered in the Eurobarometer, World Value and other surveys, and our own EURONAT survey, gives some indications but is not entirely conclusive in assessing the adequacy of these three positions. Basically, there is an agreement that a European identity is still generally weak (Hettlage 1999). Thus, when measured as an alternative form of identification to a national identity, Europe evokes much less attachment and loyalty than the nation. Furthermore, in the last decade European attachment has even slightly weakened, as shown in recent Eurobarometer results. This appears to support the first theoretical position of the continuing primacy of national identities. However, when measured, as in the recent Eurobarometer surveys, as two different but not exclusive forms of identification, there is a considerable attachment to Europe among peoples of Europe, even though its weight is significantly weaker than the attachment to a nation, region and locality. Measured in this way, it seems both national and European identities have been developing in parallel, although the patterns of development differ from country to country (Citrin and Sites 2004, Haller 1999). These findings make the third hybridity model more plausible, but they neither falsify the primary salience of national loyalties nor exclude a future strengthening of European attachments.

The conventional discussions of European identity, as fruitful as they may have been, have been limited to the European Union and its current member-states in the geographical boundaries of Western Europe. With the break-down of Soviet communism in Central and Eastern Europe, the end of the Cold War division of the European continent and the progress of the eastern enlargement of the European Union, these conventional parameters of the European identity debate are no longer tenable. Moreover, in addition to the original political conception of Europe (i.e. Europe as the EU), a second basic meaning of Europe has come to the surface: a cultural-civilizational identity of Europe. This was more or less suppressed and latent during the Cold War period, but has manifested itself at the end of the Cold War. This European cultural-civilizational identity has been at the core of the wish of the postcommunist countries in Eastern and Central Europe to 'return to Europe'. It has also been central to the aims of the West European countries to reunify the European continent. A cultural-civilizational identity is also crucial for the definition of the finalité of the European Union. At the same time, there is an obvious East-Western asymmetry. In Western Europe, a European civilizational identity is re-emerging as a cultural foundation of the European integration project, whereas in postcommunist Eastern Europe an identification with the European Union will only emerge in the course of the accession and integration.

Thus, with the opening of the pan-European space, also the axes of the debates on European identity have been transformed. Instead of the conventional two-dimensional model of national and European identity, therefore, we propose a multi-level model which takes into account national, intra-national, inter-national, European civilizational and European integrational dimensions. In methodological terms, this includes an analysis of (i) identification with the nation and sub-national units; this includes the nation's relations with the outside world as well with its political, cultural and socio-economic components; (ii) identification with Europe in its constitutive components and its external and internal boundary constructions; and (iii) identification with the European integration project and its institutionalization in the European Union in its constitutive components and its relations to the nation and Europe. This multiple model of collective identity can be summarized as follows:

Table 0.1 Collective identities in Europe: An analytical scheme

Constitutive dimensions	Relational dimensions			
	Local/regional	National	Europe	EU
Ethnic-territorial				
Religious-cultural				
Socio-economic				
Political-legal				
Political-military				

The horizontal axis deals with the relational or spatial dimensions of collective identities. This analytical multi-level model starts from the premise that collective identities are not simply tied to the nation or Europe, but made up of multiple levels of identification. National identities are, on the one hand, composed of local and regional identities which reflect ethno-national relations between the dominant majority groups and subdominant national or immigrant ethnic minorities. National identities, furthermore, do not form in isolation from each other as many theories of nationalism and national identity formation tend to presuppose. Rather, they are interrelated and include mutual boundary constructions. The same can be said of European identities. They are based on the international relations and boundary constructions between the manifold national identities and involve distinct European regional identifications. At the same time, European identities include inter-civilizational relations and boundary constructions to other civilizations such as the Islamic civilization, European-derived Russian and American civilizations and other non-European civilizations. European identities are therefore founded on these interrelated webs, and identification with the European integration process also adds both internal and external dimensions and boundary constructions.

The vertical axis represents the constitutive dimensions of collective identities which reflect the second premise that collective identities should be analyzed according to their different constitutive components. The model proposes to consider five main dimensions in particular: the ethnic-territorial, religious-cultural, socio-economic, political-legal and political-military components. The distinction of these dimensions goes parallel to similar categorizations in the theories of nationalism and national identity. For example, Anthony Smith, in his definition of national identity, distinguishes between an historic territory or homeland, common myths and historical memories, a common mass public culture, common political rights and duties of all members, and a common economy with territorial mobility (Smith 1991: 14). Shmuel Eisenstadt and Bernhard Giesen, from a different viewpoint, distinguish between ethnic-primordial, religious-cultural, and political-civic dimensions of national identity

(Eisenstadt and Giesen 1995). Two caveats should be emphasized. First, the proposed multi-level model is conceptualized as an analytical model and thus implies that national identities are composed in varying combinations of all the dimensions or components. National identities should not be essentialized or reified, since essentialization is one trap any typology of nations and nationalism, as in the case of the ethnic vs civic dichotomy for instance, may fall into. It should also be noted that these constitutive components do not fix national identities which are, after all, in a constant state of flux. The proposed analytical model should therefore not be regarded as timeless or ahistorical. Rather, it is used for analytical purposes to determine the persisting and changing features of the multi-level collective identity components and their interrelations in each country at the present in a long-term historical perspective.

Broadly based on this analytical model of collective identity formation, the following chapters pursue, first, the task of summarizing the main features of the historical development of the entanglement of national and European identities in each case. The time period under examination spans from the beginning of modern nation-state formation to the present. The chapters start with the historical foundations of the national and European identity web in early modern Europe; they continue with their formation and development during the nineteenth and early twentieth centuries in the modern age of nationalism; they follow changes in national and European identities between the two World Wars and the division of Europe during the Cold War era; and they analyze particularly their transformations after the end of the division of Europe in the last decade and outline the impacts of the European integration process, first in the Western European countries and then, in *statu nascendi*, in the postcommunist East Central European countries. The model is then employed to make sense of the findings from nine cases. It therefore enables us to reach a more nuanced overview of the historical processes of collective identity construction in each country.

At the same time, the proposed model helps us with comparing the findings from the case studies. A large number of comparative investigations into national identities and nationalism in Europe, and their relations to the nation-state formation, democratization, status of ethnic minority or citizenship regimes, have been carried out and have contributed to the understanding of these issues. However, they are often limited in their comparative methodology, chiefly because they tend to resort to an inductive approach. The proposed model is designed to redress this shortcoming and to allow a systematic comparison between the varying trajectories of national-European identity webs. In line with works by Charles Tilly (1984), Theda Skocpol (1984) and John A Hall (1999), the EURONAT project takes an analytical-generalizing and variation-finding approach while paying attention to the cultural dimension and related interpretive and constructivist modes of analysis.

2. A Comparative Framework for the Analysis of the Historical Formation of National-European Identity Webs

The comparative framework that guides the analysis of nine case studies combines four distinct areas of the historical development of collective identities in Europe. First, it considers the various typologies of nationalism and national identity formation in Europe. This is mainly conducted in relation to history and historical sociology of European nationalism. Secondly, it takes up the various attempts in historical sociology and political science to map and explain the varying types of state formation, nation-building and democratization as a historical-structural basis of collective identity formation. Thirdly, it examines attempts in historical sociology and cultural history to analyze comparatively the development of the meanings of Europe in relation to national identities within the context of the European civilization. And fourthly, it incorporates some approaches in political science, international relations and comparative sociology to explain the different forms of European identity which have arisen as a consequence of the impact of the European integration process on national identities or the Europeanization of national identities.

There have been different attempts to classify the varying forms of nationalism in Europe. A common ground, here, is the ideal-typical distinction by Anthony D Smith (1986; following Kohn 1944) between the Western European civic-territorial type of nationalism and the Eastern European ethnic-demotic type of nationalism. Although it is quite useful as an ideal-typical distinction (Brubaker 1992), the difficulty of this dichotomy begins when it is taken as the basis for real-types of nationalism in Europe. In this case, a question has been raised whether this is a structural distinction which is resistant to geographical movement and historical change. As the main protagonists of this debate have proposed (Brubaker 1999), the alternative option is to take these ideal-types as two major co-existing components of national identity formation and to consider, as we propose in our multi-level model, other socio-economic, cultural and political components as well. From that perspective, the Western European national identities comprise not only political-civic, but also ethnic, cultural and socio-economic elements. This is clear in the British, Italian and Spanish cases, as we shall see later. Conversely, as the Polish and Hungarian cases in this volume powerfully point out, the Central and Eastern European nations are not only characterized by ethnic-demotic, but also political and socio-economic as well as cultural features. A comparative framework of collective identity formation must therefore include the historically changing multi-dimensional combination of the ethnic, cultural, socio-economic and political components of nationalism and national identities.

Regarding the political dimension in the comparative map of European nationalism, the German historian Theodor Schieder (1992; also Alter 1985 and Hirschhausen and Langewiesche 2001) has proposed four types of nationalism, taking into account the different paths of nation-state formation in Europe: (i) the Western European form of state-led nationalism as in England, France or Spain, where the formation of states preceded nationalism and national identity formation; (ii) the Central European form of unifying nationalism as in Italy or Germany, where nationalism and nation-building led to the formation of nation-states; (iii) the East Central European form of separatist nationalism as in the cases of Poland, Czechoslovakia, Hungary or also Greece, where the formation of nations and nationalism resulted in the separation of nations from the overarching Empires; and (iv) the Eastern European form of Empire-contracting nationalism as in Russia/Soviet Union and Turkey/Ottoman Empire, where nationalism evolved within established traditional Empires and transformed the overarching Empires into nation-states. This typology of nationalism corresponds with the historical sociology of state formation and nation-building in the works of Ernest Gellner (1993) and Stein Rokkan (1980) who have distinguished between four main routes of nation-state formation in Europe: (i) the Western European zone, where early state formation went hand in hand with early nation-building or cultural homogenization; (ii) the Central European zone, where an overarching legal and cultural imperial framework resulted in late forms of nation-state formation; (iii) the East Central European zone, where the hegemony of Empires enabled only late-late forms of nation-state-building; and (iv) the Eastern European zone, where Empires lasted into the twentieth century and limited homogenizing forms of nation-state building.

The typologies of Rokkan, Schieder and Gellner focus primarily on the processes of state formation and nation-building, but they do not explicitly include the processes and timing of democratization in these four zones as they should do. Another significant limitation of these typologies is the missing military dimension in state formation that has been analysed by Tilly (1990), and we will consider it as a geopolitical-relational component in the following discussion. Following Barrington Moore (1967), Rueschemeyer, Stephens and Huber-Stephens (1992), as well as Juan Linz and Alfred Stepan (1996), the different zones of nation-state formation are connected to different routes of democratization and thus have an impact on the weight of the political-civic component in nationalism and national identity.

This political-institutional dimension of nation-state formation and democratization is intertwined with the other aspects of nationalism and national identity formation, such as ethnic-territorial, religious-cultural and socio-economic elements. Regarding the ethnic-territorial component, according to Krejci and Velmisky (1981), the Western European cases show low ethno-national conflict potentials due to early state-building, cultural homogenization through centralized educational institutions as well as acculturation of ethno-national minorities to the hegemonic nation-state. The only exceptions are the few cases in the Atlantic peripheral zone such as Ireland or the Basque country. In Central Europe, the ethno-national conflict potential has been much higher, due to the 'lateness' of nation-state building and a conflictive ethno-national mobilization in overlapping settlement structures. In East-Central Europe, this ethno-national conflict potential has been the highest, due to the late-late forms of nation-state formation in overlapping settlement structures and the organic nature of separating nationalisms. In the parts of Eastern Europe which were under imperial rule, ethnic-national conflict potentials have been lower, due to the overarching continuity and predominance of the imperial core that managed to demobilize ethno-national conflicts through military-political force and cultural-assimilative attraction. The intensity of ethno-national conflicts, in turn, correlates with the process of democratization. Ethno-cultural homogenization is a crucial prerequisite of democratic pluralization and more civic forms of nationalism, whereas ethno-cultural conflicts tend to enhance organic forms of national integration or more ethnic forms of nationalism.

Regarding the religious-cultural components, there is a close relation between religion, language, ethnicity and nation-building (Hastings 1997), but these relationships differ depending on the type of religion involved. In a simplified manner, one can distinguish four basic religious zones in Europe. The first grouping is found in the North-western corner of Europe, in which Protestantism (both Calvinism and Lutheranism) is dominant with a small Catholic minority. The second group is found in South-Western Europe as well and Central Europe, which consists of pre-dominantly Catholic countries. The third group is comprised of Russian Orthodox countries and the fourth groupings have been under the influence of Orthodox Christianity as well as Islam largely due to the Ottoman Empire. Each type of religion has exercised different kinds of influence on the nation-building, democratization and national identity formation processes. The Protestant Reformation has been generally a major impulse for sovereign nation-state building, but Calvinistic Protestantism has been more conducive to democratization and civic-plural nationalism, whereas Lutheran Protestantism tended to support forms of state authoritarianism. Catholicism was for a long time rather a limiting factor in nation-state formation and at the same time hindering democratization. It was only in the second half of the twentieth century that it became a major force of democratization in Southern European authoritarian regimes and in Eastern European communist regimes. Christian Orthodoxy supported early on ethno-national formations, but at the same time its ceasaro-papist structure went in hand with authoritarian regimes.

Finally, closely connected to political-institutional environments and religious cultures, economic developments clearly differed in the different zones of nation-state formation and religious cultures. In the modern age, capitalism and industrialization developed first and most vigorously in the North-Western Protestant zone and then seized the West- Central European part where Protestantism and Catholicism are more mixed. The Catholic countries in South-Western, Southern, Central and East-Central Europe fell behind. Economic development was even worse in the Orthodox-Christian and Islamic/Orthodox zones. At the same time, it mattered whether or not an economically backward country was able to use its strong state as a promoter of capitalism and industrialization. Economic development, depending on its connection to a socio-cultural context of a market/civil-society or an interventionist state, stood in ambiguous relation to national identity formation. In Calvinist North-Western Europe, the rise of capitalism promoted also democratization and a more civic form of national identity. In Lutheran North-Central Europe, it went hand in hand with authoritarian absolutism and authoritarian forms of nationalism. In Catholic Europe, capitalism became intertwined with corporatist social institutions and authoritarian forms of nationalism, and in Orthodox-Christian Europe with the autocratic state and organic forms of nationalism.

The discussion has not yet focused on the relational determinants of collective identity formation. Nations, nationalisms, and national identities have not been formed in isolation, but in interaction with each other in the broader context of the European civilization and its boundary constructions vis-à-vis other civilizations. The different political trajectories are interrelated with each other within the overarching European inter-state system and its power balances. The different cultural and religious zones are interconnected by cultural exchange, perceptions and boundary constructions. Differing economic developmental processes and trajectories include not only different forms of interregional, inter- and transnationational exchange, but also different, continuing or changing, economic hierarchies of core, semi-peripheries and peripheries. In other words, the geo-political, geo-cultural and geo-economic location of a nation within European civilization, broadly defined, has an impact on the historical formation of national and European identities. Moreover, on these historical foundations, the form and timing of inclusion into the European integration process shapes and transforms the European level in the construction of collective identities.

A European identity has been formed on the foundations of the European civilization and its boundary construction in opposition to other civilizations. In a comparative-civilizational perspective, Shmuel Eisenstadt (1987) has seen the specificity of European civilization in its structural and cultural pluralism. The structural pluralism refers to the multiple processes of political centre formation, and with them the formation of a European inter-state system and international power balances. The cultural pluralism refers to the multiple religious and cultural sources of European civilization such as Judaism, Hellenism and Christianity as well as the differentiation of Christianity, its cultural secularization by Renaissance, Reformation and Enlightenment and its crystallization in varying national cultures. At the same time, the European civilizational complex should not be seen as a fixed entity, but as a moving process of construction and reconstruction of self-definition and boundary-setting (Delanty 1995). In this European civilizational context, the meaning of Europe in each national identity is therefore shaped by the geo-structural and geo-cultural location of a national state, society and culture within the European civilization. And the meaning of Europe in each national identity moves with changing inter-national and inter-civilizational relations, self-definitions and boundary constructions.

In the context of these power conflicts and balances in the European inter-state system, two factors are particularly important for shaping the meaning of Europe in national identities. One factor relates to the power position of each nation-state within the European inter-state system. On the one hand, there are big and more powerful nation-states, on the other there are small, less powerful and often victimized nation-states. The big states of the Western European zone were at the same time leaders in colonial Empire-building overseas, the big ones in Central Europe simultaneously continental imperial powers and the big states in Eastern Europe continuing traditional Empires. As a consequence, the small states in Western, Central and particularly in East Central Europe became victims of great power politics. The other factor relates to the geographical position within European civilization. The states at the Western fringes of European civilization formed imperial bridges to their overseas Empires, the states at the Northern fringes formed their own Nordic identity, the states at the Southern fringes crystallized around a Mediterranean identity, the states at the Eastern fringes formed a Eurasian identity, and only the continental European states were locked in the middle of the European civilization. Therefore, some nation-states have alternative images to Europe while some do not.

The political and military power position of a European nation-state is linked to its state capacity to mobilize socio-economic, technical-scientific and political-military resources (Mann 1993). Of particular importance here are the economic power relations based on stages of economic development and economic hierarchies of core, semi-periphery and periphery relations. In late medieval Europe, the Central European city-belt zone (Rokkan 1980) was economically the most advanced region in Europe, but it was, at the same time, unfavourable for the formation of strong states. In early modern Europe, instead, the Western European states, supported strongly by the rise of the Atlantic economy, were able to take the lead as economic, political and military powers. In East Central and Eastern Europe, the traditional empires, despite their economic backwardness, were able to expand their imperial power. These economic centre-periphery relations were then transformed by the rise of the Central European region under the leadership of unifying Germany from a moderately backward to the industrially most advanced region, challenging Western Europe and increasing the centre-periphery imbalances in the East. Though failing to further expand its continental European hegemony because of the two World Wars, Germany maintained, nonetheless, its relatively predominant economic power position during the second half of the 20th century. At the same time, East-Central and Eastern Europe, under the hegemony of the Soviet Union, embarked on programmes to change its peripheral position by a state-induced industrialization strategy, but in the end it failed to catch-up with the Western European core and thus experienced a detour from periphery to periphery (Berend 1996). As a result, a *longue duree* pattern of concentric circles of semi-peripheral and peripheral relations around the Western European core remains the basis of the European integration project. Also, collective identities in each nation-state are shaped by its position in this centre-periphery matrix of the European economy.

At the core of the geo-cultural relations in Europe, its self-definitions and its boundary constructions, are the different types of religion in the context of the cultural pluralism or diversity in Europe. The external boundary constructions of European civilization are primarily determined by religious and civilizational differences and distinctions. European civilization is defined first and foremost as a Christian civilization in contrast to the Islamic civilization. It is also defined in opposition to other non-European civilizations, but also to European-Christian derivatives such as American and Russian civilization, the cases in which different forms of Christianity have played a crucial role. These external boundary constructions have continued with secularization processes within Christianity, contributing to new secular-religious oppositions between 'enlightened' Europe and non-European religious civilizations. In addition, the major internal boundary constructions within the European civilization follow the major religious-cultural zones. One of the lasting divisions in Europe is the distinction between Western and Eastern Christianity, but the opposition between Catholic and Protestant Europe also plays an important role. Here, secularization processes do not replace these distinctions, but are superimposed on them. Furthermore, as nations and national identities are often built on particular types of religion and therefore are infused by religious identities and missions, the international relations between nation-states often carry religious meanings and boundary constructions. Co-religious nations are less inclined, and nations with different religions are more inclined, to international conflicts. Finally, these religiously infused external and internal boundary constructions are combined with religious and cultural hierarchies, leading to the formation of superiority and inferiority feelings. This has been the case between Christianity, Islam and Judaism, between Western Christianity and Eastern Christianity as well as between Protestantism and Catholicism. These religious hierarchies are now complemented by oppositions between Enlightenment and religion, science and superstition, secularist and religious belief systems. Thus, the form of European identities in each nation-state is also shaped by its position within this European geo-cultural matrix of religious and secular identities and boundary constructions.

The European identities that are formed during the European integration process are deeply embedded in the multi-dimensional matrices of European civilizational identity outlined above. The European integration process proceeds in the forms of interactions between the multiple European nation-states and the evolving European multi-level polity. The European orientations, attitudes and attachments in each national collective identity have also been constructed in the interactions between the European civilization and the European integrational identity dimensions. Of particular importance here is the position in the European political/military power hierarchy as a big or small state, a great or dependent power, a former colonial or still imperial power or a former peripheral and colonized one. In all these instances different attitudes and images of the format of a European polity can be detected. Equally important are such factors as: the position within the socio-economic core-periphery matrix as a leading and advanced national economy or a dependent and backward one; the structure of economy – post-industrial, industrial or agrarian; or the type of capitalism – a rather liberal, corporate or state-regulated; and the related expectations and impacts regarding an integrated European economy regulated by the European Union. Moreover the position within the European geo-cultural matrix of religious and cultural zones and hierarchies is significant. So the predominant religious and secular as well as national and political cultures shape the orientations and images of the European integration project. The cultural-moral hierarchy patterns related to the traumas of World War II and the Holocaust and the roles as perpetrators or victims play a role in the relationship to the European integration project. On the foundations of a European civilizational identity, all the embedded political, economic and cultural dimensions participate in and shape the forms of a European integrational identity.

Finally, the timing of inclusion into the European integration process and the length of experiences with it need to be considered. There are crucial differences in European integrational identities depending on when the member-state in question joined the process. For the early West-Central European founding members (often known as the Six), the emerging European Community was first and foremost their own and a rather limited sectoral integration project. After the destructions of World War II, the integration project functioned as a rescue of the substantially damaged and weakened nation-states (Milward 1992). Accordingly, national and European identities went largely hand in hand. For the early North-Western European liberal adjusters such as Denmark and the UK, the European Community was politically and economically already too important to stay away from. At the same time, the accession strengthened liberal-capitalist orientations within a more corporatist European integration project, involving conflicting relationships between more liberal and corporatist European identities. Inversely, the middle adjusters of Southern Europe, such as Greece and Spain, represented regimes in transition from authoritarianism and peripheral-backward economies. At this stage, the European integration framework was much further advanced, imposed upon rather than shaped. In addition, Europe had acquired a different meaning: catching-up with an economically, socially and politically modern Europe. Then, the late adjusters of Northern Scandinavian Europe (plus Austria) joined an already quite established European edifice in the form of the European Union, membership realized due to the end of the Cold War which eroded their traditional neutral position between Western and Eastern Europe. At the same time, as economically well advanced newcomers, they wanted to strengthen the European Union by their own social, social liberal and social-democratic value orientations. Finally, the late-late adjusters from East-Central and South-Eastern Europe represented, after the break-down of the Soviet Empire, the postcommunist transformation societies for whom membership in the European Union materializes not only the return to Europe, but also catching-up with Western European forms of market capitalism, welfare states and liberal democracies. At the same time, joining the European Union implies also a conflicting relationship between the just won national sovereignty and the semi-sovereign inclusion in a transnational European polity.

3. The Case Studies

It is probably appropriate at this stage to reiterate what has been said earlier: the proposed framework is a framework – it is a skeleton. It does not claim to be the 'essentials' of the entangled webs of national and European identities, and should not be seen as such. Although we cannot outline a 'decisive' pattern of entanglement of national and European identities, since the patterns are varied, it is probably useful to explore some of the issues that are repeatedly discussed in the following chapters as a way of providing an overview.

Britain and the Rest

When looking at the overall pattern of entanglement of national and European identities, it is clear from the cases assembled here that one is not replacing another. This is perhaps a truism but each chapter refutes the lingering popular myth of a Europe destroying existing national identity. However, if we focus on the willingness to acknowledge having European identity, there is still a divide between Britain and the rest. Despite the fact that Europe remains its significant other, people of Britain are markedly reluctant to admit to have a European identity layer in their identity structure. On the other hand, the others are much happier in admitting they are European as well as national. Of course there is a variation. Some cases such as the Italian shows a combination of rather weak national identity and a strong orientation with Europe while others such as the Greeks with a strong sense of national identity with a positive view of Europe. The chapters on the newly acceded countries show that despite ideological implications of joining Europe, people there are not subsuming their national identity under European identity. As far as the nine case studies can show, however, the British appear to be more indifferent to Europe than others. This seems to confirm the conventional wisdom that Britain's Atlantic orientation has made it different from others. This is certainly a point that needs to be explored further through comparison with other 'Euro-sceptic' countries such as Norway, Denmark and Sweden.

Religion

If not Britain's Atlantic orientation, can religion explain this divergence? As argued above, religion is no doubt an important element in the process of national identity formation. Moreover, as it has been time and again pointed out, Europe was once conceived as Christendom. It is reasonable to expect for religion to emerge as a powerful factor that could explain the patterns of entanglement. The chapters assembled here, however, do not provide a clear-cut picture. As predicted, each chapter picks up religion as one of the important factors in the formation of national identity. However, when one examines the relationship between religion and how a particular nation perceives Europe, the picture is not clear. For instance, the Greeks are Christian but Orthodox Christian, and Orthodoxy's place in the idea of Europe is less clear than that of Catholicism. There is no doubt that Orthodoxy was, and probably still is, what makes Greeks distinct in the South Eastern corner of Europe. But Europe is often seen as something representing the secular, and sometimes the Orthodox Church speaks against what come out of a secular Europe. In short, while Orthodoxy does make the Greeks European in relation to the Turks, it does not necessarily make them more, or less, European than other Christian nations. The Poles, Hungarians and Spaniards are mainly Catholics, and the idea of being 'the defender of the faith' in the face of Islam and Islamic empires (either in the form of Turks or Arabs or peoples of the 'new world') had a significant effect on their national identity formation and maintenance. Does it mean that they are more European than others? The answer given by the chapters of this volume appears to be negative. The ways they are European are also shaped by other factors. It is not a question of either Catholicism or Protestantism. In the cases of predominantly Protestant nations in this volume (the Czechs with a distinctive Protestant history and the British with Anglicanism), the ways national and European identities are interrelated show more difference than similarity. In the cases of the Germans and Austrians, the role of religion becomes even more complicated because of the mixture of Catholicism and Protestantism and because of the legacy of the Holy Roman Empire.

The apparent lack of explanatory power of religion in examining the relationship between national and European identities may need to be reviewed in the context of secularization. This is certainly a huge topic that requires much more space to investigate, but a direction to which any study following this volume may consider pursuing. The degree of secularization, if it can be measured at all, and its historical development contrasted with the historical development of national and European identities may clarify what role religion plays in this arena.

Compensation/Aspiration

The case studies have shown that, except in Britain, the EU or membership of the EU often functions as a means of overcoming certain shameful pasts or shortfalls in the present. In the case of Spain, becoming a member of the EU symbolizes the completion of the long process of democratization and modernization of Spanish society which was tarnished by Franco's dictatorship. For the Greeks, membership of the EU represents part of the process of modernization of Greek society, again regaining respectability after the experience of generals' dictatorship. In Italy the EU is seen as a means of putting the fascist past behind and a remedy for national ills in the present. In Germany, the EU is seen as the same as Western Europe, an entity to which post-war Western German identity is intricately tied. The Poles endorsed membership of the EU as a means of ensuring future prosperity. The Czechs and the Hungarians also perceive the EU as a model to aspire to and an entity to which they need to belong in order to secure their standings in the world.

One of the common threads that bind these eight countries is that all of them have experienced dictatorship, fascism or some kind of authoritarian regime in the twentieth century. And the EU as a distinct entity from much fuzzier 'Europe' appears to provide a means to compensate their immediate past which contains disturbing elements. As pointed out in the Spanish chapter, because of this, European identity which is now merged with EU identity has acquired a moral aspect. Read from this angle, European identity, which may have been based more on Christianity or imperial expansion to the 'new world', has gained a positive trait by the birth and expansion of the EU. EU identity, on the other hand, could not have started without the pre-existing ideas of Europe. Here, we can witness another transformation of European identity with the EU having emerged as an increasingly concrete entity.

The compensational aspect of EU identity that appears to be firmly superimposed on European identity probably explains why the British are an exception in this volume; they did not need compensation in this form. In order to test this hypothesis, as mentioned above, a further comparative work that includes the Nordic countries would be beneficial.

A Final Point

Before closing these introductory remarks, a methodological point should be made which has a far-reaching implication. When one goes through the following nine chapters it transpires that the authors of the chapters tend to focus on the discursive dimension in examining the paths of nation and national identity formations. There are probably two major reasons why this has been the case. The first is a familiar problem in social science: a nation is a social construct without a definite shape, weight or any measurable properties, and therefore the discursive approach – focusing on what is talked about in what way by whom and when – perhaps offers the surest ground on which we can build our understandings. Whether a nation is a fact, a real existence or not is an argument that is beyond the scope of the current volume. We have set out with an assumption that, although we have not explicitly agreed whether a nation is a real existence, it is sensible to assume that most people in the world consider the existence of a nation as a fact or act as if they believe it is a fact. Secondly, this tendency to turn to discourse analysis is partly explained by the methodological limitation that historical sociology always confronts. As John Goldthorpe has stated, historical sociology has to work with the evidence that happens to have survived to this date; we cannot go out to produce new historical data (Goldthorpe 1991). What has survived often takes the form of writing, and if we are working from the writings that have survived, employing the discursive approach is not only sensible but also indispensable. However, discourse is significant for us in so far as it influences people's actions and behaviour, and therefore although we have made the most of the discursive approach, we do not claim that the current volume is a work on discourse. This is a product of our efforts to stretch the limit of historical sociology.

References

Alter, Peter (1985), *Nationalismus*, Frankfurt/M.: Suhrkamp.

Axtmann, Roland (1999), *Globalization and Europe*, London: Routledge.

Berend, Ivan (1996), *Central and Eastern Europe: Detour from the Periphery to the Periphery*, Cambridge: Cambridge University Press.

Brubaker, Rogers (1992), *Citizenship and Nationhood in France and Germany*, Cambridge, Mass: Harvard University Press.

Brubaker, Rogers (1999), 'The Manichean Myth: Rethinking the Distinction between 'Civic' and 'Ethnic' Nationalism', in Kriesi et al. (eds), pp. 55-72.

Citrin, Jack and John Sites (2004), 'More than Nationals: How Identity Choice Matters in the New Europe', in Herrmann and Risse (eds).

Delanty, Gerard (1995), *Inventing Europe*, London: Routledge.

Deutsch, Karl (1979), *Tides among Nations*, New York: Free Press.

Eder, Klaus and Bernhard Giesen (eds) (2001), *European Citizenship: National Legacies and Transnational Projects*, Oxford: Oxford University Press.

Eisenstadt, Shmuel (1987), *The European Civilization in Comparative Perspective*, Oslo: Scandinavian University Press.

Eisenstadt, Shmuel and Bernhard Giesen (1995), 'The Construction of Collective Identity', *Archive sociologique europeenne*, 36, pp. 72-102.

Flora, Peter, Stein Kuehnle and Derek Urwin (1999), *State Formation, Nation-Building and Mass Politics in Europe: The Theory of Stein Rokkan*, Oxford: Oxford University Press.

Gellner, Ernest (1983), *Nations and Nationalism*, Oxford: Blackwell.

Goldthorp, John (1991), 'The Uses of History in Sociology: Reflections on Some Recent Tendencies', *British Journal of Sociology*, 42(2), pp. 211-230.

Haas, Ernst (1964), *Beyond the Nation-State: Functionalism and International Organisation*, Stanford, CA: Stanford University Press.

Hall, John A (ed.) (1998), *The State of the Nation: Ernest Gellner and the Theory of Nationalism*, Cambridge: Cambridge University Press.

Haller, Max (1999), 'Voiceless Submission or Deliberate Choice? European Integration and the Relation between National and European Identity', in Han-Peter Kriesi et al. (eds), pp. 263-296.

Hastings, Adrian (1997), *The Construction of Nationhood: Ethnicity, Religion and Nationalism*, Cambridge: Cambridge University Press.

Herrmann, Rick and Thomas Risse (eds) (2004), *Transnational Identities: Becoming European in the EU*, Lanham, MD: Rowman and Littlefield.

Hettlage, Robert (1999), 'European Identity – Between Inclusion and Exclusion', in Kriesi, et al. (eds), pp. 243-262.

Hirschhausen, Ulrike and Dieter Langewiesche (eds), (2001), *Nationalismus in Europa: West- und Osteuropa im Vergleich*, Goettingen: Vandenhoek and Ruprecht.

Kohli, Martin (2000), 'The Battlegrounds of European Identity', *European Societies*, 2 (2), pp. 113-137.

Kohn, Hans (1944), *The Idea of Nationalism*, New York: McMillan.

Krejci, Jaroslav and Viteszlav Velimsky (1981), *Ethnic and Political Nations in Europe*, London: Croom Helm.

Kriesi, Hans-Peter et al. (eds) (1999), *Nation and National Identity: The European Experience in Comparison*, Zuerich: Rueegger.

Lepsius, Rainer M. (1998), 'Die Europaeische Union: Oekonomisch-politische Integration und kulturelle Pluralitaet', in: Reinhold Viehoff and Rien Segers (eds), pp. 201-222.

Linz, Juan and Alfred Stepan (1996), *Problems of Transition and Consolidation of Democracy. Southern Europe, Latin America and Eastern Europe*, Baltimore, MD: The Johns Hopkins University.

Loth, Wilfried and Wolfgang Wessels (eds) (2001), *Theorien europaeischer Integration*, Opladen: Leske and Buderich.

Malmborg, Mikael af and Bo Stråth (eds) (2002), *The Meaning of Europe*, Oxford: Berg.

Mann, Michael (1993), *The Sources of Social Power*, Cambridge, MA: Cambridge University Press.

Mann, Michael (ed.) (1990), *The Rise and Decline of the Nation-State*, Cambridge, MA: Cambridge University Press.

Milward, Alan (1992), *The European Rescue of the Nation-State*, London: Routledge.

Milward, Alan (2000), *The European Rescue of the Nation-State, 2nd ed.*, London: Routledge.

Morre, Barrington (1967), *Social Origins of Dictatorship and Democracy: Lord and Peasant in the Making of the Modern World*, London: Allen Lane.

O'Neill, Michael (1996), *The Politics of European Integration*, London: Routledge.

Pagden, Anthony (ed.) (2002), *The Idea of Europe: From Antiquity to the European Union*, Cambridge: Cambridge University Press.

Rokkan, Stein (1980), Eine Familie von Modellen fuer die vergleichende Geschichte Europas, *Zeitschrift fuer Soziologie*, (9)2.

Rueschemeyer, Dietrich, Evelyne Stephen-Huber and John Stephen (1992), *Democracy and Capitalist Development*, Chicago: Chicago University Press.

Schieder, Theodor (1992), *Nationalismus und Nationalstaat*, Goettingen: Vandenhoek and Ruprecht.

Skocpol, Theda (ed.) (1984), *Vision and Method in Historical Sociology*, Cambridge, MA: Cambridge University Press.

Smith, Anthony (1986), *Ethnic Origins of Nations*, Cambridge, MA: Cambridge University Press.

Smith, Anthony (1991), *National Identity*, Reno, NE: Nebraska University Press.

Smith, Anthony (1996), *Nations and Nationalism in a Global Era*, Oxford: Oxford University Press.

Tilly, Charles (1984), *Big Structures, Large Processes, Huge Comparisons*, Cambridge, MA: Cambridge University Press.

Tilly, Charles (1990), *Coercion, Capital, and European States AD 990-1990*, Cambridge: Blackwell.

Chapter 1

A Balancing Act: British State and Nation Formation and 'Europe'

Atsuko Ichijo

Introduction

National identity can never be a clear-cut phenomenon but the British case poses an even more complex question in discussing its identity. The question is: what are we looking at? The full name of the UK is the United Kingdom of Great Britain and Northern Ireland, which took its current form in 1922 as a result of Irish independence. Until the Union of Great Britain and Ireland in 1801, there were two separate independent states: Great Britain and Ireland. Going back further, until the Union of England and Scotland of 1707, there were two independent kingdoms on the largest island of the British Isles – England and Scotland, although since 1603 both had been ruled by the same monarch. A little further back, Wales was formally incorporated in England in 1536 although it was for long under *de facto* English rule since the 14th century. Due to the historical circumstances, the UK has at least four constituent nations: English, Scots, Welsh and Irish. In addition, there are a large number of ethnic minorities, both white and non-white, in the present day UK.[1] The issue of national identity in this polity is indeed complicated.

What I propose to do, in this limited space, is to concentrate on the Anglo-British polity, a fusion of England which has been a dominant force in the British Isles and Britain which came into a formal existence with the Union of 1707. This should allow us to appreciate the complexity of the British reality while acknowledging the dominance of the English perspective in the formation of Britain's identity and its relationship with Europe.

---

[1] According to the latest available census result (conducted in 2001), 7.6 per cent of the UK population classified themselves as non-white.

1. The Formation of Britain: The State and Nation

Great Britain as a state formally came into existence with the Union of England and Scotland in 1707, when the Scottish parliament agreed to vote itself out of existence, and the Westminster, i.e., English parliament was refashioned as the British parliament. While England and Scotland were independent states until the union, whether the English or the Scots constituted a fully fledged nation by then is a matter of controversy which lies outside the scope of this chapter. The idea of Britain or Great Britain had been around for a while albeit more as a geographical category than a political unit. For instance, in 1474, when a marriage between the daughter of Edward IV of England and the son of James III of Scotland was proposed, one of the declared purposes of the plan was to advance the peace and prosperity of 'this Nobill Isle, callit Gret Britanne' (Hay 1956: 61). John Mair, a Glaswegian educated in Paris, published *Historia Majoris Britanniae* (History of Greater Britain) in 1520 declaring that although there were two kingdoms on the island, those who lived there were 'Britions' (Robbins 1998: 4). However, the process of producing Britons can be argued to have started in earnest when James VI of Scotland succeeded the English Crown in 1603. He styled himself the King of Great Britain, France and Ireland, and is known to have manoeuvred to bring about the formal political union of England and Scotland (Murdoch 1998; Kearney 2000). Although the Stuart dynasty did not succeed in bringing about the political union of three kingdoms (England, Scotland and Ireland), the period between 1603 and 1707 was formative in creating the British state and nation: the idea of parliamentary sovereignty, for instance, was reaffirmed by two revolutions. Moreover, England, Scotland and Ireland were for once united, admittedly by force, under Oliver Cromwell to form the godly Commonwealth (1649-1660). As a consequence of this, Protestantism was firmly established as the principle that bound the country, except in Ireland. The idea of Britain which was thus developed had a sectarian tone, i.e., it was the country of Protestants.

Forging Britons, as Linda Colley put it, was not a smooth process (Colley 1992). Although Scotland went into the Union with England voluntarily, there was much popular dissent to the Union as well as to the Hanoverian regime which had been installed in 1688. Those who supported the deposed Stuarts planned to regain the Crown in 1715 and 1745. The 1745 Jacobite Rising was the last civil war fought on the British soil. Although the Jacobite army was initially successful, the much modern army of King George II won and a severe punishment for the Jacobite supporters followed. The main casualty was the Highlands way of life; bagpipes were banned, and so was the wearing of weapons. The suppression was followed by Highland Clearance in which landlords forced crofters to leave the land in order to secure pasture for sheep. In other words, Highland society was one of the most visible casualties of the formation of the British state.

Having quelled internal dissent by the mid-18th century, post-union Britain was involved with many wars, not in Europe but overseas. The Seven Years' War (1756-63) confirmed Britain's status as the dominant colonial power at the expense of France. The Treaty of Paris of 1773, which concluded the war between Britain and France, allocated Quebec, Florida, Minorca, further parts of

India and West Indies to Britain. Although Britain lost the Thirteen Colonies as a result of the Wars of American Independence (1775-83), the British overseas territory kept expanding especially in Asia.

In the meantime, the British state was consolidating its position as the one and only world power due to the Industrial Revolution. The world's first steam engine was invented in 1712, and the invention of the flying shuttle revolutionalized the cotton industry. By the end of the 18th century, the Industrial Revolution was clearly making its impact felt. British manufactured goods dominated the world market for a few decades in the 19th century, and as a consequence, Britain was dubbed as the 'Workshop of the World'.

It is perhaps worthwhile to add another viewpoint in relation to the formation of the British nation and state. A group of historians now argue that it would be more helpful to see the British state as a union state or Unionist state, not as a unitary state like post-revolutionary France (Eastwood *et al.* 1997).[2] It did not have an all-abiding constitution or a strong centralizing tendency. Therefore, the Scots were left to get on with their distinct educational and legal systems and their Church intact.[3] Moreover, there was not an all-Union working environment which could have helped to forge a strong sense of being British amongst elite (except the military) until well into the 19th century; engineers, lawyers, doctors and clergy continued to operate in their 'national' or regional frameworks (Brokliss 1997). The Unionist British state worked precisely because it did not ask too much from its subjects: what was demanded was 'loyalty to the Crown, obedience to Parliament, tolerance of Church establishment, and acceptance of English as the primary public language' (Eastwood *et al.* 1997: 194-5). According to these historians, Britishness, which came about as a consequence of the Union of 1707, emerged much later than Colley suggested; and it was largely institutional. There were no conscious attempts by the British state to create and promote a hegemonic cultural British identity. as Colley pointed out, during the wartimes, some patriotic sentiments, especially in the form of Franco-phobia, were heightened. However, the historians are at pains to point out that Britishness was something juxtaposed upon existing identities and was not a primary identity for many.

The relationship with Ireland was another issue that Great Britain as a union state tried to solve. Ireland, like Wales, was never politically united; this arguably made it vulnerable to threats from outside. After the Reformation in England, because it was a Catholic country, Ireland became a potential threat to England. England, and at times Scotland too, tried to subjugate Ireland by means of military campaigns and plantation over years. In a sense, England, and later Great Britain, as the *de facto* ruler of Ireland, was always looking for the optimal solution for the troubled relationship with Ireland. Great Britain gave Ireland an independent parliament in return for their support at the Wars of American

---

[2] The distinction between a union state and a unitary state derives from the work by Stein Rokkan and Derek Urwin. For more discussion, see Mitchell (1996: 38-9).

[3] Davis argues that since there were two established churches – Anglican and the Church of Scotland – and no unified legal system, the United Kingdom could not have been a nation-state (Davis 1999: 1039).

Independence, for instance. However, given the deepening confrontation between Catholics and Protestants and the impeding threats of invasion by Napoleon, the British government decided to form a union with Ireland which would enable them to rule it directly. Thus, in 1801, the United Kingdom of Great Britain and Ireland was born. Another symbol of Britishness, the Union Flag, was redesigned to incorporate the red saltire of St Patrick in the same year. The Catholic Emancipation Act of 1829 was arguably another step in forging Britons, this time inclusive of Catholics and Irish, albeit up to a point.

The 19th century is said to have witnessed Britain in its prime. Britain came through the Napoleonic Wars of 1803-15 victorious, thus consolidated its position as the greatest power in the world. Its colonies kept expanding and Queen Victoria was crowned the Empress of India in 1876. To the outside world, Britain represented modernity, and the Great Exhibition of 1851 and the Diamond Jubilee of Queen Victoria in 1897 were occasions of celebrating British success. Internally, successive reform acts (1832, 1867, and 1884) eventually extended franchise to adult males, allowing the masses to have a say in the way Britain, or more precisely at that time, the United Kingdom of Great Britain and Ireland, was run.

The Irish continued to be a problem for the UK state. As a result of the 1885 General Election, the Irish Home Rule party held the balance of power in the House of Commons. The then prime minister Gladstone introduced a home rule bill in 1886 in a bid to keep the unity of the UK; the bill was subsequently defeated. The defeat of the bill could be interpreted as the retreat of the all-inclusive Britishness which could accommodate all denominations, and the shift to a more ethnic, more English idea of Britishness in the late 19th century (Kearney 2000). But the home rule debate refused to disappear. The second bill was introduced in 1893 and defeated in the House of Lords. The third one introduced in 1912 became law in 1914, but with the outbreak of the First World War, it was suspended and then abandoned. By the time of the introduction of the third bill, the idea had grown to 'Home-Rule-All-Around' which included some devolution measures for Scotland and Wales as well as English regions (Bogdanor 1999: 44).

The 20th Century

The First World War is often described as having killed a Liberal Britain since it coincided with the rise of the Labour party and the rapid decline of the Liberal party. The UK was a member of the Allied Powers, and came out of the long, traumatic war victorious. One can perhaps single out two effects of the First World War on the British state and on Britishness. The War, firstly, reinforced the sense of Britishness. There were several dimensions to the newly emerged unity of the country. Conscription was one of them; English, Welsh, Scots and Irish fought as British. The loss was felt across the UK; it was not confined to a certain area or class. The First World War established some rituals which are still practiced today. Remembrance Sunday, for instance, was institutionalized to commemorate the war dead after the First World War, and so was the Poppy appeal. Even today, from late October until Remembrance Sunday in November, one still sees politicians,

TV personalities, and people in the street wearing a poppy, whose significance is widely recognized, and the Remembrance Sunday ceremony is televised. Whether or not they still have a mass resonance, these rituals are repeated to symbolize the unity of the nation, and by so doing, the state. The War had another effect on the British state and nation: Irish independence. Following the Easter Rising of 1916, Irish nationalists formed the Irish Free State in 1922 and seceded from the UK, though leaving the six counties in the north as part of the UK. This settlement was the cause of the so-called 'Troubles', the conflicts between the Protestant (Unionist) and Catholic (Nationalist) communities in Northern Ireland. It was also a birth of the current UK – the United Kingdom of Great Britain and Northern Ireland, and Britishness arguably lost a large part of its Irish dimension as a result of this.

The Second World War was also significant in terms of British identity as well as the future of Britain's relationship with Europe as we shall see later in this chapter. In 1940, when France was occupied by Nazi Germany and before the participation of the USA, Britain literally stood alone in the face of the advancing undemocratic force. It is suggestive in our investigation into the British attitudes to Europe that what is often referred to as 'Britain's finest hour' was experienced during the confrontation with the Axis power, when Britain was defending freedom and democracy on its own. In this vision, the continent was occupied by the evil powers of fascism and Nazism while the British Isles were seen as the last bastion of freedom and democracy. One can detect a strong Anglo-British element in this vision that the English (and occasionally British) are people of freedom. Also some influence of racialist thinking seems to have set in to replace the religion; the British/English love freedom because they are Anglo-Saxons (McLeod 1999). When the USA joined the war as a response to the Japanese surprise attack on Pearl Harbour in 1941, the UK forces fought with the Americans. This appears to have consolidated the idea that Britain has a special relationship with the US, which would have some effect on the relationship between Britain and Europe in the postwar era. The Second World War was important in the way it conditioned the ideas about Britain. The ideas that Britain was different from the continent, that the British constituted an Island race, and that it stood for democracy were reinforced during the war and they were circulated in the country through Winston Churchill's speeches, history books and newspapers.

In the 1950s, the world surrounding Britain was changing fast. Although the UK was on the winning side of the Second World War, its status as the world major power did not last long. From the 1950s, its colonies started gaining independence. As the empire withered, so did the power of the British state on the international stage. At the Suez Crisis of 1956-57, in which Britain and France tried to prevent Egypt from nationalizing the Suez Canal by mounting a military intervention, Britain was effectively told by the US to stop the war. The British economy was slowing down compared to those of the continental countries, the US and Japan, and in 1967, the government was forced to devalue the pound.

Immigration became an explosive issue as the economy slipped into recession and stagnation. There were times in the past when immigration was an important issue: immigrants from Ireland in the 19th century and Jews fleeing persecution in continental countries in the interwar period were once political issues (Mason 2000: 19-22). However, the postwar situation was different from earlier times since immigration became a race-relations issue (Schwarz 1992; Mason 2000). This is not to underplay anti-Semitism before 1945. It is simply a recognition that the majority of immigrants arriving after WWII were involved in a different social and power relationship from the Irish and Jewish people. In the 1950s, in order to compensate for the labour shortage, British companies and organizations actively recruited workers from the Commonwealth; the effort by the London Transport in West Indies is one of the well-known examples. It is worth noting that, for these companies, recruiting in the Commonwealth was a relatively easy option given that the British Nationality Act of 1948 had guaranteed people in the Commonwealth the right to enter, work and live in the UK freely (Mason 2000: 25). Probably because immigrants from the Commonwealth were much more visible than those who constituted earlier waves of immigrants, such as Poles and Italians, anti-immigrant feelings soon intensified and manifested themselves in incidents like the Notting Hill riots of 1958. Hostility to and uneasiness about immigration from the Commonwealth fed into a series of immigration acts (1962, 1968 and 1971; 1981 Nationality Act) which increasingly worked to prohibit legal immigration and to restrict citizenship by the 'partiality', i.e. blood principle. Immigration has been a significant issue in postwar Britain. Enoch Powell's notorious 'rivers of blood' speech of 1968 in which he warned of an imminent race war in Britain is still often evoked in the discussion of race relations. This is not a place for a detailed discussion of the merits and effects of these acts in contemporary Britain. However, it is fair to argue that because of these legislations, the preciously implicit link between Britishness and being white has become apparent. This has invited many attempts to redefine Britishness as we shall see shortly, and the number of dimensions contemporary Britishness has multiplied as a result.

There is also an issue of Europe. The details of Britain's relations with Europe will be discussed later, and it should suffice to state that the British politicians and policy makers as well as many British people did not consider the initiative for European integration relevant to them for a long while. When Britain woke up to the fact that it was now a middle-sized country at the edge of Europe, not a major power, Europe became a threat (Ellison 2000). Since Britain joined the European Economic Community, Europe has been seen as a threat to its parliamentary sovereignty and national identity itself.

Devolution

At the end of the last century, two more significant developments took place. The Labour government which came into power in 1997 held referenda on devolution in Scotland and Wales, and went on to implement it. In the meantime, for the first time ever, the proportion of the population who feel that the monarchy would not survive for a long time exceeded those who believe in the continuity of the monarchy.

That monarchy is an old institution in Britain and its condition may prove to be another indicator of the state of Britain. However, devolution has arguably had much more profound effects on the British state and therefore on British national identity than the recent royal scandals (Nairn 2000; Parekh 2000; Bagdanor 1999; Curtice and Heath 2000).

The demand for more autonomy for Scotland and Wales re-entered the political arena between the late 1960s and the early 1970s when votes for nationalist parties, the Scottish National Party (SNP) in Scotland and Plaid Cymru in Wales, surged. During the late 1960s, the SNP's electoral performance started to improve, and at the 1970 General Election it acquired 11 per cent of the vote cast in Scotland and secured one seat in Westminster; at the February 1974 election, it secured 22 per cent of the Scottish vote and sent two MPs to London; and at the subsequent October 1974 election, the SNP gained 30 per cent of the Scottish vote and the number of MPs jumped to eleven. Plaid Cymru was also coming out of obscurity, and at the February 1974 election, it gained 10.7 per cent of the Welsh vote and sent two MPs, and at the October election, it secured 10.8 per cent and three seats. At the face of the rise of nationalism in Scotland and Wales, the then Labour government was forced to hold referenda in 1975 to ask if voters in Scotland and Wales would like to have their own legislative bodies. The result from Wales was a clear no, but the Scottish result was very close. Although more 'yes' votes were cast than 'no' votes, because of a high proportion of absentees, the result was declared 'no', and the devolution seemed to have died.

The nationalist parties performance from the late 1970s to 1980s was miserable, but the Conservative government which came to power in 1979 nonetheless continued with so-called 'administrative devolution', in which some competence of governmental departments was handed over to the Scottish and Welsh Offices. Mrs Thatcher was seen by many in Scotland and Wales as the embodiment of a narrow-minded, market-oriented conservatism, a quality which was then linked to English nationalism in these people's mind. Her programme of revitalizing the British economy by injecting the virtue of privatization offended a more collectivist and corporatist ethos of the Scots and Welsh, as well as people of North England. When the Labour Party came to power in 1997, it held another round of referenda in Scotland and Wales, and later in London, about a Scottish Parliament, a Welsh Assembly and a Greater London Assembly. The result from the Scottish referendum was a clear endorsement of the setting up of a Scottish Parliament with a power to raise or lower the income tax by 3 per cent. The Welsh result was much more ambiguous but it was declared that the Welsh voters supported the idea of a Welsh Assembly, and the London result also indicated that the majority of those who voted wanted to have an assembly. The elections for the Scottish Parliament, Welsh and Greater London Assemblies took place in the following year, and in 1999, the Scottish Parliament 'reconvened' after almost three hundred years and the Welsh and London Assemblies were opened.

Those who supported devolutionary measures based their argument on democracy: they argued that it was only democratic to have these parliaments and assemblies when people wanted it. In this way, the Labour government has positioned devolution as one of the cornerstones of their project of 'modernizing'

Britain – regeneration of democracy. However, there was fierce opposition to devolution, especially from the Conservative Party, for fear that it might lead to the break-up of Britain. While the Labour and Liberal Democrat devolution supporters argued that devolution was necessary to stem the flow of nationalism and that devolution was a means to strengthen the Union, the Tory opponents voiced their fear that devolution would turn out to be a slippery slope for independence especially for the Scots. A few years passed since political devolution was officially implemented and the jury is still out. The anxiety that Britain may break up persists.

2. Dominant Discourses of Nationhood

Britishness may be a relatively new identity, but in many respects it has incorporated a lot from English identity, which has a longer history. This is largely due to the fact that England has always been the most dominant component in the British isles in terms of size, population and power. Therefore the discussion of Britishness is coloured by several themes which derive from English identity. These include the idea that the English and therefore the British are a chosen people; constitutional liberties which have been won through a series of stages from Magna Carta to the Glorious Revolution; common law which has gradually evolved; hostility to European powers cultivated through English confrontation with Spain and France, and so on. Other undercurrents are the idea that the British are an island race (which justifies its isolation or exceptionalism), and that the UK is a global player with its status as a nuclear power and a permanent member of the UN Security Council (which reflects the past status of the UK as the world power).

    The dominant idea of Britishness by far is that it is a civic identity. It is civic because it is not ethnic; it did not organically grow out of a pre-existing entity, but was forged or constructed through institutions such as the Parliament and monarchy and wars against France, as Colley has pointed out (Colley 1992). This argument tends to play down the English influence on British identity. Following this line of argument, British identity is sometimes labelled as a state identity, an attachment to the state, not to the people (McCrone 1997). Bernard Crick has even declared that British identity 'does not correspond to any real sense of a nation' since there is no British nation in the way there is the French nation (Crick 1991: 97). These deliberations are put forward in a recognition that Britishness and Englishness should be separated; and Britishness in contrast to Englishness is presented as institutional, state-centred, and non-ethnic. It is also a statement against the conventional historical approach where history of Britain more often than not means history of England.[4]

    British identity as a non-ethnic one is a useful tool in explaining some phenomena. First, the idea is frequently utilized by scholars working on Scottish and Welsh nationalism in explaining the dual identity structure which is often

---

[4] For critique of this long standing conflation of England and Britain, see Davis (1999).

observed in Scotland and Wales. Various surveys have reported that the majority of the Scots and Welsh see themselves as both Scottish/Welsh and British though with some differences in emphasis.[5] One of the explanations is that there is a division of labour between British identity (civic and political) and Scottish/Welsh identity (ethnic and cultural). Although in the Scottish case, it is possible to argue that Scottish identity is as civic and institutional as the British one, British identity as a civic identity is held to offer some clues in understanding the complexity of the identity issues.

The same logic can be applied to the understanding of the second- and third- generation of immigrants. That they would call themselves 'Black British' or 'Asian British' is often held to be indicative of the civic or institutional nature of British identity. Since British identity is an institutional, inclusive one, so the argument goes, everyone can be British. In this case, again, Britishness is contrasted to Englishness, which is supposed to be ethnic and therefore exclusive.

The other aspect of British identity which also follows Colley's thesis of Britishness is that British identity is essentially imperial. Colley stresses the role of the British Empire in forging Britons as a common project where the English, Scots and Welsh (and Irish) could work together (Colley 1992). The importance of the Empire, along with wars and intermarriages, in formulating British identity is widely recognized by historians (Davis 1999: 911-2). From this angle British identity is therefore informed by imperialism, which suggests that it has an element of the idea of white superiority, or what we may call racist aspect.

The idea that being British implies being white is widely taken up by literature especially in the field of race relations. In this light, Britishness is exclusive and exploitative, and something that has to be changed in order to create a better British society. The racist aspect of Britishness has recently been drawing a lot of attention, largely due to two official reports. The Macpherson Report (1999), which looked into the circumstances surrounding a murder of a black teenager, Stephen Lawrence, by a white gang in 1993, loudly condemned the police for being 'institutionally racist'. The accusation that the police, one of the key institutions of the state, was institutionally racist attracted enormous media coverage, and the Government swiftly published action plans to eradicate institutional racism from public services. The debate on Britishness sparked by the MacPherson Report was taken further by another government commissioned report on the future of multi-ethnic Britain by the Runnymede Trust, published in 2000. The report stated that Britishness does carry an unspoken, racial connotation, and given that Englishness cannot be an alternative because of its overt association with being white, the current notion of Britishness needs to be revised to be more inclusive and genuinely multicultural (Runnymede Trust 2000: 34-9).

The current dominant discourses on Britishness are focusing on two opposing aspects of Britishness. Different aspects are illuminated in different

---

[5] For an example of such survey results, see McCrone (1997). The usual complaint is that the English cannot distinguish being English and British. They tend to describe themselves as 'equally British and English' while a large proportion of Scots and Welsh opt for 'More Scottish/Welsh than British'.

contexts, which points to the fact that national identity is not homogeneous but a complex phenomenon. It poses different questions according to the socio-historical circumstances in which the people in question find themselves. One can also detect a strong aspirational element in these discussions: the shared understanding appears to be that ethnic based identity should be overridden by civic based identity in order to ensure inclusiveness.

3. Relations with Europe: A Brief Overview

The history of the UK/Britain's relationship with Europe is a long and eventful one, but what characterizes it most is the prevailing image of 'Europe as an elsewhere' (Passerini 2000: 10). This detachedness was well captured by Winston Churchill's statement: 'We are with but not of Europe' (Lord 1998: 23). There is another famous episode of a British newspaper running a story entitled 'Fog in the Channel, Europe cut off'. It is true that these islands which constitute today's UK have been deeply involved with the Continent: the Roman invasion, Vikings raids, the Norman conquest of 1066, countless wars with forces of the Continent, and the Reformation, to name but a few.[6] There have also been intense intellectual exchange and trade between the two. However, partly because of the geography,[7] and partly because of the UK's imperial past, 'Europe as an elsewhere' seems to describe best the underlying tone of the UK-Europe relationship. It is worth noting here that in the British context, the EU and Europe are largely conflated; both belong to 'somewhere else'. Some intellectuals and politicians can articulate the difference between the two, but this differentiation does not make strong impacts on the discussions of the UK-Europe relationship.

The British attitudes to the process which has led to the birth of the European Union could never be described as enthusiastic. Although Britain was a driving force behind setting up the Organisation for European Economic Co-operation in 1948, which was to administer Marshall Plan announced a year earlier, it did not show much interest in the establishment of the European Coal and Steel Community (ECSC) in 1951. It also did not take part in the negotiations which eventually produced the Treaty of Rome of 1957. Alarmed by the progress on the custom union of the European Economic Community, the UK proposed an alternative idea of international economic co-operation in the form of the European Free Trade Association (EFTA), which did not have an explicit political dimension. Austria, Denmark, Norway, Portugal, Sweden, Switzerland and the UK became the signatories of the EFTA Convention in 1960.

---

[6] For a good overview of the history of the relationship between Britain and the continent, see Black (1994).

[7] Although it has been pointed out by many scholars that the sea was not an obstacle to communication in the pre-railways age, in the present discourse on Britain and Europe, Britain as 'an island race' is often cited as a reason for a perceived distant relationship between Britain and 'Europe'. See Shore (2000), Radice (1992) and Thomas (1991) for this popularised version of history of Britain and Europe.

In the following year, 1961, however, the Conservative Macmillan government, disturbed at the progress made by the six, submitted the first application to join the EEC. In 1963 President De Gaulle of France vetoed UK membership of the EEC on the basis that Britain was not yet a suitable candidate. An interesting aspect of the first application was that by September 1957, well before the submission of the application, 'many people in Britain were under the impression that Britain was already a member [of the EEC]', but at the same time, 'the majority had not even heard of the EEC' (Spence 1976: 19). The British public opinion during the Macmillan initiative was largely favourable of membership (Spence 1976: 20).

The Vietnam war and the crisis in Rhodesia finally pushed the Labour Wilson government to put the second application to join the EEC in May 1967. It was swiftly vetoed by President De Gaulle in November. Further negotiation for the British entry had to wait until President De Gaulle stepped down in 1969, and the return of the Conservative government led by Edward Heath in 1970. The European Community opened membership negotiations with Denmark, Ireland, Norway and the UK in June 1970, and in January 1972, the UK signed the Treaty of Accession together with Denmark, Ireland and Norway; in January 1973, the UK became formally a member of the EC.

In the meantime, a Labour government, which was more hostile to the EEC, came to power with a promise to renegotiate the terms of entry to the EEC in 1974, and the renegotiations concluded in 1975. In June the same year, the British government held a referendum over the renegotiated terms of entry, and with the turn-out of 65 per cent, the majority (67 per cent) voted 'yes', thus confirming British membership at least in a legalistic sense.

Even with its membership of the EEC confirmed, the UK has been described to be a 'reluctant European' (Gowland and Tuner 2000), or as playing the 'politics of detachment' (Bulmer 1992). The UK has never been keen on any development which might lead to a further transfer of sovereignty to European institutions. The most visible representation of an 'awkward partner' has been Margaret Thatcher. Her Bruges speech, delivered in September 1998, is widely seen as a wholehearted attack on the process of European integration.[8] Although her successor, John Major adopted a far less hostile attitude to the European project, his policy was 'wait and see': hardly a positive policy towards Europe. In the meantime, the Labour Party abandoned its overtly hostile stance to the EC while the Tory Party, which was traditionally more pro-Europe, came to be seen as more hostile to Europe (Hearl 1994). When the Labour government came to power in 1997, it quickly signed the Social Chapter and styled itself as a new leader of Europe. However, the ultimate issue – the euro – divides the Eurozone and Britain, and the image of Britain being an odd existence still prevails (Barker 2001).

---

[8] Perhaps, the best known section of her speech is: 'We have not successfully rolled back the frontiers of the state in Britain only to see them re-imposed at a European level, with a European super-state exercising a new dominance from Brussels.'

This much is reflected in public attitudes towards Europe. According to the successive *Eurobarometer* surveys, British respondents are 'reluctant Europeans'.

Table 1.1 National and European identity: The UK and the EU average, 1996-2003 (%)

(figures in brackets show the EU average)

	European only	European and nationality	Nationality and European	Nationality only
1996	5 (5)	6 (6)	26 (40)	60 (46)
1997	6 (5)	3 (6)	29 (40)	57 (45)
1998	5 (4)	4 (7)	27 (43)	62 (43)
1999	3 (4)	3 (6)	24 (42)	67 (45)
2000	3 (4)	3 (7)	27 (49)	62 (38)
2001	2 (3)	4 (6)	22 (44)	71 (44)
2002	4 (4)	4 (7)	28 (48)	62 (38)
2003	3 (4)	4 (8)	24 (44)	64 (40)

Source: Eurobarometers 45-59.

Although the percentage of the British respondents identifying themselves as exclusively European does not differ much from the EU average, a clear difference is shown in the categories of 'British first, European second' and 'British only'. The EU average figures show that on average people in the EU tend to profess to a dual identity structure with an emphasis on their nationality. However, the British are not forthcoming in admitting a European element in their identity; more than 60 per cent have been consistently declaring that they are British, no more, no less. The *Eurobarometer* surveys have also shown that the British respondents hold less favourable views of the EU than others. The gap between the politicians' attitudes to the EU and Europe and those of the electorate is not wide in contemporary Britain.

4. The British as Reluctant Europeans: Some Explanations

Geopolitical Conditions

The fact that the UK was not defeated or occupied in the Second World War is argued to have particularly affected British attitudes at the start of the current process of European integration (Gowland and Turner 2000; Shore 2000; Maitland 2001: 2-3; Bell 1996; Haseler 1996: 60). It did not need as much as some continental countries the assurance of peace and stability which the process of European integration promised. Moreover, British politicians were under the influence of the idea of the UK being the 'third force' in the postwar world, standing shoulder to shoulder with the USA and the Soviet Union, and they thought a deeper involvement with Europe could undermine its status. Despite its economic and military decline which started in the late 19th century, the politicians and policy makers at the end of the war still saw the UK as a global player. There were a few postwar developments which allowed the UK government to hang on to the idea of being a global player: the status of a permanent member of the United Nations Security Council and the successful development of nuclear weapons. In order to maintain its increasingly unrealistic position of a global player, the UK government tended to play down the significance of the European development in assessing its national interest.

Another, and interrelated with the first, source of British reluctance to Europe was the Commonwealth (Gowland and Turner 2000; Shore 2000: 170-2; Maitland 2001). The Commonwealth today is a collection of 54 countries with most of them being ex-British colonies, and acts as a forum for international co-operation. It was given an official and legal status in 1931 (Maitland 2001: 1). At the end of the war, the Commonwealth was politically, economically and emotionally significant to the UK population. First, it was indispensable in the idea of the UK being the 'third force'. Even today the Commonwealth covers about 30 per cent of the world population, and it was thought that the weight of this huge organization would enhance the British status in the world stage. The Commonwealth with its multi- racial, ethnic and cultural character was also ideal PR material in publicizing the UK's intention to bring about peace and prosperity in the world, not only in Europe (Ward 2001).

The Commonwealth was also an important trading partner of the UK. By 1950, 47.7 per cent of Britain's total export went to the Commonwealth while 41.1 per cent of Britain's total import came from the Commonwealth. On the other hand, between 1938 and 1948, the share of export to the Six in the total British export fell from 21.7 per cent to 16.7 percent, and the share of import from the Six from 18.6 per cent to 13.1 per cent (Gowland and Turner 2000: 86). Of course, this was largely due to the formation of bloc economies as response to the Great Depression of the 1930s and the peculiarity of the wartime economy. However, it is clear that at the end of the war and well into the 1950s, the Commonwealth was far more important to British economy than the Continental countries.

Thirdly, there was the issue of emotion which strengthened the geopolitical case of not joining the process of European integration. The Commonwealth contributed to the UK's war efforts in terms of goods and soldiers and it is argued that the British political elite and people in general felt gratitude to the Commonwealth, and therefore could not forsake it for a new future in Europe; in this aspect, the EEC represented selfishness in pursuit of economic benefits, while the Commonwealth symbolized higher moral loyalty (Maitland 2001: 3). It is also important that a large section of the population had some kind of ties – family, business, intellectual – with Commonwealth countries, which could have affected their perception of the European project and Britain's role in it.

A special relationship with the United States is another factor which has been exercising considerable influence over British foreign policy and public opinion. The idea of a special relationship with the US also feeds into the idea of Britain as the third force and a global player, and therefore it has exercised a prolonged influence on the way in which British foreign policy has been formulated. Many politicians, policy makers and some lay people thought and, to some extent, still think, that 'Going into Europe' might undermine this cherished special relationship with the USA. Ironically, the US wants the UK in Europe, a fact which is now increasingly recognized by policy makers and politicians of the UK, but is not necessarily shared by the majority of the British public (Rachman 1998).

Historical Conditions: English Experiences

The necessity of focusing on Anglo-Britishness becomes clear when one looks into the historical conditions of the British reluctance to European integration in comparison to Scottish attitudes. To put it simply, the contemporary Scots are less hostile to European integration than the British in general (Ichijo 2004). Since British identity was forged through the wars with France, Protestantism and participation in the Empire, Anglo-British and Scottish views should be based on the same foundation vis-à-vis the continent. Because Scotland and England have shared most historical experiences since the union of 1707, especially those of external relationship, the fact that there is divergence suggests that the major reason should be found in their pre-Union histories, rather than the postwar geopolitical reasons.

Set in the English perspective, it can be argued that the present Anglo-British view of European integration reflects historical English antagonism towards the continent (Haseler 1996; Ash 2001; Condren 1999; Bell 1996). On the whole, for the English, Europe is somewhere else to which England does not belong. However, historians have now begun to stress the European past of England, that England was very much involved with and influenced by the affairs of the continent (Davis 1999; Kearney 1989; Black 1994). The invasions of the Romans and subsequently the Anglo-Saxons, Vikings, and the Norman conquest, all demonstrate that Great Britain was not isolated in the North-Western corner of the area which we can roughly call Europe. However, the conventional view has it that the Hundred Years War with France (1337-1453) marked the change of the scene. The English army left French soil in 1453, and when Calais was lost to the French in 1558, England did not make any further attempt to conquer the continent and concentrated on its maritime expansion. It has also been pointed out that the English Channel was increasingly seen as the defence line, not as a link to the continent in the 16th century, thus encouraging the emergence of the island metaphor (Lambert and Heuser 1999).

It was in the following period when the idea of Great Britain as an island separated from the Continent, and that of English, and later British, exceptionalism evolved (Ash 2001; Haseler 1996). The gradual strengthening of the parliament in relation to the power of the monarch, the Reformation, revolutions which established the principle of parliamentary sovereignty, all took place in this period. The people of the continent, especially the French, became an important 'Other' for the English to form the idea as to who they were and who they were not. Europe became 'a theatre, a means of showing Britain's status and significance'

(Condren 1999: 18).[9] In what way were the English different, then? The points of reference were 'the slow, steady organic growth of institutions, of Common Law, Parliament, and a unique concept of sovereignty, vested in the Crown in Parliament' (Ash 2001: 6). Furthermore, the idea of freedom became entrenched in British institutions (Robbins 1998: 133-5). These have translated into the idea that the English are freedom lovers who are democratic and who respect commonsense. The continent, especially revolutionary France was, on the other hand, where extremism ruled and despotism reined in the English eye.

The idea of English exceptionalism was further reinforced by another idea: the English is God's elect (Haseler 1996: 20; Greenfeld 1992) The idea was mobilized by a series of historical actors: Oliver Cromwell was one of them. Indeed, in 1559, a bishop declared that God was English, suggesting the view that 'the English people was chosen, separated from others and distinguished by God' was in fashion (Greenfeld 1992: 60-1). The English were a special people in their mind. This implies that foreigners from the continent were inferior to the English, an idea which conditioned the underlying tone of English and Anglo-British understandings of Europe. This idea is especially pronounced vis-à-vis France, and a certain anti-French feeling still prevails (Haseler 1996). When De Gaul vetoed the UK's application for membership of the EEC, it appeared to testify to the received wisdom that the Anglo-French relationship was conditioned by 'deep-seated suspicion and mistrust on both sides' (Gowland and Turner 2000: 142). The Anglo-British view of Europe is therefore underpinned by certain antagonism which emerged and has been maintained through the history.

It is not this chapter's intention, however, to argue that the English have historically been, and are now, entirely anti-European. There is a wealth of evidence to demonstrate that English fascination with the continent also has a long history; the custom of grand tour whereby children of the well-off class finished off their education with an extended tour of the continental countries is one example. In the 18th century, at the height of Enlightenment, the intellectual and social exchange between England (and Britain as a whole) and France was lively, and 'cultivated Englishmen' would express their Francophile tendency without any inhibition (Newman 1987: 1-2). What is stressed here is that the traditional English hostility to European countries and people is a significant element in colouring the contemporary Anglo-British attitudes to European integration, which comes out stronger than English affinity with the continent.

Conclusion

The chapter has outlined the paths that the British state and nation have taken up to the present and how they relate to the issue of Europe. What has become clear is that despite current British reluctance in embracing the EU, Britain's state and

---

[9] From the Anglo-British perspective, 'Britain' in this quote is understood to refer to 'England'. Another example of the messiness one encounters when investigating the UK case.

nation formation and re-formation have been intertwined with the developments in continental Europe. Although not many contemporary Britons admit that they have a European identity, Europe has been in various ways a significant other for Britain. This is probably inevitable because of the geographical fact that the British Isles are in Europe. Trade, commerce, military interaction, intellectual exchanges and population movements between Britain and the continent have been ultimately conditioned by this geographical fact. The continent was naturally the first place people of the British Isles would interact, and despite Britain's expansion to the West and the formation of a special relationship with the USA, Europe has never ceased to be something that Britain has to reckon with. One cannot grasp the nature of British identity without reference to Europe, despite the popular myth that says otherwise.

References

Ash, Timothy Garton (2001), 'Is Britain European?', *International Affairs*, 77(1), pp. 1-13.

Baker, David (2001), 'Britain and Europe: The Argument Continues', *Parliamentary Affairs*, 54, pp. 276-288.

Bell, Philip (1996), 'A historical cast of mind: some eminent English historians and attitudes to Continental Europe in the middle of the twentieth century', *Journal of European Integration History*, 2(2), pp. 5-20.

Black, Jeremy (1994), *Convergence or Divergence?: Britain and the Continent*, Basingstoke: Macmillan.

Bogdanor, Vernon (1999), *Devolution in the United Kingdom*, Oxford: Oxford University Press.

Brockliss, Laurence (1997), 'The professions and national identity', in Brockless and Eastwood (eds), pp. 9-28.

Brockless, Laurence and Eastwood, David (eds) (1997), *A Union of Multiple Identities: the British Isles, c.1750-c.1850*, Manchester: Manchester University Press.

Bulmer, Simon (1992), *United Kingdom and EC Membership Evaluated*, London: Pinter.

Colley, Linda (1992), *Britons: Forging the Nation 1707-1837*, London: Yale University Press.

Condren, Conal (1999), 'English Historiography and the invention of Britain and Europe', in Milfull (ed.), pp. 11-27.

Crick, Bernard (1991), 'The English and the British', in Crick (ed.), pp. 90-104.

Crick, Bernard (ed.) (1991), *National Identities: The Constitution of the United Kingdom*, Oxford: Blackwell.

Curtice, John and Heath, Anthony (2000), 'Is the English lion about to roar? National identity after devolution', in Jowell et al. (eds) pp. 155-174.

Davis, Norman (1999), *The Isles: A History*, Basingstoke: Macmillan.

Eastwood, David; Brockliss, Laurence and John, Michael (1997), 'Conclusion: From dynastic union to unitary state: the European experience', in Brockless and Eastwood (eds), pp. 193-212.

Ellison, James (2000), *Threatening Europe: Britain and the Creation of the European Communities, 1955-58*, Basingstoke: Macmillan.

Gowland, David and Turner, Arthur (2000), *Reluctant Europeans: Britain and European Integration, 1945-1998*, Harlow, Essex: Longman.

Greenfeld, Liah (1992), *Nationalism: Five Roads to Modernity*, Cambridge, MA: Harvard University Press.

Haseler, Stephen (1996), *The English Tribe: Identity, Nation and Europe*, Basingstoke: Macmillan.

Hay, Denys (1956), 'The use of the term "Great Britain" in the Middle Ages', *Proceedings of the Society of Antiquaries of Scotland 1955-1956*, 89, pp. 55-66.

Hearl, Derek (1994), 'Britain and Europe since 1945', *Parliamentary Affairs*, 47(4), pp. 515-529.

Ichijo, Atsuko (2004), *Scottish Nationalism and the Idea of Europe: Concepts of Europe and the Nation*, London: Routledge.

Jowell, Roger and Hoinville, Gerald (eds) (1976), *Britain into Europe: Public Opinion and the EEC, 1961-75*, London: Croom Helm.

Jowell, Roger et al. (eds) (2000), *British Social Attitudes, the 17th Report*, London: Sage.

Kearney, Hugh (1989), *The British Isles: A History of Four Nations*, Cambridge: Cambridge University Press.

Kearney, Hugh (2000), 'The importance of being British', *Political Quarterly*, 71(1), pp. 15-25.

Lambert, Andrew and Heuser, Beatrice (1999), 'The silver sea between Britain and her European identity', in Petricioli and Varsori (eds), pp. 23-44.

Lord, Christopher (1998), '"With but not of": Britain and the Schumann Plan, a reinterpretation', *Journal of European Integration History*, 4(2), pp. 23-46.

McCrone, David (1997), 'Unmasking Britannia: The rise and fall of British national identity7, *Nations and Nationalism*, 3(4), pp. 579-596.

McLeod, Hugh (1999), 'Protestantism and British national identity, 1815-1945', in van den Veer and Leumann (eds), pp. 44-70.

Maitland, David (2001), 'Britain, the Commonwealth and Europe: an Overview', in May (ed.), pp. 1-8.

Mason, David (2000), *Race and Ethnicity in Modern Britain*, second edition, Oxford: Oxford University Press.

May, Alex (ed.) (2001), *Britain, the Commonwealth and Europe: The Commonwealth and Britain's Application to Join the European Communities*, Basingstoke: Palgrave.

Milfull, John (ed.) (1999), *Britain in Europe: Prospects of Change*, Aldershot: Ashgate.

Mitchell, James (1996), *Strategies for Self-government: The Campaign for a Scottish Parliament*, Edinburgh: Polygon.

Murdoch, Alexander (1998), *British History 1660-1832: National Identity and Local Culture*, Basingstoke: Macmillan.

Nairn, Tom (2000), *After Britain: New Labour and the Return of Scotland*, London: Granta.

Newman, Gerald (1987), *The Rise of English Nationalism: A Cultural History 1740-1830*, Basingstoke: Macmillan.

Parekh, Bhiku (2000), 'Defining British national identity', *Political Quarterly*, 71(1), pp. 4-14.

Passerini, Luisa (2000), *Europe in Love, Love in Europe: Imagination and Politics in Britain between the Wars*, London: I. B. Tauris.

Petricioli, Marta and Varsori, Antonio (eds) (1999), *The Seas as Europe's External Borders and their Role in Shaping a European Identity*, London: Lothian Foundation Press.

Rachman, Gideon (1998), 'Britain's European dilemma', *The Washington Quarterly*, 21(3), pp. 175-190.

Robbins, Keith (1998), *Great Britain: Identities, Institutions and the Idea of Britishness*, London: Longman.

Runnymede Trust, the (2000), *The Future of Multi-Ethnic Britain: Report of the Commission on the Future of Multi-Ethnic Britain*, London: Profile Books.

Schwarz, Bill (1992), 'England in Europe: reflections on national identity and cultural theory', *Cultural Studies*, 6(2), pp. 198-206.

Shore, Peter (2000), *Separate Ways: The Heart of Europe*, London: Gerald Duckworth & Co.

Spence, James (1976), 'Movements in the public mood, 1961-75', in Jowell and Hoinville (eds), pp. 18-36.

Thomas, Hugh (1991), *Ever Closer Union: Britain's Destiny in Europe*, London: Hutchinson.

van den Veer, Peter and Leumann, Hartmut (eds) (1999), *Nation and Religion: Perspectives on Europe and Asia*, Princeton, NJ: Princeton University Press.

Ward, Stuart (2001), 'A matter of preference: the EEC and the erosion of the old Commonwealth relationship', in May (ed.), pp. 156-180.

Chapter 2

Germany: From *Kulturnation* to Europeanization?

Michael Minkenberg

Introduction

From a comparative perspective, the German case of nation-building diverges from both a 'Western model', in which nation-building was preceded by state building and accompanied by the emergence of a common civic culture and ideology, and an 'Eastern model' of very late or even blocked nation-building and the prevalence of cultural and ethnic nationalism.[1] As is well known, the German path to national unity and the subsequent national identity is characterized by its heavy emphasis on the German *Kulturnation* which, after unification in 1871, resulted in the myth of an ethnic community of Germans, or *Volksnation*. At the same time, democratization processes from above (the introduction of the most liberal electoral law at the time) and below (the push of the working class for integration and recognition) resulted in the emergence of the legal-political equality of members in the framework of the ethnic concept of citizenship enshrined in the 1913 nationality code. Thus the main characteristics of the German case are:

- the polycentric form in different regional political centers and ethnic cultures;
- the interconnection of these ethnic groups in a common high language and culture;
- the imperial framework of the Holy Roman Empire of the German Nation; and
- the continuation of this polycentric form of ethno-genesis into modern nation-building on the basis of the common culture and a federal structure.

What follows is a two-step analysis of the German path of nation building. The first step contains its contextualizing in a European framework of ideal type trajectories according to regional, geo-political economic and cultural zones (see introduction), with particular attention paid to the long-time issue of shifting

[1] This chapter is based on a joint text by the author with Willfried Spohn and Daniel Becker, published in *Representations of Europe and the Nation in Current and Prospective Member States: The Collective State of the Art and Historical Reports.* Bruxelles: European Commission, 2003, pp. 86-126. The author is grateful to Willfried Spohn and Daniel Becker for their comments and contribution to bringing about this chapter.

boundaries and territory (until 1990). The second step attempts the analysis of the entanglement of current (post-war) German identity with its European context, both in terms of Europe at large and the European Union as a supranational institutional framework for national politics.

1. Historical Patterns of Nation Formation in Germany

The Road toward a Unified German Nation-State

The process of German nation-building emerged from a polycentric form of ethno-genesis with overarching linguistic and cultural commonalties within the framework of the Holy Roman Empire of the German Nation (Conze 1992, Dann 1996). The Protestant Reformation and Catholic Counterreformation strengthened the aristocratic rulers and fostered the development of absolutist states. At the same time, the translation of the Bible into vernacular German unified the German language. On these linguistic and religious bases, German literature, art and philosophy as well as church and popular songs emerged in the 17th and 18th centuries and created the German *Kulturnation* – those who were able to speak the German language and participated in the values of humanistic *Bildung* (see Meinecke 1908). This polycentric form of ethnogenesis and state formation constituted a major obstacle towards a unified German nation-state.

The major force to disrupt the entropy of the imperial polycentric order did not come from inside, but from outside. The French Revolution created the modern democratic nation-state and exported this model to Continental Europe by the Napoleonic Wars. Many reformers and revolutionaries in Germany sympathized with the French Revolution and, especially in the West of the Holy Roman Empire, cooperated with Napoleon to dissolve the Empire and to modernize the larger and centralizing absolutist states. There is a certain paradox in this development, however. In the so-called liberation wars against French dominance in Germany, the principles of the French Revolution were turned against Napoleonic France itself; and even if the first beginnings of what would later develop into a German nationalist movement grew out of these wars, their primary result was a strengthening of the absolutist states against the cause of a united German nation-state.

German nationalism, then, emerged not only as a resistance movement against a foreign power, but soon turned into an opposition movement against the still mostly absolutist governments in the more than 30 quasi-sovereign German states, too. With the tide of events, German nationalism, which was never a wholly coherent ideology, changed and was transformed from one code to another, thus mirroring the problems of defining the boundaries of a German nation which remained prominent during the 19th century (see Giesen 1993). Whatever its transformations over time, however, two main currents or layers can be made out as distinctive features of German nationalism. The first layer was the political dimension of German nationalism. Here the French revolutionary model gave the orientation towards a sovereign, centralized and strong nation-state able to end the semi-dependency on France and play an equal part in the European state order. The French revolutionary model also included the orientation towards a parliamentarian, democratic and constitutional nation-state – both in a more radical revolutionary direction as well as in a more liberal-conservative orientation.[2] The second layer of German nationalism was cultural. This included a linguistic basis – the German speaking regions (except those in the West already belonging to other nation-states such as Switzerland, the Netherlands or France) – and a cultural basis – the German *Kultur* as a superior value orientation against the Western materialistic civilization (Elias 1969, Mosse 1978).

Both layers were not a structural essence, but a historically developing political-cultural configuration. As a consequence, a tension between the political nation and the cultural nation evolved. On the one hand, the German *Kulturnation* implied a great German solution which was not only unacceptable to the other great powers in Europe, but was also opposed to the three-tiered political structure between the German *Bund*, Prussia and the Habsburg Empire. On the other hand, any realistic form of political unification – in the form of centralized German Bund, a combination of the German Bund plus either Prussia or Austria – implied a major political restructuration of the traditional dynastic states in Germany, but also remained insufficient as compared to the common German *Kulturnation*. These tensions were of crucial importance after the unification of Germany.

The decisive moment in the process of German nation building came when in the revolution of 1848 the *Frankfurter Nationalversammlung* attempted to institutionalize a unified national state first against the established dynasties and then in cooperation with the Prussian king. The effort failed, not merely because of the political powerlessness of the democratic movement, but also because of the inherent contradictions and difficulties in defining the territorial borders of a unified Germany without destabilizing the European state order and including other nationalities against their will. The defeat of the *Nationalversammlung* as well as the expulsion and domestication of many participants of the national-democratic movement through the traditional political powers in Germany, Prussia and Habsburg Austria, closed the chapter of unifying Germany through German democracy from below. Instead, Prussia as the growing economic and military power took the lead in the unification of Germany. In three wars against Denmark (1864), Austria (1866), and France (1870/71), the German Empire was founded on 'iron and blood' and on a compromise between Prussian dynastic interests and German democratic-liberal nationalism (Nipperdey 1991, Wehler 1995).

The territorial question constituted an unsolved problem until the very recent past. The answers to the famous question in the *Xenien* of Goethe and

---

[2] It should be noted, nonetheless, that the drive for German unification among the early liberal theoreticians and politicians, such as Karl von Rotteck and his circle, was less forceful than usually assumed. Mediated through their reading of Kant, these 'enlightened liberals' (Blänkner 1998) were also influenced by English trans-atlantic thought as well the Scottish Enlightenment. Thus their main focus, quite influential until the eve of the 1848 revolution, was based more upon a 'democratic' constitution than on a unified German nation-state.

Schiller (1796) 'Deutschland! Aber wo liegt es?'[3] showed great variation. It is well-known that the assembly of the *Paulskirche* defined the German territory, finally, along the borders of the German League (*Deutscher Bund*). Accordingly, Czechs, Slovenians, many Italians and a few Danes were asked to elect deputies to the Frankfurt parliament, whereas no one had the idea to also include Alsatians or Lorrainers (cf. Brandt 1987: 116f.). During the time of the first German national state, they also were included, as well as the Polish majority of the population in Posen and Western Prussia, whereas the Germans in the Habsburg Empire remained excluded.

Instead of revolution and civil war, then, it was violence in the form of war which assumed a central function in German nation building. During the Napoleonic Wars from 1806 to 1815, German national sentiment was articulated on a broader basis for the first time. The so-called 'unification wars' of 1864, 1866 and 1870/71 resolved the territorial problem in favour of a *Kleindeutschland* excluding the Germans in the Habsburg Empire, favouring a Prussian-Protestant predominance within the Empire. One of the most severe consequences was a far-reaching disassociation of the national and the democratic idea. This course towards a German union accentuated the role of war and violence as a unifying factor in the process of nation-building, and added the 'congenital defect' of a lack of democratic legitimacy to the German variant.

The German Empire (1871–1945)

The successful implementation of the 'small German solution' produced an imbalance between the predominantly Prussian North and the South, which had fought, three years before the Empire was founded, against Prussia at the side of Austria. This territorial tension was intensified by the *Kulturkampf* in the 1870s and relaxed only after the separation of the two German states after 1945, and a reorganization of the Federal Republic in federal and party political terms. Moreover, the internal tensions of the German nation-state became aggravated because of the international and geopolitical consequences of its foundation. The existence of the German Empire meant a thorough change of the traditional power balance of the European state order (Calleo 1978). A strong, unified state had emerged in the centre of Europe, challenging the power balance between the great powers at the fringes of Europe. And with the transition from Bismarck to William II, the transition from European *Realpolitik* to German *Weltpolitik* lay at the core of the coming World Wars.

The crucial 'deficiency' of the German national state in comparison with other Western democracies was, without any doubt, its lack of democratization.

---

[3] 'Germany! But where is it?' quoted in Jeismann (1992: 27), according to whom the answer of the time was rooted, at most, in a geographic, but not a political, concept of Germany. If one takes into account the settlement structures of Germans in Mid- and Eastern Europe and the several multinational states with a German majority in the population, and especially the inexact borders, one can, however, conceive of the question as an expression of a political as well as a geographic, i.e. territorial, indistinctness.

Even though there was a constitution in most of the German states since 1848, it was precisely the failure of the assembly of the *Paulskirche* that reinforced the illiberal elements. A number of basic political rights were introduced only in 1867 with the foundation of the Northern German League (*Norddeutscher Bund*), which, at the time, contained the most liberal suffrage in Europe and which, later, would be adopted for elections to the Reichstag as well. However, the continued existence of the Prussian three-class electoral system until 1917, the repressive approach towards civil rights during the *Kulturkampf* and under the socialist laws, as well as the limitation of freedom of expression and the lack of responsibility of the executive towards the electorate, all showed that this made no difference whatsoever to the authoritarian nature of the new regime and the continuing disassociation from the national state and democracy.

In this context of nation building, a concept and self-image of a nation emerged in Germany, which is generally regarded as the prototype of an ethnically defined cultural nation (cf. Minkenberg 1998, ch. 2). As such, it is neither associated with a (national) state, nor an originally democratic legitimation, but relates to the German people as a community (cf. Brubaker 1992: 9f.; Greenfeld 1992: 358-371). This self-assessment, as well as the widespread characterization of the German nation as a 'cultural nation', proves, however, to be problematic (cf. Dann 1995). First of all, Germany can hardly be regarded as a prototype of a nation in which ethnic community, the idea of a nation, and the national state coincide. Moreover, one must take into account that the concept of the 'cultural nation', as Meinecke introduced it with regard to the German development, refers primarily to a shared culture – which, in Meinecke's view, mainly means a shared religion. There is no mention in his writings either of a people or a spirit of the people (cf. Meinecke 1908: 3; Dann 1995: 71).

The nation-building process culminated in the German law issued in 1913, regulating membership in the Empire and the state (Reichs-und Staatsangehörigkeitsgesetz). This law codified the idea of ethnic homogeneity of the German nation, which is inherent to the concept of the community of the people (*Volksgemeinschaft*), and which finally found its expression in a popular – that is, racist – form of politics. This law not only swept away the liberal conception of the nation from 1848, but also replaced the equally liberal Prussian citizenship law of 1842, which had not been based on ethnic criteria, but had taken into account the reality of a state constituted by two peoples (see Brubaker 1992: 63). From now on, there applied a definition of German nationality which was solely based on the right of origin, the *ius sanguinis*. This development, however, had not at all been clearly determined by Herder and the romantic period, but was characterized by open situations. There had been, after all, a numeric majority in the German parliament (Reichstag) consisting of SPD, National Liberals and liberals who advocated a regulation similar to the French citizenship laws. But the authoritarian construction of the Empire prevented it from being put to practice. It was only a small step from this law to the racially based (*völkisch*) definition of the German nation, which provided legitimacy not only for the war against the Western powers from 1914 onwards, but also for the special, partly anti-modernist, course Germany took into modernity. Likewise, close to this law was the criticism of any liberal form of politics, including the rejection of the Weimar Republic (cf. Mommsen 1990: 87-105).

During the course of World War I, the *Reich* had finally become a full parliamentary system. Interestingly enough, this transformation could be achieved without a formal amendment of the text of the constitution, simply by parliamentary procedure (Eschenburg 1963). However, the transformed monarchy (which had, during the course of the war, effectively been replaced by some sort of military dictatorship) could not survive the armistice at the end of a lost war. For a short time, illiberal, extreme German nationalism was retreating, giving way to the constitution of the Weimar Republic which was at that time considered to be the most liberal constitution in the world. In terms of contemporary transition research, the Weimar Republic was even a consolidated democracy (Merkel 1999).

However, it had two structural limitations which would, under the conditions of the world crisis in the late 1920s, lead to the destruction of the Weimar Republic and its replacement by the Nazi dictatorship. The first was the lack of democratic nation-building and the growing (re-) mobilization of a humiliated authoritarian and totalitarian German nationalism. The Peace Accord of Versailles, which blamed sole responsibility for the outbreak of World War I on Germany and forced the German delegation to accept significant cessations of territory, partial occupation of the *Reich*, and high amounts of reparations payments, became the most important focus and source of anti-system propaganda of the radical right (Lepsius 1966; Winkler 2000). The second structural limitation was the still unbroken power position of the old élites in state and society, who did not accept the Weimar Republic as a legitimate form of government and worked for a restoration of a monarchical or dictatorial regime. In this context, the strong constitutional position of the President – originally conceived of by Max Weber as a counterweight against democratic populism – became a gateway for anti-system policies when the aging archconservative General von Hindenburg was elected as head of state in 1925. This is not to say that Hindenburg's victory sealed the fate of the first German republic; quite to the contrary, Hitler's appointment as chancellor seemed to be an inconceivable option until well into January 1933 (Jasper 1986). By this time, however, the only constitutional organ that was left intact as a power base was the presidency, inhabited by an ailing man who had never wanted to become a politician in the first place. Thus the republic had become a hollow construction, a 'power vacuum' (Bracher 1971).

On the eve of the 'German Revolution' (Mosse 1978), Germany seemed to be on the verge of civil war, an image to which the National Socialists had contributed to a considerable degree. National Socialism was a totalitarian-racist movement, but integrated various forms of authoritarian political nationalism, broad sentiments of cultural-missionary nationalism and streams of Protestant and Catholic religious nationalism. On this basis, it excluded and finally annihilated the Jews, discriminated against all other minor races and nationalities and suppressed all independent democratic, liberal, socialist and communist currents that seemed to threaten the unity of the German nation. As a result, the process of German nation-building found an ethnic-national coherence as never before, but at the same time this *völkisch* definition excluded also the German pluralist and democratic elements and thus again split the German political nation (Winkler 2000).

The "Greater Germany" and its hegemony over Europe that Nazism aspired to and finally created in World War II was based on the legacy of the Roman German Empire and the German *Kulturnation*. This was the core legitimacy basis of Nazism for its aggressive foreign policy and warfare in order to create a European racial order. At the same time, on the grounds of its racist totalitarian ideology, Nazism transgressed not only the moral boundaries and territorial borders of the German *Kulturnation*, but also led to the catastrophic destruction of Germany itself. This was also the moral and political starting point of the resistance movement against Hitler. As a consequence, German nationalism in its political and cultural currents collapsed with the German nation as a political and cultural order. But paradoxically, this collapse and traumatization of national identity occurred on the basis of an ethnically and culturally enormously more integrated nation, and as a result of the warfare, the common fate, the extinction of ethnic minorities and the resettlement of the *Reich* Germans inside Germany.

Post-War Divided Germany, 1945-1990

The collapse of Nazi-Germany and the subsequent occupation of Germany by the Allies, the division of Germany in four zones and the expulsion and resettlement of the *Reich* Germans from the East were accompanied by a collapsing German nationalism. This collapse of German nationalism was not only a reflection of the complete military defeat of Nazi Germany, but also of the destruction of the traditional belief in the destiny and superiority of the German nation. Although the war had in the end homogenized the German ethnic settlement space, the missionary belief in the German *Kulturnation* as well as in the restoration of a strong German nation-state were destroyed by Nazism's 'total warfare'. In post-War Germany, therefore, German nationalism existed *politically* in the will of the surviving Weimar democratic spectrum to re-build a new democratic Germany and *culturally* in the wish to be morally re-accepted and re-respected in cooperation and reconciliation with the Allies. After World War II, unlike after World War I, there was no resentful and humiliated nationalism, but rather a broken and traumatized nationalism. However, with the division of Germany into two states, the West German Federal Republic and the Eastern German People's Republic, German nationalism and national identity followed two different paths (Kleßmann 1986; Winkler 2000).

In West Germany, the German nation existed as a political wish and moral obligation for a reunified and democratic nation-state. Not only did the 'reunification imperative' receive a prominent part in the preamble of the West German (provisional) constitution, but it also resonated amongst the West German population, at least until well into the 1970s. The imagined territorial boundaries of this future reunified German nation-state remained for some time oriented to the borders of the German Reich in 1937, but increasingly and by a growing number of West Germans, adjusted to the present Oder-Neisse border and unofficially recognized by the West German *Ostpolitik* of Brandt and Kohl. Nonetheless, the division of Germany, the deepening of the East-West antagonism, the construction of the Berlin Wall, and the diverging development of West and East Germany increasingly weakened the common, pan-German national bond over time, giving way to a genuine 'West German historical consciousness' (Wolfrum 1999). The unified political nation became more and more remote, a distant and utopian aim for the future. Still, the acceptance of two states was more a tribute to the reality of the Cold War rather than a consequence of the development of separate West German nationalism that would have propagated the creation of a West German nation (Kleßmann 1986; Winkler 2000).

The increasing loyalty to the West German constitution (*Verfassungspatriotismus*, or constitutional patriotism) was a result of the widespread experience of the well functioning West German political order supported by its internationally secured peaceful development, its economic dynamism (*Wirtschaftswunder*, or economic miracle) and its welfare system. But this widespread acceptance of a democratic-federal order never stood in contrast or opposition to the German nation. Rather, the German nation in its West German *gestalt* became politically transformed in a civic-territorial nation as a partial reality and a future aim. At the same time, as emphasized here, the formation of a (West) German political-democratic identity was accompanied and influenced by the widening public discourse calling on Germans to come to terms with the past. In essence, this moral public discussion was driven by and resulted in a reconstruction and redefinition of the German *Kulturnation* (either formally denied or acknowledged). The West German survey research has pictured these political and cultural elements of West German national identity formation over the decades very well. The identification with Germany increased over the years, but in comparison with other European nations the positive identification remained relatively low. The indicators for national pride show that West Germans had a low but rising level of national pride and self-esteem. The characteristic descriptive term in the eighties was the troubled or hurt nation (Noelle-Neumann 1984). The question remains, however, whether being German meant, by the 1980s, being West German to the inhabitants of the Federal Republic, thus establishing West Germany as a nation-state in its own right.[4]

In East Germany, the German nation remained the frame of reference for national identity (Schweigler 1972). In ethnic-territorial terms, there is some evidence that though the GDR was forced to recognize the Oder-Neisse border, the imagined boundaries of national territory only slowly adjusted to the new realities. In political terms, the dominant layer identified the German nation with a socialist Germany. Yet the socialist GDR was seen only as a transitional state towards a future pan-German socialist nation. The construction of the wall therefore was depicted not as fostering of the division of Germany, but as a temporal security

---

[4] Arguments in this direction can be found, for example, in Fulbrook (1999) and especially Wolfrum (1999), who can convincingly show that the intra-German systemic competition enhanced the development of two rather distinct political cultures and 'national' identities in the two German states vis-à-vis each other.

measure for socialist Germany on East German soil with a future perspective of a common socialist Germany. Economic success and political stability after the wall had been built contributed to the legitimacy of the GDR system. However, the official image of the GDR was constantly questioned and finally undermined by the alternative model of the West German more prosperous and more liberal nation.

The German *Kulturnation* also went a different course: in East Germany the feeling of moral guilt never developed in the same way as in the West. As a suppressed political current in Nazi Germany, East German communism never saw itself responsible for the Nazi past. Instead, the official picture painted by GDR propaganda let the East German state end up on the side of the 'winners of history' (a figure of thought which was in itself very German rather than dialectical) (Kittsteiner 1994). Rather, it saw itself and not the Jews as the main victims of Nazism, and relegated the Holocaust to a marginal aspect of the past and thus had no problems in participating in Soviet-communist anti-Zionism and anti-Semitism. The best way to come to terms with the past was to build socialism on German soil. From this perspective it was then also unproblematic to include the good legacies of the German political and cultural history into the East German national identity. These included Luther and the Protestant Reformation, Frederick the Great and Prussian enlightened absolutism, Bismarck and the first German nation-state as well as the classical German cultural tradition and its continuation in German socialist humanism. It can therefore be argued with some reason that the GDR had become the 'more German' of the two states by the end of the 1980s (Winkler 2000: vol. 2, 619; Fulbrook 1999: 155). Again, it has to be noted that these dominant cultural elements in East German national identity formation were opposed by subdominant currents (particularly in the East German literature circles and Protestant milieus), but they came to the fore only after German unification (Kaelble and Kocka 1994).

2. German National and European Identities

Two Countries, One Nation? The Construction of National Identities in Divided Germany

The division of Germany into two states, as it developed with the unfolding of the Cold-War between the Western Allies and the Soviets, had first not been accepted on the basis of a common and self-evident German national identity (Westle 1999a, b; Winkler 2000). With the construction of the Berlin Wall in 1961 this pan-German identity became questioned and public and scholarly debates on the relationship between the German nation and the two German states started in the 1960s and 1970s.

The pan-German consensus of a common German nation eroded further in the 1980s when parts of the left and liberal spectrums in West Germany publicly renounced any further attempts at bringing about German unification. In East Germany, too, the Communist leadership started to mobilize the German national heritage for GDR patriotism. By the end of the 1980s, people in the Federal Republic had developed a distinctive notion of a West German identity, even though the Berlin Wall remained a thorn in the side of a sleeping pan-German consciousness. Had the civil rights movement in the GDR not succeeded in peacefully overthrowing the SED regime, West Germans would probably have had no great difficulty with further accommodating to the status quo (Wolfrum 1999). And when the motto of the East German resistance movement changed from 'We are the people' to 'We are one people', this may only partially be related to the still lingering feelings of pan-German national consciousness. It may well have had to do with a more pragmatic notion: namely, that the West German model had proven to be more successful. There is evidence that the calls for unification were motivated more by material needs and wishes that the devastated GDR economy could no longer meet, than by feelings of belonging together and having a common history and ancestry (see Merkel/Liebert 1991). This is underscored by the fact that West Germans became far more reluctant to embrace their newly regained brethren in the East when it became clear that unification would mean sacrifices for both sides of the former iron curtain (Görtemaker 1999: 770-777).

In order to better understand the phenomenon that Jürgen Kocka (1995) has aptly called 'unification crisis' (*Vereinigungskrise*), we need to shed some light on the principal debates (or non-debates) that shaped the development of two rather distinct notions of historical consciousness and national identity in the two German states. At least since the student movement at the end of the 1960s had succeeded in putting it on the public agenda, the burden of the Nazi past was a prominent feature in political debates in the Federal Republic. These debates culminated in the 1980s, beginning with the clumsy management of Ronald Reagan's visit to Germany in April 1985, and continuing with the critically acclaimed speech delivered by president Richard von Weizsäcker on the occasion of the 40th anniversary of the end of World War II (Reichel 1999: 231-254): the latter reached a first climax in the 'historians' debate' over the uniqueness of the Nazi annihilation of the Jews (Historikerstreit 1987; Maier 1988), and went on to quarrels about a speech held by Philipp Jenninger, president of the Bundestag, at the 50th anniversary of the 9 November 1938, nation-wide pogrom (Reichel 1999: 269-279). This culture of discourses about the Nazi past continued somewhat unabated in the 1990s, although some changes in rhetoric and connotation can be made out (the following, see Becker 2001).

On the West German side, two main positions crystallized in the public and scholarly debates until the late 1980s. A left-liberal, social-democratic and green spectrum, articulated first by Dolf Sternberger (1982) and later, and in a much more 'metaphysical' way, by Jürgen Habermas (1990), wanted to ground West German patriotism solely on the loyalty to the West German constitution (*Verfassungspatriotismus*); whereas the opposition conservative-liberal camp articulated by Lübbe (1989) or Nipperdey (1990) emphasized also the salience of German culture and history. Although both camps shared basic democratic value orientations, they denounced each other as nationalists – either 'positive' or 'negative'.

To a lesser extent, German history between 1933 and 1945 also played an important role in the political culture in the GDR, albeit in a less sophisticated form of official anti-fascism (Grunenberg 1991). It is not altogether clear whether the grand narrative which placed the GDR in the position of the highest level of German national development could command as much support as the 'negative' or 'positive' West German identity. However, we follow Mary Fulbrook's (1999: 155) thesis that on the hand, the narrative plots of the official tales, and the vocabulary in which they were phrased, do not in the main appear to have been so perfectly ingested and digested as to be generally reproduced as unquestionable truth; but on the other hand, the underlying moral of these tales, that one had little or nothing to be ashamed of, does appear to have achieved broad popular resonance. Hence, East Germans appear to have felt in the main no need to be 'ashamed to be a German' (even if, at the same time, they did not swell with pride at being 'citizens of the GDR').

One Country, Two Nations? Problems of National Identity after Reunification

With the unification of Germany, there is now a general trend in the public and scholarly debates to reconcile the ethnic-cultural and political civic dimension of the German nation. As a consequence, the major oppositions between the political and cultural constitutions are tuned down, but also complemented by a revitalized nation of the German nation as a solely ethno-cultural community (Westle 1999a, b).

In this context, it is important to note that the unification of Germany finally brought about a basic congruence of nation and state. For the first time in the history of German nation-building and state formation, the ethnic-linguistic settlement space of the German population as well as the cultural self-definition coincided with the political borders of the German state. Due to the resettlement of millions of Germans from the East after World War II and the reflow of ethnic Germans (Aussiedler) from Eastern Europe in the 1980s and 1990s, as well as to the separate national path of the German Austrians, any German irredenta nationalism has ceased to exist. At the same time, the originally missionary German cultural nationalism based on the German *Kulturnation* has been transformed into a moral self-critical attitude towards any renewed misuse of the German nation. And political nationalism has overcome the authoritarian, collectivist and totalitarian attitudes in the direction of a democratic constitutional and more civic, participatory political culture.

However, the unification of Germany has also led to a stronger German national consciousness, growing national pride and a stronger identification with Germany, as well as to a strengthening of right-wing nationalism and increased xenophobia (see Minkenberg 1994, 1998). Although left and liberal intellectuals are still dominating public discourse to great extent, voices calling for a 'healthy' national self-confidence and an end to self-accusation and political self-restraint are finding a wider audience and a positive reputation. This re-nationalization of German national identity has nonetheless been accompanied by the continuation of a self-critical discourse on German national identity (Westle 1999b). In these debates, the old West German principal oppositions between the anti-nationalist and pro-nationalist intellectual camps were still visible. But on the whole, on the basis of a consolidated German nation-state and a more self-assured German identity, the debates became less principled and more pragmatic.

Despite the common pan-German national identity, the division between the two forms of national identity in West and East Germany continued to exist and have crystallized in mutual boundary constructions (see Minkenberg 1993). These two German identities are not two different regional identities, but two forms of national identity based on the different historical legacies and their reconstruction under the different social and political conditions in both parts of Germany. One of the starting points of this division of identities was the unequal form of national unification. Although the majority of the East Germans voted for it, the East German political, economic and cultural systems were all reconstructed according to the West German model (disregarding the need for a reform of this system which had been articulated in West Germany in the 1980s). Attempts at taking the call for a new, all-German constitution (laid out in the West German Basic Law and considered as desirable at the round table talks before the first, and last, free elections to the East German parliament), were soon muted by the pressures of day to day politics (cf. Görtemaker 1999: 773). Hence, a political and cultural expropriation of East Germany took place. In addition, the socio-economic development of Eastern Germany, despite its relative success, has not really been catching up with the West German economy. For East Germany, a dual economy is characteristic. One half of the East German economy and population participates in the growth dynamic of the West German and European economic development; the other half is excluded with stagnating economic growth, high unemployment rates and continuing migration flows from the East to the West. As a consequence, the enormous financial transfers and the corresponding dependence of East on West Germany continue (see Kitschelt/Streeck 2004).

In this context, the two German national identities show interesting differences. According to a study by Bettina Westle (1999a), the following differences can be observed. First, German national pride is conspicuously lower than in other European nations. At the same time, national pride in East Germany is higher than in West Germany. Westle's analysis shows that East German pride was relatively high in 1989/90, decreased considerably through the transformation crisis 1990-1993, but then overtook again the West German level. West German national pride was traditionally low, fell even more after German unification, but then showed a slow movement of self-assurance. Second, the components of East and West German national identity also differ. On the one hand, East Germans show a stronger ethnically based identification with the nation than West Germans do. As often observed, the East Germans are 'more German' than the West Germans (cf. Minkenberg 1993). As Westle demonstrates, the East Germans feel more closely attached to their town and region as well as to the former GDR than the West Germans do to their respective regions and to the former Federal Republic (Westle 1999a: 181-183). At the same time, West Germans identify more with the political-legal system, constitutional law and the social security system, whereas the East Germans are more proud of scientific, cultural and sports achievements (ibid., 185). Finally, the types of nationalism have a different composition. Whereas in West Germany strong and moderate anti-nationalism has more weight, in East Germany strong patriotic and nationalistic positions are more widespread (ibid., 189).

These findings also correspond to the differing attitudes towards foreigners and immigration. Whereas in West Germany a multicultural society in which ethnic minorities are accepted in keeping their distinct traditions can gain more support, in East Germany the emphasis is more on assimilating ethnic minorities into German culture. This corresponds to stronger xenophobic attitudes towards and violent acts against foreigners in East Germany than in West Germany (Minkenberg 2004; Westle 1999a: 189-192).

German Attitudes toward the European Union

In this context, the formation of West German national identity was from the beginning closely connected to Western Europe. The political stabilization of the Federal Republic, the preservation of peace in confrontation with Soviet communism, the economic reconstruction and regained economic prosperity, and the moral re-acceptance by and reconciliation with the West – all this was also closely intertwined with European integration. As in other West European countries, the West German identification with Europe was a gradual process and never replaced the building-up of a new German national identity. At the same time, because of the low national pride and self-esteem, this growing European component had a particular weight in West German identity. This contrasts the West German case to most other West European cases and justifies the statement by Max Haller (1999) that the strong German identification with Europe can be interpreted as a re-compensation for a weak national identity.

However, also here with German unification, a certain and mostly unnoticed re-composition of the relation between the German and European components in national identity has set in (cf. Spohn 1995). As in other West European countries, German national identity (when the nation is measured as one form of identification besides Europe or the region and home town), moves in a parallel with an identification with Europe. However, when measured as an alternative (see Table 2.1), the national components in German identity have become stronger and the European components stagnated or even slightly weakened. In other words, with German unification the stronger German self-esteem has also diminished the compensatory identification with Europe. This view is reinforced by an East-West comparison. In the GDR, Europe could not provide a compensatory function until 1990; but even in 2000, clearly more East than West Germans identify with the nation only, while identification with Europe is weaker in the East than in the West.

**Table 2.1 Change in national and European identification, Germany, 1993-
2000**

(2000: West and East), (per cent identifying with...)

	1993	1994	1995	1996	1997	1998	1999	2000	'00(W)	'00(E)
Nation only	42	31	38	51	49	49	49	40	38	47
Nation/Europe	45	45	46	37	35	38	38	46	47	43
Europe/Nation	9	15	10	7	9	9	8	9	9	8
Europe only	4	9	6	5	7	5	4	5	5	3

Source: Eurobarometers 40 – 54 as in Westle (2003: 464, 478). The all-German figures for
2000 are recalculated based on the separate figures for West and East Germany due to an
inconsistency in Westle (2003).

The Western German identification with Western Europe and European
integration, however, does not cover the whole meaning of Europe in German
national identity. In a divided form, German national identity not only include East
Germany as a part of the German nation, but also implied the relation to Eastern
Europe. In West Germany, underneath a strong anti-communism in political
culture, the same *motif* of peace and reconciliation vis-à-vis the West was also
present vis-à-vis the East. This reconciliation motivation was at the heart of the
new *Ostpolitik* since Willy Brandt, and it lays also at the core of the moral mission
after the collapse of communism to develop a new peace order in Eastern Europe
and to promote the Eastern Enlargement of the European Union. Still in communist
East Germany, the dominant official layer was a strong identification with the
Communist East, but also on the mass level a re-evaluation of German attitudes to
the Eastern neighbors took place. On this backdrop, in present East Germany there
is a special sense to find a European peace order with Eastern Europe in contrast to
a lower identification with the Western European based European Union.

European Elements in German National Identity

A general feature of the public and scholarly debates on German national identity
was, and to a diminishing degree still is, the moral and political emphasis on the
internal predicament of the German nation and only secondarily the issue of the
relationship between the German nation and Europe and other European nations.
To many foreign observers, the German discourse on national identity has been
characterized by soul-searching, moral and political vagueness and suspicion in its
anti-nationalist identification with Europe. The German-British sociologist, Ralf
Dahrendorf, articulated this international concern when he criticized the lack of a
stable political definition of German national interests in relation to Europe
(Dahrendorf 1990). Nevertheless, two main elements in the relationship between
Germany and Europe in West German identity discourse can be distinguished.

On the one hand, there has developed a consensus in the West German
political elite that Germany can morally and politically be renewed only in
integration with the West, Western Europe and particularly France. This was the

basic premise from Adenauer's *Westpolitik* to the foundation of the European Economic Community, the accession to NATO and the policy of deepening European integration by the Brandt/Schmidt and Kohl/Genscher governments. On this basis, the Kohl government also pressured for the deepening of European integration as a counterbalance against German unification. On the other hand, this political elite position was accompanied by a public and scholarly discourse that emphasized the moral renewal of Germany in reconciliation with its European neighbors on the basis of a European culture. This German moral and cultural Europeanness continued the cosmopolitan elements of German classical cultural nationalism, but this time without any claim of German cultural superiority, and rather in a fusion between German and European culture. Indeed, until German unification, the crystallizing German political and cultural orientations to Europe imagined an identity of Germanness and Europeanness. Only in unified Germany, this fusion is differentiating into its German and European elements in a clearer definition of a distinct German national position within and vis-à-vis Europe (Jarausch 1997).

Conclusion

It has been shown that the German case of nation-building combines different trajectories, most notably a 'Western model' (state-building before nation-building and civic identities) and an 'Eastern model' (late nation-building and ethno-cultural identities). The resulting tensions between civic and ethnic identities survived various regime changes and were carried over into divided Germany after World War II. After unification in 1990, German national identity is not only internally divided into West German and East German identities, but also externally in its European components. Regarding the weight of Europe in relation to the nation, the region and the home town, Western German national identity is more European and less ethnic than the East German counterpart. But this relates to the dimension of European integration or a European integrating identity in German national identity. At the same time, the support for the Eastern enlargement of the European Union is until to date slightly higher in East Germany than in West Germany. This difference reflects an expression of the higher attachment of East Germans to a peace order with Eastern Europe in terms of a European civilizational identity and less of an attachment to the European Union; the West Germans tend to identify more with the Western European based European Union and fear more the implications of the Eastern enlargements for Germany. It remains to be seen whether or not the progressing social and political unification of Germany will continue or even out the East-West differences in the German identity web of European and national entanglements.

References

Becker, Daniel (2001), *Verhandlungen mit der Vergangenheit: Der Holocaust in der deutschen politischen Kultur*, 1989-1999, Masters Thesis, European University Viadrina Frankfurt (Oder).

Blänkner, R. (1998), 'Verfassung als symbolische Ordnung: Zur politischen Kultur des Konstitutionalismus in Deutschland 1790-1840', in François (ed.).

Bracher, Klaus D. (1971), *Die Auflösung der Weimarer Republik: Eine Studie zum Problem des Machtverfalls in der Demokratie*, Düsseldorf: Droste.

Brandt, Harm-Hinrich (1987), 'The Revolution of 1848 and the Problem of Central European Nationalities', in Schulze (ed.), pp. 107-134.

Brubaker, Rogers (1992), *Citizenship and Nationhood in France and Germany*, Cambridge, MA: Harvard University Press.

Calleo, David (1978), *The German Problem Reconsidered: Germany and the World Order, 1870 to the Present*, Cambridge: Cambridge University Press.

Dahrendorf, Ralf (1990), 'Die Sache mit der Nation', *Merkur* 44(10/11), pp. 823-834.

Dann, Otto (1996), *Nation und Nationalismus in Deutschland, 1770-1990*, Munich: Beck.

Elias, Norbert (1969), *Über den Prozeß der Zivilisation*, Frankfurt/Main: Suhrkamp.

Eschenburg, Theodor (1963), *Die improvisierte Demokratie: Gesammelte Aufsätze zur Weimarer Republik*, München: Piper.

Etienne François (ed.) (1998), *Marianne – Germania: Deutsch-französischer Kulturtransfer im europäischen Kontext / Les transfers culturels France-Allemagne et leur contexte européen 1789-1914*, Vol. 1, Leipzig: Leiziger Universitätsverlag.

Fulbrook, Mary (1999), *German National Identity after the Holocaust*, Cambridge: Polity Press.

Giesen, B. (1993), *Die Intellektuellen und die Nation: Eine deutsche Achsenzeit*, Frankfurt/Main: Suhrkamp.

Görtemaker, Manfred (1999), *Geschichte der Bundesrepublik Deutschland: Von der Gründung bis zur Gegenwart*, Munich: C.H. Beck.

Greenfeld, Liah (1992), *Nationalism: Five Roads to Modernity*, Cambridge, MA: Harvard University Press.

Grunenberg, Antonia (1991), *Antifaschismus – ein deutscher Mythos*, Reinbek: Rowohlt.

Habermas, J. (1990), *Die nachholende Revolution*, Frankfurt/M.: Suhrkamp.

Haller, Max (1999), 'Voiceless Submission or Deliberate Choice: European Integration and the Relation between National and European Identity', in Kriesi et al. (eds), pp. 263-296.

Hanson, Steve and Spohn, Willfried (eds), *Can Europe Work? Germany and the Reconstruction of Postcommunist Societies*, Seattle, WA: Washington University Press.

Historikerstreit (1987), *Die Dokumentation der Kontroverse um die Einzigartigkeit der nationalsozialistischen Judenvernichtung*, Munich: Piper.

Jarausch, Konrad (ed.) (1997), *After Unity: Reconfiguring German Identities*, Providence, RI: Berghahn Books.

Jasper, G. (1986), *Die gescheiterte Zähmung: Wege zur Machtergreifung Hitlers 1930-1934*, Frankfurt/Main: Suhrkamp.

Kaelble, Hartmut and Jürgen Kocka (eds) (1994), *Sozialgeschichte der DDR*, Göttingen: Vandenhoeck & Ruprecht.

Kershaw, Ian (1999), *Hitler, 2 vols.*, Stuttgart: Deutsche Verlagsanstalt.

Kitschelt, Herbert and Wolfgang Streeck (eds) (2004), *Germany: Beyond the Stable State*, London: Frank Cass.

Kittsteiner, Heinz-Dieter (1994), 'Die in sich gebrochene Heroisierung: Ein geschichtstheoretischer Versuch zum Menschenbild in der Kunst der DDR', *Historische Anthropologie*, 2, pp. 442-461.

Kleßmann, Christoph (1986), *Die doppelte Staatsgründung: Deutsche Geschichte 1945-1955*, Göttingen: Vandenhoeck & Ruprecht.

Kocka, Jürgen (1995), *Vereinigungskrise: Zur Geschichte der Gegenwart*, Göttingen.

Kriesi, Hanspeter, et al. (eds) (1999), *Nation and National Identity: The European Experience in Perspective*, Zürich: Verlag Rüegger.

Lepsius, Rainer M. (1966), *Extremer Nationalismus: Strukturbedingungen vor der National-Sozialistischen Machtergreifung*, Stuttgart: Klett.

Lübbe, Herrmann (1989), 'Patriotismus, Verfassung und verdrängte Geschichte', *Die neue Gesellschaft/Frankfurter Hefte*, 36(5), pp. 408-415.

Maier, Charles (1988), *The Unmasterable Past*, Cambridge: Cambridge University Press.

Merkel, Wolfgang (1999), *Systemtransformation*, Opladen: Leske + Budrich.

Merkel, Wolfgang and Liebert, Ulrike, (eds) *Die Politik der deutschen Einheit*, Opladen: Leske + Budrich.

Meinecke, Friedrich (1908), *Weltbürgertum und Nationalstaat*, Berlin: R. Oldenbourg.

Minkenberg, Michael (1993), 'The Wall after the Wall: On the Continuing Division of Germany and the Remaking of Political Culture', in *Comparative Politics*, 26(1), pp. 53-68.

Minkenberg, Michael (1994), 'German Unification and the Continuity of Discontinuities: Cultural Change and the Far Right in East and West', *German Politics*, 3(2), pp. 169-192.

Minkenberg, Michael (1998), *Die neue radikale Rechte im Vergleich: USA, Frankreich, Deutschland*, Opladen: Westdeutscher Verlag.

Minkenberg, Michael (2004), 'The Politics of Citizenship in the New Republic', in Kitschelt and Streeck (eds), pp. 219-240.

Mommsen, Wolfgang (1990), *Der autoritäre Nationalstaat*, Reinbek: Rowohlt.

Mosse, George (1978), *The Crisis of German Ideology: Intellectual Origins of the Third Reich*, New York: Fertig.

Nipperdey, Thomas (1990), 'Die Deutschen wollen und dürfen eine Nation sein', *Frankfurter Allgemeine Zeitung*, 160, p. 10.

Nipperdey, Thomas (1991), *Deutsche Geschichte 1866-1918: Machtstaat vor der Demokratie*, Munich: Beck.

Noelle-Neumann, Elisabeth and Renate Köcher (1984), *Die verletzte Nation*, Stuttgart: Deutsche Verlagsanstalt.

Schieder, Theodor (1992), *Nationalismus und Nationalstaat*, Göttingen: Vandenhoeck & Ruprecht.

Schulze, Hagen, (ed.) (1987), *Nation Building in Central Europe*, New York: Berg.

Schweigler, Gerhard (1972), *Nationalbewußtsein in der BRD und der DDR*, Düsseldorf: Bertelsmann Universitätsverlag.

Spohn, Willfried (1995), 'United Germany as the Renewed Center in Europe: Continuity and Change in the German Question', in Hanson and Spohn (eds), pp. 79-128.

Sternberger, Dolf (1982), *Verfassungspatriotismus*, Bonn: Insel.

Wehler, Hans-Ulrich (1995), *Deutsche Gesellschaftsgeschichte 1849-1914*, Munich: Beck.

Westle, Bettina et al. (eds), pp. 175-198.

Westle, Bettina (1999b), *Kollektive Identität im vereinten Deutschland: Nation und Demokratie in der Wahrnehmung der Deutschen*, Opladen: Leske & Budrich.

Westle, Bettina (2003), 'Europäische Identifikation im Spannungsfeld regionaler und nationaler Identitäten', in: *Politische Vierteljahresschrift*, 44(4), pp. 453-482.

Winkler, Hans August (*2000*), *Der lange Weg nach Westen: Deutsche Geschichte*, 2 vols. Munich: Beck.

Wolfrum, E. (1999), *Geschichtspolitik in der Bundesrepublik Deutschland: Der Weg zur bundesrepublikanischen Erinnerung 1948-1990*, Darmstadt: Wissenschaftliche Buchgesellschaft.

Chapter 3

Austria: From Habsburg Empire to a Small Nation in Europe

Willfried Spohn

Introduction

In the present, Austria in its relation to Germany is an autonomous and self-conscious nation. Accordingly, the predominant propensity in the social, political and to some extent also historical sciences has been to project the Austrian nation as a primordial entity into the past (e.g. Bluhm 1973, Katzenstein 1976). This projection, however, presents an objectivist fallacy (Bruckmüller 1996). In early modern Europe, Austria had ascended to the double political center of the German Roman Empire as well as the Habsburg Empire and, despite the expansion and relocation of the Habsburg Empire to the East, remained so until the dissolution of the German Roman Empire under the impact of the French Revolution and the Napoleonic European wars. Under those circumstances, the emerging modern nationalism in Austria since the early 19th century oscillated between an Empire-oriented, regional Austrian as well as pan-German nationalism. In the 1848 revolution, the German Austrians, though with tensions, were an integral part of the pan-German Frankfurt Parliament. After the defeat of the Habsburg army against Prussia in 1866, the ground was prepared for the unification of Germany under Prussian hegemony and the closer unity between Austria and Hungary as the double centre of the Habsburg Empire. At the same time, the growing German-Austrian nationalism developed still in the triadic form of an Empire-preserving, regional Austrian as well as pan-German nationalism. When after World War I the Habsburg Empire collapsed, the First Austrian Republic defined itself as an Austrian nation, but at the same time as an integral part of the German Reich (though hindered by the victorious Allies to join it). And when the Nazi Third Reich annexed Austria in 1938, about two thirds of the Austrian population saw this as a fulfillment of national aspirations. Only with the experience of Nazi totalitarian dictatorship and its collapse in World War II was the ground prepared for a separate formation of an Austrian nation and national identity.

On this historical background, I propose to view the post-War II development of an Austrian national identity as an Empire-contracting nationalism, separating from its double imperial legacy of the Habsburg as well as the German empire. In the following, I will analyze in three steps the transformation of the Habsburg imperial identity to an Austrian national identity and its relation to

Europe. Firstly, I will present an historical-sociological outline of Austrian Empire-contracting nation-building and national identity formation until 1945. Secondly, I will analyze the construction of Austrian national identity after 1945/55 and its reconstruction after the end of the Cold-War system. Thirdly, I will interpret the related changes of Austrian collective identity in its interconnections to Europe and the European integration process.

1. A Historical-Sociological Outline of Austrian Nation-Building and National Identity, *c.* 1500-1945

Following Anthony Smith's historical-sociological approach to nation-building and national identity, it is crucial to view modern nation-building as a historical continuation of the preceding process of ethno-genesis interwoven with modern state formation (Smith 1992). This historical-sociological approach contrasts with primordialist positions assuming modern nations as an unfolding of a pre-given ethnic basis as well as with modernist positions conceptualizing modern nations as a by-product of modern state formation. Within this framework, Anthony Smith proposes an ideal-typical distinction between the Western civic-territorial, vertical route and the Eastern ethnic-demotic, lateral trajectory of nation-building. With others (Brubaker 1998, Greenfeld 1998), however, I consider this ideal-typical distinction conceptually and historically far too dichotomous and therefore propose two corrections. Regarding the process of ethno-genesis, on the one hand, I assume following Conze (1992) that it includes also, in Eastern Europe, political forms of aristocratic incorporation. Regarding the process of state formation, on the other hand, I propose to distinguish, instead of two, four main zones of state formation: the Western European Atlantic zone, the Central European imperial city-belt zone, the East Central European peripheral and the East Eastern European imperial zone. In this comparative framework, the Austrian like the German case of nation-building belongs to the second zone, combining a polycentric form of ethno-genesis and an overarching high culture within a fragmenting imperial roof.

Within the context of the polycentric ethno-genesis of the German-speaking regions and the overarching political framework of the German Roman Empire, the Austrian lands – first upper and lower Austria, then including Styria and Carinthia and later Salzburg (the province of Burgenland only became part of Austria in 1921) – had been characterized since the early middle ages by several specific features. In territorial terms, the Austrian lands originated from an expansion of German settlement to the South and East, which formed a border region first in competition with Slavic and Hungarian kingdoms and later also with the Ottoman Empire and the Islamic civilization. In ethnic composition, the Austrian lands combined eastward migrating German people, Alemanni and Bavarians (developed during the fifth and sixth century out of various Germanic tribes and the local Roman/romanized population), and westward migrating Slavic and Hungarian people. In this sense, the Austrians did not form one ethnic group like the Saxons or Swabians, but an ethnic conglomerate held together by a common political estate order from the middle ages to the modern period.

(Bruckmüller 1996: 155-199; Grothusen 1974; Kann 1993:17-30; Zöllner 1990: 39-110).

Also within the overarching framework of the German Roman Empire, the Austrian lands had a special position. The Habsburg dynasty, regionally concentrated around the Austrian territories, became since the high middle ages (first temporarily and then constantly) the emperor of the Holy Roman Empire of the German Nation. In the modern period, in addition, the Habsburg dynasty expanded its sphere of domination both to Western and East Central Europe, creating in the early modern period a world empire. In this three-tiered function of a regional, German imperial and world imperial power, the Habsburg Empire only partially contributed to Austrian state formation. Although with the decline as a world power, the Habsburg Empire consolidated more its Austrian imperial core with an East Central European multinational focus, it never became an absolutist state as a proto-modern nation-state like France, Prussia or the German territorial absolutisms. Austrian state formation was thus, until the dissolution of the German Roman Empire in 1806, a mixture between a regional state administration plus estate order and an imperial state holding together a multi-national empire (Kann 1993; Zoellner 1990). Moreover, regarding its position within the German-Roman Empire, the more the Habsburg dynasty consolidated its East Central European empire, the more it lost its core position within the German regions.

Two major geopolitical and socio-cultural developments in the modern era contributed to this Easternization of the Habsburg Empire. First, the rise of the Atlantic economy through France and Great Britain weakened the Habsburg-led Spanish colonial empire and, in addition, early modern state formation in Western Europe happened often in opposition to the Habsburg sphere of influence. At the same time, the Western expansion of the Ottoman Empire forced the Habsburg dynasty to concentrate on the Eastern frontier and contributed to the consolidation of the East-Central European based Habsburg Empire. Second, the Protestant Reformation contributed substantially to weakening the Habsburg imperial center within the German-Roman Empire. The Protestant North German state as well as the Protestant-Catholic South and Western German absolutist states increased their independence from the imperial roof and thus at the cost of the Habsburg imperial center. And in addition, the Protestant Reformation and the Habsburg-led Catholic (Counter-)Reformation divided the German-speaking lands not only between predominantly Protestant and Catholic regions but also between an imperial Catholic Habsburg-oriented part and a proto-nation-state Protestant and Prussian-oriented part (Kann 1993; Heer 1981).

Modern nationalism in German Austria, as in the whole of Germany, emerged in orientation and reaction to the French Revolution, the Napoleonic wars in continental Europe, the dissolution of the Holy Roman Empire, and the modernizing reforms of the German absolutist states. Unlike the case of German nationalism identifying with the strongest and most modern neo-absolutist German state, Protestant Prussia, however, Austrian nationalism emerged as a mixture between Austrian and Great German components (Heer 1981; Langewiesche 1999; Sheehan 1987). On the one hand, the Austrian components consisted of imperial as well as regional layers. The imperial layer, shaped in the previous Theresian and

Josephine reform era, was strengthened through the separation and restoration of the Habsburg Empire under Metternich. German Austrian aristocrats and middle class intellectuals such as Count Johann von Hormayr or Foreign Minister Count Philipp Stadion propagated an Austrian political nation, an Austrian cultural nation, as well as an Austrian European nation. At the same time, a strong resistance movement against Napoleon in Tyrol under the leadership of Andreas Hofer articulated also an Austrian regional popular identity (Heer 1981). But characteristically, both aristocratic and popular layers did not connect with each other in a shared Austrian nationalism.

On the other hand, a Great German nationalism also emerged under the impact of the French revolution and the Napoleonic wars. This Austrian-German nationalism shared with German-German nationalism the democratic-anti-dynastical national orientation emulating the French model of a modern democratic nation-state. At the same time, it had in common a German cultural nationalism based on German high culture that had developed since the second half of the eighteenth century in opposition to the Habsburg aristocratic court culture (Heer 1981; Sheehan 1987). Goethe, Schiller, Lessing, Kant and Herder, often against the direction of their cosmopolitan-European thinking, became icons also in German Austria. Moreover, a Protestant-Evangelical anti-Catholic sub-current, an open or secret identification with Protestant Prussia seen as a more tolerant, democratic and modern German nation-state, played an important role in the emerging pro-German attitudes. Further, a romantic, even chiliastic orientation towards Germany and Prussia emerged. It played a particular role in the German and German-Austrian youth and student movements evolving in the first half of the 19th century (Heer 1981).

Both layers, the Austrian and the German ones, were present in the formation of German-Austrian national identity in the Metternich era. The aristocratic elite of the Habsburg Empire, as particularly Count Metternich himself, continued to be oriented to the multi-national imperial identity of Austria. However, due to the anti-democratic and restorative features of the Habsburg political system, the emerging educated middle classes defected increasingly from an identification with the multi-national empire and became instead oriented to German liberal-democratic and cultural nationalism (Heer 1981; Sheehan 1987). In the *Vormärz*, the liberalizing period before the 1848 revolution, both intellectual currents became more articulated. Austrian writers like Ignaz Kuranda praised Habsburg Austria and the Austrian nation, whereas German-Austrian poets like Alfred Meissner or Moritz Hartmann made a plea for the unification with Germany. In the 1848 revolution which was breaking out also in Vienna and other German-Austrian and Habsburg cities, a Great-German nationalism became more pronounced. The German liberal and social democratic movement demanded 'a democratic monarchy, popular sovereignty and closest connection with Germany, even at the price of giving up Austrian independence' (Heer 1981: 199). In the Frankfurt Parliament, the Austrian democratic delegates were divided between Austrian-Habsburg and Great-German positions. At the same time, the German delegates were in a majority and started in their predominantly pro-Prussian orientation to exclude the German Austrians. As a result, the constitutional crown was offered to the Prussian king who however declined the honor. But despite Austria's exclusion, also after the defeat of the 1848 revolution, the pro-German orientations remained strong – not least because of the authoritarian, non-constitutional and pro-Catholic policies in the following restoration era under Count Schwarzenberg and Emperor Franz Joseph (Heer 1981; Sheehan 1987). At the same time, the larger part of the German-speaking middle classes displayed an interest in the continuation of the Empire, since they either held a prominent position in the imperial army and bureaucracy or depended as entrepreneurs on the access to the imperial markets. Thus, larger parts of the middle classes backed the counter-revolution as soon as the continuity of the Empire was put into question, and they aligned themselves with the neo-absolutist regime course after 1849 (Bruckmüller 1996).

The decline and final dissolution of the Habsburg Empire was basically caused by the rise of Central European nationalism (Barkey and von Hagen 1997; Good and Rudolph 1992; Gumplowicz 1909; Kann 1993). The first important step in this direction was the unification of Italy that led to the loss of Habsburg's Northern Italian provinces in 1859/60. The second major blow was the defeat of the Habsburg army against Prussia in 1866 that ended Habsburg Austria's imperial influence in Germany. As a consequence, the Habsburg Empire turned more eastward and was restructured as a dual monarchy in which Austria shared the imperial power with Hungary. But this dual imperial structure only accelerated the nationalistic claims of the many other small nations within the Habsburg Empire. The nationalist movements in the Czech, Slovak, Polish and Romanian lands were growing against Habsburg's imperial structure and at the same time the national wars of independence in the Balkan countries led Habsburg to extend its imperial power further to the South East (Kann 1964). Against this internal erosion, there were only few reformers in the Habsburg political elite structure who envisioned a transformation of the imperial structure into a more decentralized and democratic federation of nations which could have potentially contained a nationalistic break-up of the empire (Bauer 1924). Instead, the imperial elite under Emperor Franz Joseph tried to suppress the nationalistic and democratic claims and thus prepared the final collapse of the Habsburg Empire after the military defeat in World War I (Heer 1981).

In the Josephine pre-War era, the predominant layer of an Austrian identity was characteristically still more connected to the preservation of the Habsburg Empire and less oriented to an Empire-contracting Austrian nationalism confined to the German-Austrian lands alone. As compared to the growth of other peripheral nationalisms in the Habsburg Empire, a specific Austrian patriotism or nationalism had been the weakest of all. If it existed, then it was primarily in the form of a Great German-Austrian identity that was identical with the multinational Empire and carried by the imperial aristocracy, the imperial state administration, the army and the empire-oriented bourgeoisie, which benefited from the state institutions and economic opportunities the Empire offered. Underneath this imperial identity, two other layers of an Austrian identity, more latent than manifest, can be seen. On the one hand, there emerged a more regional Austrian identity which became articulated in form of the Catholic Social Party as one of the

Austrian-based political parties in the imperial party system. On the other hand, a Great-German nationalism continued and even strengthened after the defeat of Habsburgs against Prussia in 1866 (Heer 1981). This is a paradox, considering the foundation of the Bismarckian German Empire without Austria and the growing power of Imperial Germany vis-à-vis a declining Habsburg. However, it was precisely the stronger, more modern, economically more developed, politically more democratic, Protestant, anti-Catholic and secular Prussian Germany that became increasingly more attractive and a basis of identification for rising German nationalism in German Austria.

There were several reasons for this growing German nationalism in German Austria. First, the educated middle classes continued to share a German cultural nationalism, the belief in German language and culture as the basis of a unified German nation. For example, the academic elite at German-Austrian universities, often from Germany, were mostly oriented to German science and culture; most student associations were strongly German nationalistic; and also the emerging cultural associations and sports clubs connected first to liberalism and then to socialism were oriented to the parallel movement culture in Germany (Heer 1981; Langewiesche 1999). Second, the emerging political parties were also in their majority oriented to the German model. This was true for the left-wing democratic political specter, first the Liberal Party and later the Social-Democratic Party. This was also characteristic of the emerging right-wing specter, first the German National Party and then also the radical all-German and anti-Semitic movement (Heer 1981). Third, the background for the pro-German orientation of the majority of political parties was the basically authoritarian and ultramontane character of the Habsburg regime as well as the rise of nationalism in the non-German nations of the Habsburg Empire (Kann 1964; Lemberg 1950). For the various German nationalist currents, the Habsburg regime represented a backward, anti-democratic and anti-national regime, whereas Germany embodied a modern, democratic as well as national order.

The growing strength of this Great-German nationalism on the left as well as the right of the political spectrum came to the fore after the military defeat of Imperial Germany and the Habsburg Empire in World War I, and its dissolution by the formation of independent nation-states. The First Austrian Republic, founded on 30 October 1918, was officially named German-Austria, and the national assembly at its first gathering on 12 November voted unanimously for a state law that declared German Austria as an integral part of the German Republic. The Germans did the same in Bohemia and Moravia. Referenda in Tyrol and Salzburg voted with 99 per cent for the unification with Germany. An attempt at unification with Switzerland was made by Austria's most western province Vorarlberg. But the Allies did not permit the voluntary *Anschluß*; they forbade in the St. Germain Peace Treaty in 1919 the use of the name of German Austria; and they prohibited further public referenda. Under those circumstances, it became unrealistic to insist officially on unification with the German Reich. Underneath official politics, however, German nationalism began to radicalize. German Austrian Social-Democracy continued to aim at a Great-German democratic republic. The German Nationals and later the Austrian National Socialists continuously propagated the unification of Austria with the German Reich. Only the Christian Social Party, which came to power in 1922, accepted the international conditions and became the center of an emerging Austrian-Catholic nationalism. With the increasing polarization between left and right wing parties, it established an Austro-fascist dictatorship in 1934, yet was unable to prevent the annexation of Austria by Nazi Germany (Erdmann 1988; Heer 1981).

The basic reason for the predominance of a German nationalism in the First Austrian Republic was the unbroken belief in German language and culture as the basis for a Great-German nation-state on the left as well as on the right. The Social Democrats as inheritors of liberal-democratic nationalism presented the left wing version of this Great German cultural nationalism. For the Austrian Social Democratic leaders such as Victor Adler, Otto Bauer, Karl Renner, Friedrich Austerlitz or Julius Braunthal, Germany represented the country of humanism, culture, education and the progress of humanity. The belief in it explains the first positive evaluation of Hitler's annexation of Austria by the Social-Democratic leadership. In the right-wing versions of this German cultural nationalism, as in the German Nationals and the National Socialists, the democratic-liberal elements were replaced by authoritarian and totalitarian political components, but on the same basis of a belief in the superiority of the German people, including the German Austrians. In its radical versions, as in the German-Austrian Hitler himself, German cultural nationalism became transformed in a chiliastic belief in the Holy German Reich (Heer 1981).

In contrast to these varieties of German nationalism, the Austrian nationalism of the Christian Social Party and its social and political carriers was rather weak and developed more firmly only during the course of the First Austrian Republic. It articulated, in particular, mentalities of the countryside and the mountains against the city, and regional and local identities as well as a Catholic culture. The transition to the authoritarian Dollfuß/Schuschnigg regime was thus only motivated not by the struggle against left and right wing radicalism, but also by the insistence on an independent Austrian-German nation vis-à-vis the German Reich. But characteristically even this Austrian nationalism in its Social-Catholic leadership remained ambivalent between a separate Austrian and a pan-German orientation. Thus, the 'German way' of the Dollfuß/Schuschnigg regime was by no means prepared to defend Austrian sovereignty against Hitler's annexation policy. In a still independent survey in early 1938, about 60 per cent of the Austrian population supported a German *Anschluß*, and in the referendum following the *fait accompli* of the annexation and prepared with huge propaganda efforts 99 per cent voted for it (Heer 1981). It took the experience of Nazi dictatorship, the repression of all political opponents, the political reorganization and disempowerment of Austria and, not least, the catastrophic warfare, to finally undermine the predominant Great-German orientations and identifications and to thus prepare the way for a separate Austrian identity.

2. The Constitution of a Separate Austrian Nation and National Identity (1945-2000)

The separation of Austrian national identity from its German legacies and components developed in the framework of the imposed occupation order by the victorious Allies. To begin with, Austria was restored to the borders of 1937 and divided in four occupations zones with a special status for Vienna. A provisional government composed of the Socialist, the People's (former Christian Social) and the Communist parties and again with Karl Renner as chancellor, was formed, and after the first elections in 1946, was followed by a grand coalition of ÖVP and SPÖ with Leopold Figl (ÖVP) as chancellor and Karl Renner (SPÖ) as president. In 1955 Austria regained full national independence and sovereignty with the foundation of the Second Republic of Austria on the basis of the State Treaty with the Allies. The Treaty restored Austria to the borders of January 1938, prohibited the unification with Germany, and prescribed a perennial neutrality of the Austrian foreign policy. The political system was characterized by a continuation of grand coalition governments until 1966, then followed by changing ÖVP and SPÖ governments. The power in the country was thus divided between the two political camps, fostering a corporative power sharing between them (*Proporzsystem*). With the formation of an independent, democratic and economically stable Austrian state, there gradually developed also an independent and separate Austrian national identity. The traditional antagonisms between a Great-German and an Austrian nationalism were finally overcome by an integrating Austrian identity (Bluhm 1973).

The integrating formation of an Austrian identity must be understood as a process rather than as an immediate outcome of World War II and the collapse of the Nazi German Reich. Regarding the political party spectrum, the newly found Austrian People's Party (ÖVP), as the follower of the Christian Social Party, most forcefully supported an independent non-German course. Also the Communist Party (KPÖ), following the directives of Stalin (but gaining only 4 per cent in the 1946 elections) propagated an independent Austrian nation-state. The Social Democrats (SPÖ) with their leader Karl Renner still adhered for a while to a pan-German republican ideal, but soon gave it up under the new realities of an independent Austria and a partitioned Germany. Only the Freedom Party (FPÖ), representing particularly Protestant voters, continued with a diminishing influence the German national tradition. Regarding the policy of the emerging Austrian state, the conscious aim was, in contrast to the First Republic, to build an Austrian nation and to form and deepen an Austrian identity. There were continuous efforts to institutionalize national symbols, to nationalize the universities, to re-write school books and to develop a public discourse on Austrian history and heritage. This did not happen without continuous conflicts, as the public scandals and historical debates demonstrated, but at the same time these efforts were an integral part of a growing Austrian national identity (Bruckmüller 1996).

As in the German case, a crucial role in the construction of an Austrian national identity was played by coming to terms with the past. Supported by the perception and policy of the Allies, Austria was seen and saw itself as a small nation which had become victimized by the forced annexation through Nazi-Germany (Bruckmüller 1996; Wodak 1999). The de-nazification policy of the Allies helped to support this perception, and for the majority of Austrians the de-coupling from their former Great-German identification was accompanied by the construction of this self-perception. As a consequence, the predominant form of coming to terms with the past consisted of the suppression of, rather than a moral confrontation, with the past. This attitude of suppression was originally also prominent in the West German case, but here the moral confrontation with the past was much more difficult to avoid, and the cultural dynamics of this moral confrontation unfolded in the reconstruction of German national identity. Thus, the negation of the active role of Austrians in the Third Reich remained a predominant feature of Austrian national identity in the Second Republic.

The separation of an Austrian national identity from the Great-German heritage included also a separation from the cultural legacies and moral components of the German *Kulturnation.* The Austrians defined themselves, due to the ambiguities of the national meaning of the German cultural legacy, primarily as a *Staatsnation* and, at the same time, substituted gradually the German *Kulturnation* with an Austrian *Kulturnation.* This substitution included a purification of the German and Habsburg imperial components, the re-definition in a small-Austrian sense, and the transformation of regional and local traditions to national cultural salience. But the former German *Kulturnation* remained a layer of Austrian national identity either in its ethnic-*völkish* or in its cultural enlightenment components.

An emphasized social basis for the constitution of a separate Austrian national identity facilitated the successful development of the Austrian economy and welfare state. Traditionally, the Austrian and particularly Viennese economy profited from the Habsburg imperial center, but as compared to the economic dynamics of Imperial Germany, the Austrian economy remained rather backward. After the collapse of the Austrian Empire, the First Austrian Republic was shaped by a continuation of this economic backwardness and was, in addition, afflicted by the economic depression in the inter-War period. Against this historical background, the economic development in the Second Austrian Republic was characterized by economic modernization and continuing growth, and growing welfare and social security. All this contributed to not only the political stability of the Austrian state, but also the growing identification with the Austrian nation.

The gradual crystallization of a separate Austrian national identity, despite its internal ambiguities, can be indicated by the continuous surveys undertaken since 1955 in order to monitor its successful development. So in 1956, in response to the question: 'Do you think that we are a group of the German *volk* or are we a separate Austrian *volk*?', only 49 per cent answered that they belong to a separate Austrian *volk*, whereas still 46 per cent responded to be part of the German *volk*. The percentage of those who identified with Austria as a nation then continuously increased and finally stabilized at a level of 80 per cent (Bruckmüller 1996: 61).

Table 3.1 Austrian national consciousness 1964-1993 (%)

	1964	1970	1977	1980	1987	1989	1990	1992	1993
A is a nation	47	66	62	67	75	79	74	78	80
A starts to feel as one	23	16	16	19	16	15	20	15	12
A is not a nation	15	8	11	11	5	4	5	5	5
No answer	14	10	12	3	3	3	1	2	2

Source: Brückmüller (1996: 65).

On the foundations of an integrated Austrian nation, the collapse of the Soviet communist empire and the accompanying geo-political sea-change in Europe have affected Austrian national identity in several ways. First, there has been a further consolidation of an Austrian political national identity with diminishing tensions between the Austrian and German cultural components. Second, a contributing factor to the consolidation of Austrian national identity has been the growing political and cultural pluralization of the Austrian nation. Thirdly, of importance here has been the rising impact of immigration and (im)migrant ethnic minorities and, as a reaction, the transformation of the traditionally Great-German oriented right-wing nationalism into an Austrian neo-nationalism.

The development of Austrian national identity in the decade after 1990 has been characterized by a further consolidation. By taking the above indicator of Austrian national consciousness from 1990 to 1995, it can be observed that those who think that Austria is a nation grew from 74 per cent in 1990 to 78 per cent in 1992, 80 per cent in 1993 and 85 per cent in 1995; whereas those who think that Austria is not a nation in the same period first increased from 5 per cent in 1990 to 9 per cent in 1992, but then fell again to 5 per cent in 1993 and 4 per cent in 1995 (Haller 1996: 67). Although it is interesting to note that the transition period in 1989/1990 marked a certain crisis in Austrian national identification, the long-term trend of a further consolidation of an Austrian national identity is obvious. According to another survey in 1995, 51 per cent feel very strongly attached to Austria, 31 per cent strongly, and 6 per cent only weakly, whereas 9 per cent feel attached to German nationality and 3 per cent to other nationalities (Haller 1996: 66).

This consolidation of an Austrian national identity corresponds to a further increase in the high degree of Austrian national pride, seen in an international comparative perspective. According to a survey in 1989, 53 per cent of the Austrian population were 'very proud' and 'proud' as compared to the United States with 87 per cent, Great Britain with 58 per cent, France with 42 per cent, Switzerland with 31 per cent and Germany with 21 per cent (Plasser and Ulram 1993: 40). In 1995, the percentage of those being 'very proud' and 'proud' of Austria had even risen to 67 per cent, whereas only 20 per cent were little or not at all proud of Austria. In a study of 17 to 19 year-old Austrians, those 'very proud' and 'proud' of Austria in 1995 were even 87 per cent, in contrast to those not very proud and not proud at all (Langer 1998: 163). Regarding the dimensions of Austrian national pride, Austrians were particularly proud of Austrian sports, the social security system, science, history, culture and art, whereas the pride of Austrian politics and democracy was less pronounced (Haller 1996). In other words, the national identification with history and culture as well as economic development and social welfare is stronger than that with the political-civic components of the Austrian nation.

Secondly, the growing consolidation of an Austrian national identity after 1990 was accompanied by an increasing dissolution of the traditional corporate power sharing between ÖVP and SPÖ by an increasing pluralization of the political system through the growth of the FPÖ and the Greens. Of particular importance here was the conspicuous increase of the votes for the FPÖ during the 1990s, leading in 1999 to the current coalition government of ÖVP and FPÖ, though the votes for the FPÖ fell again considerably in 2002 (cf. Plasser, Ulram, Sommer 2000). At the same time, it is important that the degree of national identification with Austria as a nation increased in all parties. As a survey on national consciousness and party preference conducted in 1987 and 1993 shows, the great majority of voters for all parties now share an Austrian national identity, and only a small part of the voters still support a German or German-Austrian or regional identity (Bruckmüller 1996: 65). This is also true of the FPÖ under the leadership of Jörg Haider, who during the 1990s has increasingly substituted the Great-German legacy for an Austrian national identity. Along with this transformation, the German-Austrian ambiguities in the conception of an Austrian *Kulturnation* also became reduced, indicated by an increasing trend to see Austria not only as a *Staatsnation*, but also as a *Sprachnation* (Bruckmüller 1996: 65).

Thirdly, the other side of the growing consolidation of an Austrian national identity is the diminishing role of internal boundaries vis-à-vis historical minorities, and the strengthening importance of external boundaries vis-à-vis the increasing number of immigrants. Whereas traditionally the (however small) Slovenian, Croatian and Hungarian minorities as well as the South-Tyrolian question in Northern Italy played a conflictive role in Austrian national identity, they have now been replaced by the growing influx of immigrant minorities and their impact on Austrian national identity. There lived 9.4 per cent foreigners in Austria in 2000, particularly from ex-Yugoslavia, Turkey and in growing numbers also from Eastern Europe and non-European countries. As a reaction, xenophobic fears and rejections of foreigners have increased in the Austrian population; according to a survey in 1996, about one half of the Austrian population display negative attitudes (Haller 1996). These fears have been politically mobilized particularly by Jörg Haider and have enabled the FPÖ's conspicuous rise in Austrian politics. At the same time, many social organizations such as the industrial and labor organization also share these xenophobic sentiments. As compared to Germany, one of the crucial reasons for this is the lack of, or less impact of, a critical reassessment of the Nazi past and thus a stronger cultural and political continuity of traditional (anti-)foreign stereotypes.

3. Austria, European Integration and Austrian European Identity (1945-2000)

The historical foundations of Austrian European orientations were closely related to the geopolitical location of the German-Austrian lands as an imperial center of the German-Roman Empire as well as of the multi-national Habsburg Empire within the European state order. With the fragmentation of the German-Roman Empire after the Reformation and the rise of the Atlantic great powers, as well as the relocation and consolidation of the Habsburg Empire in East Central Europe, the Austrian European orientations basically oscillated between Western and Eastern-oriented Great-German identities. As the core Roman-Catholic power in Central Europe, the Habsburg Austrian European orientation crystallized moreover as anti-Protestant and anti-Prussian in its Western direction as well as anti-Ottoman/Islam and anti-Russian/Christian-Orthodox in its Eastern direction. Further, the more the Habsburg Empire became backward vis-à-vis Western Europe, the Western European direction became orientated towards a defensive European power equilibrium, whereas the direction vis-à-vis even more backward Eastern Europe combined with an imperial Catholic and German cultural mission. After the dissolution of the German-Roman Empire, with the further reduction of Habsburg's influence in Germany and its parallel geopolitical shift towards an East Central European multi-national empire, the basic coordinates of Habsburg-Austrian European orientations continued. But the Western European balance of power orientations became more defensive, and the Eastern European imperial-missionary orientations more offensive. The further erosion of the Habsburg empire through the rise of nationalism, the exclusion from Germany and the internal power shift within the Habsburg Empire towards Hungary and the other evolving nations, however, transformed these coordinates of European orientations also. On the basis of the growing Great-German nationalistic orientations in Habsburg Austria and of the strengthening political bonds between Imperial Germany and the Habsburg Empire, the anti-Western defensive and the Eastern imperialistic missionary attitudes intensified. Habsburg's imperial multi-culturalism was progressively replaced by a Great-German cultural-imperialistic German orientation to *Mitteleuropa*. After the collapse of the Habsburg Empire, German-Austrian identity was torn between an Empire-contracting national identity and an Empire-restoring identity in either a civic-republican or an ethnic-dictatorial form. After the experience and collapse of the totalitarian Nazi Great-German Reich, Austrian collective identity finally constituted itself as an Empire-contracting national identity separating from its Great-German past.

In the context of the post-WW II division of Europe and the constitution of an independent and separate Austrian nation-state, the formation of an Austrian national identity went together with a radical change in its European orientations. On the one hand, in a parallel to the democratization of Austrian state and society, there emerged predominantly pro-Western and anti-Soviet attitudes, but at the same time in social-Christian and social-democratic rather than Western-liberal orientations. On the other hand, there evolved the political-cultural shift from a Great-German imperial to a separate Austrian identification with a small state at the front-lines between Western and Eastern Europe. This constellation facilitated the national attraction to the imposed neutrality status of an independent Austrian nation. Austria and its major political and cultural forces identified themselves as a neutral, small nation in Europe between West and East in geo-political as well as socio-political terms. This neutrality doctrine was one of the foundational principles of Austria's 'national rebirth' and became part of the constitutional law of 1955, which declared 'the purpose to keep for ever its national independence and to guarantee the inviolability of its state territory...her eternal neutrality'. (Cited in Wodak 1999: 156). This neutrality doctrine was not only a constitutional principle on paper but became part of the predominant Austrian identity. Thus, in a survey on the components of national pride in 1989, 87 per cent of the Austrian population were 'proud' and 'very proud' of Austrian neutrality (Bruckmüller 1996: 70). Under these conditions, and despite its predominant Western orientations, Austria remained neutral with regard to NATO and instead joined the third neutral bloc of the other small European nations. As well, despite the growing inter-connections with the dynamic, integrating Western European economy, Austria abstained from accession to the European integration project. Instead, it joined with the Scandinavian 'third way' countries the European Free Trade Association (EFTA). Only after the collapse of communism and the related sea-change in Europe did the coordinates of this neutrality doctrine start to erode.

On the one hand, the question of NATO membership emerged in all urgency with the NATO interventions in Bosnia-Herzegovina and Kosovo and triggered a domestic soul-searching on the neutrality doctrine. Whereas the Greens remained faithful to an anti-NATO course and the Freedom Party demanded a pro-NATO support, the then governing coalition between the SPÖ and ÖVP tried to keep a middle course between the neutrality doctrine and a support for the Western alliance; but an application for NATO membership was never seriously considered (Haller 1996; Wodak 1999). However, the current ÖVP/FPÖ coalition government recently stated that under the new geopolitical conditions, the constitutional neutrality doctrine in favor of a potential NATO membership should be reconsidered. On the other hand, the question of EU membership was emotionally less problematic; but the application for EU accession in 1988 required a redefinition of the neutrality doctrine, and this step was facilitated by the parallel EU application of the Scandinavian countries (Haller 1996; Wodak 1999). After a strong pro-EU campaign by the government, the accession to the European Union was then approved by about two thirds (66.52 per cent) of the population in a referendum in 1994 and was finalized in 1995. At the same time, according to a parallel survey, 78 per cent of the Austrians also insisted, despite Austrian EU membership, on the protection of national independence (Haller 1996: 97).

Thus, despite the overwhelming support for EU accession, the identification with Europe as compared to other European countries remains relatively low. As Table 3.2 shows, Austrian identification solely with the nation remained stable during the 1990s on a high level of above 50 per cent (like in Greece or Great Britain), whereas the combined identification with the nation first and Europe second even slightly fell in the same period (like in West and East Germany). At the same time, Austrian identification with first Europe and then the nation, or even with Europe alone, ranks clearly lower than in the case of West Germany, though similar to East Germany. The recent punishment of Austria for the inclusion of the right-wing xenophobic FPÖ into the current coalition government may have even further contributed to a stronger disenchantment with the European Union.

Table 3.2 Change in national and European identification, 1995-2000

	Nation alone		Nation>Europe		Europe>Nation		Europe alone	
	1995	2000	1995	2000	1995	2000	1995	2000
France	28.7	28.5	52.8	55.0	9.3	10.6	9.2	5.9
W Germany	32.8	45.6	64.5	40.1	9.3	7.1	8.3	4.9
E Germany	42.4	50.2	44.8	41.0	8.5	6.2	4.4	2.6
Italy	23.3	25.2	58.7	60.3	11.7	9.1	6.3	5.4
G Britain	55.2	66.6	32.5	27.3	4.2	4.0	4.2	2.6
Greece	52.8	55.0	41.8	39.7	4.0	4.0	1.4	1.4
Spain	43.6	27.3	45.9	59.1	6.0	8.3	4.6	5.3
Austria	53.5	53.9	36.8	35.0	7.6	7.5	2.1	3.6

Source: Eurobarometer 43.1 (1995) and 53 (2000).

Regarding the eastern enlargement of the European Union, the Austrian governments – the former SPÖ/ÖVP as well as the present ÖVP/FPÖ – have developed a special position (Spohn 2001). On the one hand, they have followed the basic parameters set by the European Union regarding the opening of the accession negotiations on the basis of the Copenhagen criteria as well as the inclusion of all ten East Central accession candidates plus Turkey. On the other hand, their emphasis is less on European functional integration and more on European political and cultural intergovernmental cooperation with a clear priority on the neighboring former Habsburg countries. The official government language emphasizes the common cultural heritage in the Danube region. (Streitenberger 1997). At the same time, the Austrian population is very little supportive of the Eastern enlargement; on the contrary, the majority of Austrians – more than any other European nation – is strongly opposed to it. According to the recent Eurobarometer surveys in 1999 and 2000, only 29 per cent of Austrians support the Eastern enlargement, whereas 59 per cent are against it (Eurobarometer 51 and 53,

2000 and 2001). These low support levels have only slightly improved recently, reflecting middle class as well as working class orientations. Thus, the Federation of Austrian Trade Unions (ÖGB), the Chamber of Labor, the Chamber of Agriculture and the Association of Austrian Industrialists (VÖI) – all agree on the demand for longer transition periods for the East Central European accession candidates in order to protect the Austrian labor market and Austrian economic interests. In particular, union leaders demand that the transition periods should be accompanied by a substantial leveling down of wage differences between Austria and the East Central European neighbors. In addition, they suggest that the structural funds of the Southern European member states should be used for that purpose. Meanwhile, there is a fear that the *Burgenland*, as one of the poorest Austrian border regions, will loose the EU subsidies as a consequence of financial transfers to the East Central European accession candidates. The core reason for these fears are not economic *per se*, however, but are combined with fears of rising immigration, rising labor market competition and related xenophobia (Spohn 2000).

In conclusion, the analysis of the long-term change of Austria from an imperial core region to a small nation in Europe has revealed also a characteristic transformation of the entanglements between the crystallizing Austrian national identity and related Austrian European orientations. Firstly, German-Austria as the former imperial center of the Roman-German as well as the Habsburg Empire oscillated for a long time between a more Western-Central and Eastern-Central European focus. With the increasing exclusion from Western Central Europe and the growing relocation to the East, however, the imperial identity became more defensive against the West and more expansive against the East, whereas the emerging regional nationalism identified rather with the Western unifying Great-German nationalism against the separating Eastern nationalisms. Secondly, the materialization of this Great German nationalism in the form of the Nazi Empire and its disastrous collapse was the final turning point from the former imperial Great-German identity to the separate constitution of an Austrian national identity. As a small nation in divided Europe, bordering the Soviet-communist East as well as separating from its Great-German legacies, Austria defined itself as a neutral nation between the Western and Eastern blocs – as if anxious to form its national identity without any renewed imperial domination – not only from the communist East but also from the capitalist West, the renewed German power center in Western Europe and its influence and subversion of a separate Austrian identity. Thirdly, after the collapse of Soviet communism and the related geo-political sea-change in Europe, the constitutive internal and external components of the post-WWII construction of Austrian national identity have changed. The formation of a separate Austrian national identity has become consolidated by the combined impact of a perceived growing threat of the Austrian nation by migration and the related rise of an Austrian neo-nationalism. Meanwhile, in partially giving up or re-interpreting its neutrality doctrine, Austria as a late-comer has joined the European Union and at the same time being located at the front-line of the eastern enlargement. In this double constellation, Austria's Western European orientation displays a conspicuous defensive nationalist attitude against an over-centralized,

French-German dominated European Union, whereas Austria's Eastern European orientation is characterized by propagating a cooperation of the many small, culturally close, East-Central European nations. In a sense, then, the Habsburg legacy in its defensive Western and expansive Eastern attitudes is still present in the European components of contemporary Austrian national identity.

References

Barkey, Karen and Mark von Hagen (1997), *After Empire. Multiethnic Societies and Nation-Building: The Soviet Union and the Russian, Ottoman and Habsburg Empires*, Boulder, CO: Westview Press.

Bauer, Otto (1924), Die Nationalitätenfrage und die Sozialdemokratie. 2.Aufl. Wien 1924. (erste Auflage 1907).

Bluhm, William T., (1973), *Building an Austrian Nation. The Political Integration of a Western State*, New Haven, London: Yale University Press.

Botz, Gerhard and Gerald Sprengnagel (eds)(1994), *Kontroversen um Österreichs Zeit-Geschichte. Verdrängte Vergangenheit, Österreich-Identität, Waldheim und die Historiker*, Frankfurt/M.: Campus.

Brubaker, Rogers (1998), 'The Manichean Myth: Rethinking the Distinction between "Civic" and "Ethnic" Nationalism', in Kriesi et al. (eds) pp. 55-72.

Bruckmüller, Ernst (1996), *Nation Österreich. Kulturelles Bewusstsein und gesellschaftlich-politische Prozesse*, Wien, Köln, Graz: Böhlau.

Conze, Werner (1992), *Gesellschaft, Staat, Nation*, Göttingen: Vandenhoek & Ruprecht.

Dann, Otto (1993), *Nation und Nationalismus in Deutschland 1770-1990*, München: Beck.

Erdmann, Karl Dietrich (1985), 'Drei Staaten – zwei Nationen – ein Volk? Überlegungen Zur deutsche Geschichte seit der Teilung', *Geschichte in Wissenschaft und Unterricht*, 36, pp. 671-683.

Erdmann, Karl Dietrich (1989), *Die Spur Österreichs in der deutschen Geschichte. Drei Staaten – zwei Nationen – ein Volk*, Zürich: Mannesse-Verlag.

Eurobarometer, edited by the European Commission (1995, 2000), Brussels.

Fassmann, Heinz and Rainer Münz (eds) (1995), *Einwanderungsland Österreich? Historische Integrationsmuster, aktuelle Trends und politische Maßnahmen*, Wien: Jugend & Volk.

Fellner, Fritz (1985), 'Das Problem der österreichischen Nation nach 1945', in: Otto Büsch and James Sheehan (eds), *Die Rolle der Nation in der deutschen Geschichte und Gegenwart*, Berlin: Colloquium Verlag, pp. 193-220.

Good, David and Richard Rudolph (1992), *Multinational Empire and Nationalism: The Habsburg, Russian and Ottoman Empire*, Minneapolis: Minnesota University Press.

Greenfeld, Liah (1998), 'Is Nation Unavoidable? Is Nation Unavoidable Today?', in: Kriesi et al. (eds), pp. 37-54.

Grothusen, Klaus-Detlev (ed.) (1974), *Ethnogenese und Staatsbildung in Südosteuropa*, Goettingen: Vandenhoek & Ruprecht.

Gumplowicz, Ludwig (1909), *Rassenkampf, Soziologische Untersuchungen. 2. durchgesehene und mit Anhang, enthaltend die 1875 erschienene Schrift "Rasse und Staat" vers. Aufl.* Innsbruck: Wagner.

Haller, Max (1996), *Identität und Nationalstolz der Österreicher. Gesellschaftliche Ursachen und Funktionen. Herausbildung und Transformation seit 1945, Internationaler Vergleich*, Wien, Köln, Weimar: Böhlau.

Heer, Friedrich (1981), *Der Kampf um die österreichische Identität*, Wien, Köln, Graz:

Böhlau.

Kann, Robert (1964), *Das Nationalitätenproblem der Habsburger Monarchie. Geschichte Und Ideengehalt der nationalen Bestrebungen. Vom Vormärz bis zur Auflösung des Reiches im Jahr 1918*, Wien, Köln, Graz: Böhlau.

Kann, Robert (1993), *Die Habsburger Monarchie 1648-1918*, Wien, Köln, Graz: Böhlau.

Katzenstein, Peter (1976), *Disjoined Partners. Austria and Germany since 1815*, Berkeley: Berkeley University Press.

Kriesi, Hanspeter, et al. (eds) (1998), *Nation and National Identity: The European Experience in Comparative Perspective*, Zürich: Verlag Rüegger.

Langer, Josef (1998), 'Last in, First Out? Austria's Place in the Transformation of National Identity', in Kriesi et al. (eds), pp. 153-174.

Langewiesche, Dieter (1999), *Nation, Nationalismus und Europa in der deutschen Geschichte*, Göttingen: Vandenhoek & Ruprecht.

Lemberg, Eugen (1950), *Geschichte des Nationalismus in Europa*, Stuttgart: Klett & Cotta.

Lemberg, Eugen (1964), *Nationalismus*, 2 vols., Reinbek: Rohwolt.

Minkenberg, Michael (2001), 'Haider and right-wing radicalism in Austria', in: *West European Politics*.

Pelinka, Anton (1990), *Zur österreichischen Identität. Zwischen deutscher Vereinigung und Mitteleuropa*, Wien: Überreuter.

Plaschka, Richard G., Gerald Stourzh and Jan Niederkorn (eds) (1995), *Was heist Österreich? Umfang und Wandel des Österreichbegriffs vom 10. Jahrhundert bis heute*, Wien: Verlag der österreichischen Akademie der Wissenschaften.

Plasser, Fritz and Peter Ulram (1993), *Staatsbürger oder Untertanen? Politische Kultur Deutschlands, Österreichs und der Schweiz im Vergleich*, Frankfurt/Main, Bern, New York: Lang.

Plasser, Fritz, Peter A. Ulram and Franz Sommer (eds.), *Das Österreichische Wahlverhalten*, Wien: Signum.

Sheehan, James (1987), *German History 1775-1866*, Cambridge, MA: Cambridge University Press.

Smith, Anthony (1992), *National Identity*, Reno, NE: University of Nevada Press.

Spohn, Willfried (2000), 'European Integration, Eastern Enlargement and Collective Identities. Germany, Austria, Poland and Hungary in Comparison', EUI: European Forum.

Spohn Willfried (2001) 'Europeanization, the EU's Eastern Enlargement and Collective Identities. A Western and Eastern European Comparison', EUI Working Paper.

Streitenberger, Wolfgang (ed.) (1997), *Österreichs Zukunft ist Europa*, Wien: Signum-Verlag.

Stourzh, Gerald (1990), *Vom Reich zur Republik. Studien zum Österreichbewusstsein im 20. Jahrhundert*, Wien: Wiener Journal.

Wodak, Ruth, et al. (1999), *Zur diskursiven Konstruktion nationaler Identität*, Frankfurt/M.: Suhrkamp.

Zöllner, Erich (1990), *Geschichte Österreichs*, Wien: Verlag für Geschichte und Politik.

Chapter 4

A European Spain:
The Recovery of Spanish Self-Esteem
and International Prestige[1]

Pablo Jáuregui
and
Antonia M. Ruiz-Jiménez

Introduction

Spain is one of the oldest political units in Europe. The dynastic union between Castile and Aragon comprised separate kingdoms with different legislations and autonomous institutions, as well as a multiplicity of languages. Nevertheless, all the people living in these territories were the subjects of the Spanish Monarchy, and most of them shared the Catholic religion, gradually forging an overarching 'ethno-patriotic identity' which was characterized by the fusion of religious and political identities.

However, the tensions between the Castilian centre and the peripheral nationalisms of the Basque, Catalan, and Galician regions that have characterized Spain until the present day clearly demonstrate that the Spanish state has not managed to create a fully unified nation with linguistic-cultural and emotional integration. The poverty of the state, poor communications, an inadequate education system, and the polarized divisions between liberal and conservative versions of Spanish national identity contributed to the fact that the construction of a unified nation-state was still incomplete at the beginning of the twentieth century. Only after the Disaster of 1898 did the elites seriously turn to the task of the national mass mobilization. But, as Álvarez Junco (2000: 183) has noted, 'only the Francoist regime made a determined effort at nationalisation'. As a consequence of the repression of peripheral nationalisms by Francoism, by the end of the dictatorship these movements were associated with the ideas of democracy, civilization and modernity, while 'Spanishness' or *españolismo*, became linked with the backward and brutal regime, and was hence discredited.

---

[1] We would like to thank Professors Andrés de Blas Guerrero, Paloma Aguilar and José Ignacio Torreblanca from the UNED for their valuable comments to this chapter.

This historical trajectory ultimately transformed Spain's membership of the European Union, together with the successful transition to democracy, into a potent and widespread source of national pride. The notion of 'becoming European', in the Spanish context of collective memory, essentially represented the opportunity to leave behind what was popularly known as *el atraso* ('the backwardness') of the nation's past for good. It was by 'getting into Europe' that Spain could cease to be a sort of moral outcast after decades of rejection by the leading Western European powers. 'Europe', furthermore, was seen as a chance to definitively jump on the train of Western modernity, prosperity, and progress, and as a means to secure a democratic regime. For this reason, the dominant discourses of nationhood that emerged in post-Franco Spain depicted the achievement of 'entering Europe' as an emotionally charged symbol of national resurgence. To a great extent, this is a self-representation that has continued to colour the attitudes of Spaniards towards the EU until the present day. Consequently, in the case of Spain, national sentiments have smoothly intertwined with the project of European integration.

Spain: Early Construction of the State and Weak Mass Nationalization[2]

When they married in 1479, Queen Isabella of Castile and King Fernando of Aragon unified two of the most important Catholics kingdoms in the peninsula. They assumed the task of completing the 'Reconquest' and quickly achieved the political unification of the peninsula. The borders of Spain have remained practically unchanged ever since. The union was founded on a policy of racial and religious integration that required the expulsion of those Jews and Muslims who did not convert to Catholicism, leading to the emergence of a rather homogeneous ethnic and racial mix. The state created institutions and projects commons, to all regions, and the words *España*, Spain, or the Spanish Monarchy were already used at the time. The Spanish state, therefore, can be considered to be one of the oldest in Europe. However, this does not mean that people's loyalties were national, as they in fact appear to have been above all local and/or religious. Only the elites developed a pre-national ethno-patriotism at this time.

During the modern era, identification with Spain was still centred on fidelity to the Monarchy and the Catholic religion. Neither the Habsburg nor the Bourbon Monarchies attempted to instil a sense of ethno-patriotic identity that could serve the purpose of facilitating expansion and dominion over their neighbours. The main way in which this period might have helped the initial appearance of a 'popular' national identity was through the numerous wars in which Spain was involved. As in other countries, the existence of common enemies gave rise to a common collective image. The Bourbons, moreover, also made an attempt to create national symbols to represent the state and to thus facilitate the

---

[2] This section is based on the researches by Aguilar, Álvarez Junco, Blas Guerrero, Fusi, Linz and Nuñez Seixas included in the reference section.

visual and sentimental identification of its subjects with the state. The cultural creations of this period, however, were characterized by their elitism and limited impact among the masses.

The invasion of the peninsula by Napoleon's troops and the subsequent war (1808-1814) constitutes a key turning point in the Spanish process of national integration. It is one of Spain's first modern national myths. Interpretation of the war is complex however. There was a popular component of xenophobic violence against the French invaders that might be termed 'nationalist'. But there was also a civil war, a struggle between two dynasties, both of French origin, which were supported by divided Spanish elites. The war was also an international conflict, as the two sides were backed by the armies of the two European superpowers of the day, England and France.

During the war, the Liberals tried to promote a national identity as the cornerstone of their demand for popular sovereignty, appealing to medieval regional privileges and the theory of a contract between the King and his subjects. These were the Liberals of Cádiz, inheritors of the enlightened tradition of the Bourbon Monarchy, who replaced the terms 'kingdom' and 'monarchy' with 'nation', 'fatherland' and 'Spanish people'. But the Spanish victory over the French troops brought the restoration of the *ancien régime*, paving the way for a period of political instability in which various phases of liberal ascendancy were followed by the reassertion of royal authority. Given their intermittent grip on power, the Liberals found it extremely difficult to realize their nationalist project. The financial difficulties resulting from the loss of the American empire during the 1820s made nationalist mobilization difficult when they held power. Progress was further hindered by the political demobilization of the masses under the oligarchic and *caciquil* (controlled by local party bosses or *caciques*) party system. Moreover, most power remained in the hands of the traditional oligarchies, who feared and hence avoided mass national mobilization, since in other European societies this process was associated with democratic revolutions of a type that would threaten their privileges.

Despite all these obstacles, by the 1860s, the Liberals had completed a first and fundamental phase in the construction of a new national identity (through a cultural production still more or less elitist). New 'prestige politics' (modest military expeditions in Africa) served to test the new patriotic rhetoric; it was the opportunity to show the other European nations that the Spanish Monarchy was still a great world power. But the African War also won over Catholic-conservative political sectors to the notion of nationalism. The expeditions could be interpreted as the continuation of nation's oldest foundational myth, the 'Reconquest'. Over the following decades, conservatives would insist on this interpretation of patriotic history, as the defence of Catholicism, mobilizing public opinion through a rhetoric that both affirmed national identity and called for a religious crusade. Conservatives mainly used the appeal to patriotic and national sentiments against the threat posed by socialism and social revolution, defined as anti-national.

In this context, it is not surprising, therefore, that defeat in the Spanish-American War (1898) gave rise to a strong sense of pessimism about the nation. This did not stem directly from the negative consequences that the lost of Cuba and

Puerto Rico had for Spanish political and economic interests.[3] In fact, neither was seriously harmed. The blow was not material but psychological, as it meant the end of a delusion, the imperial dream, the fiction that Spain was still one of the great European powers. Nonetheless, the negative impact of defeat was largely limited to the elites and urban population, the only educated and therefore nationalized Spaniards. It is doubtful that it had much bearing on much of the country, and particularly on the rural population. This is explained by the limited and problematic socialization of the masses in a national identity during the 19th and early 20th centuries, a reality itself attributable to a number of factors.

For most of the period, firstly, education was a monopoly of the Catholic church. The church was anti-modern and opposed mass nationalization until the 1860s. Even after that date it continued to educate people as good Catholics rather than as good Spaniards. Moreover the church always opposed state incursions into its traditional domains, such as education. When the state tried to establish its control in this sphere (through the *Moyano* Law of 1857), financial problems severely undermined the reach of its nationalization policies. However, a further problem was the lack of political will on the part of the state, which could have implemented other, less costly nationalist policies more efficiently. Before 1911 it did not establish a truly compulsory military service. Official promotion of national symbols such as the flag or anthem was weak. There was no official agreement over the Spanish flag until 1843, and it was only in 1908 that all official buildings were obliged to fly it. Moreover, the design of the flag was changed on various occasions and its legitimacy was questioned by *carlistas* (radical Conservatives) and republicans. The Spanish national anthem was not officially defined as such until the 20th century, and even now it still has no words.

The 20th Century

The first wave of mass nationalization in Spain, therefore, began in the wake of the Disaster of 1898. By the early decades of the 20th century, however, the traditional association between liberalism, democracy and nationalism had already been shattered. Although a liberal nationalist discourse continued to exist, the conservative elites turned to nationalism as an alternative to socialism and to channel social 'indiscipline'. The first serious nationalizing drive was undertaken by the dictatorship of Primo de Rivera during the 1920s. It was too late, however, for the national mobilization of the masses, by now more attracted by socialism and working-class internationalism and socialism. This conservative nationalism also acquired a new, centralist dimension, strongly opposed to emerging separatism in different regions.

After the Civil War, the Francoist regime took up a rhetoric of 'Spanishness' in which the 'Nationals' (the victors) characterized 'the enemies of Spain' (the vanquished) – that is, the Socialists, Communists and Republicans – as

---

[3] Most of Spain's colonial empire was lost during the 1820s, during the rein of Fernando VII. The territory lost in 1898 represented no more than 2 per cent of the territory Spain had once held in the Americas.

foreigners, traitors and 'bad Spaniards'. The dictatorship made unprecedented use of all the means at its disposal to socialize people into the idea of one Spanish nation: school textbooks, radio, movies, monuments, etc. This is not to suggest that were was a single, monolithic or static national discourse. Rather, we find various discourses, each with its own particularities in terms of the notion of the Spanish nation, and each of which evolved over the course of the period (see Saz Campos 2003 for a detailed description).

However, this first large-scale campaign of 'nation-building' suffered from a twofold problem, one that ultimately alienated Spanish public opinion from the idea of Spanish nationalism. First, it was exclusively Castilian and meant the repression of any other regional identities; the teaching and use of non-Castilian languages and cultures was banned outside the domestic space. Second, it was based on the intolerant Catholic-conservative tradition that rejected Spain's liberal past and exclusively represented the victors of the Civil War. As a result of the repression of peripheral nationalisms by Francoism, these movements were associated with the ideas of democracy, civilization and modernity, while 'Spanishness' or *españolismo*, became linked with the dictatorship. Above all, among the opposition parties, the identification of Spanish patriotism and symbols (including the flag) with dictatorship led them to renounce the use of nationalist discourse, or at least to keep this very vague; they even abandoned the term 'Spain' in favour of the politically more acceptable 'Spanish state'.

Peripheral Nationalisms

The emergence of Spanish peripheral nationalisms can be located in the mid-19th century. Although some nationalist authors have highlighted earlier antecedents in the Carlist Wars and the 'foralist' tradition, their analysis should be rejected, as neither Carlism nor the foralists questioned the unity of Spain. 'Foralism' developed between the 16th and 19th centuries as the ideology of those seeking to preserve the traditional privileges of the regions against the centralising policies of the state, a goal that was seen as achievable within Spain. The First Carlist War took place between 1833-1840, and the second from 1872-1876. 'Carlism' as a movement identified with a long counter-revolutionary tradition in Spain (dating from 1808), and took its name from the brother of King Fernando VII of Spain, Don Carlos. When Ferdinand died without a male heir, Carlists defended his claim to the throne against that of Isabella, the king's daughter, at the same time as they sought a return to the *ancién regime* in Spain, thereby constituting a counter-revolutionary, confessional, anti-modern and pro-absolutist movement.

The cultural movements that appeared in the mid-19th century and which can be considered the forerunners of modern peripheral nationalisms began as local literary and cultural movements. Nevertheless, until 1898 these movements did not conflict with a simultaneous sense of national patriotism: these movements were called, significantly, 'regionalist' rather than 'nationalist'. It was only after the Disaster of 1898 that some elites abandoned any hope of regenerating the Spanish state and turned inwards to the construction of autonomous regional systems. Their separatist drive lay not in the backwardness of the country, but rather in its unequal development. Tensions arose because of the lack of correspondence between the geography of economic and political power.

The movement in Catalonia originally sought autonomy, rather than independence, and enjoyed considerable electoral success from the first decade of the 20th century onwards. It was initially built on a feeling of superiority based on Barcelona's vigorous cultural life and Catalan industrial development, which was not matched by the region's political influence in Spain.

The Basque nationalist movement was much more conservative. The industrialization of Bilbao fuelled the discontent of the local petite bourgeoisie and rural inhabitants, who saw the arrival of industrial capitalism and immigration from other regions as a threat to the status quo and their way of life. The nationalism of Sabino Arana was theocratic, xenophobic and anti-liberal. Breaking with the regionalist tradition (*foralismo*) in the Basque Country, he sought complete independence from Spain, because Basques could never be true Catholics in liberal Spain.

The dictatorship of Primo de Rivera in the 1920s brought a first wave of repression of political and cultural manifestations of nationalism. It was this which gave rise to the association between peripheral nationalism and democracy that would later become consolidated among the opponents of the Francoist regime. During the 1930s, the Spanish II Republic established a decentralized structure, although Spain was defined as *one* 'integral' nation. But after the Civil War (1936-1939) the new Francoist dictatorship unleashed a much more intense wave of repression of all non-Castilian cultures, which were taken as manifestations of political dissent. Catalan nationalists continued to protest peacefully in demand for autonomy. However, in the Basque country, part of the nationalist movement moved towards the defence of armed struggle between ETA and the state.

The crucial result of all this is that the rejection of Francoist dictatorship was identified with the rejection of Spanish nationalism. Once the transition was underway (1975-1977), virtually all the political forces in Spain agreed that the old unitary framework of the Spanish state would have to be converted into a much more decentralized structure. The new democratic period has combined, therefore, a process of devolution to the so-called 'historic communities' (above all the Basque Country and Catalonia) with the decentralization of the Spanish state, which now resembles a federation with differing degrees of autonomy. Nevertheless, part of the Basque nationalist movement did not accept the negotiated solution agreed on the 1978 Constitution. This generated a lack of legitimacy in the Basque Country that still causes problems today. While part of the Basque nationalist movement evolved towards reformism and abandoned the armed struggle against the state, more radical elements developed connections with ETA and consider the use of violence as a necessity as long as the confrontation with the Spanish state continues (that is, until the Basque country is independent). This view of the problem rests on two false assumptions: first, that the current political regime in Spain (a parliamentary monarchy with a state of the Autonomies) is not democratic, but a mere continuation of the previous dictatorship; second, that the radical nationalists themselves alone represent the

'Basque working people', despite the fact that they enjoy the support of only 15 per cent of the Basque electorate.

Dominant Discourses on Nationhood

One of the earliest discourses on nationhood, initially cultivated by Liberals, was based on the myth of a 'Spanish character' which had survived for millenniums and was characterized by the stubborn affirmation of Spanish identity against foreign aggressors. It developed with the reconstruction of the popular resistance against Napoleon's troops as the *War of Independence*, a war in which the Spanish people had demonstrated their fidelity to the Spanish character against the French invaders. But this discourse was also linked to a much more ancient past, particularly the resistance of the peoples of Sagunto and Numancia against the Romans in the 2nd century AD, or the battle of Covadonga against the Muslims in the early 8th century. In this discourse, 'the people' acquired a mythical dimension, coming to represent the essence of the nation, the bearer of a spontaneous and intuitive 'national spirit', maintained precisely because of their lack of culture, and capable of defending and saving the nation at critical moments. The image of the 'the people' as the hero-fighter which saved the nation was contrasted with self-criticism of the elites, who having been corrupted by foreign knowledge, had initially collaborated with the French invaders. Liberals continued to appeal to this image over the course of the 19th century. The Republicans used the same discourse and myths intensively during the Civil War. A new re-elaboration of the myth of 'the people' emerged during the transition. Now, opinion polls reveal that Spanish citizens see themselves (together with the King) as the crucial actors in contributing to the peaceful and successful consolidation of democracy, while the political elites are believed to have played a secondary role in the success of the transition.

Another important discourse on nationhood presented Spain as the defender of the *true faith*, in this case Catholicism, first against Islam and then against the Protestant heresy. The identification of Spanish people with Catholicism appeared during the Modern Age. However, the possible evolution of a Catholic identity into a truly national identity was disturbed by the alliance between the Monarchy and the Catholic church after the *War of Independence*. The fear of losing its traditional privileges, which the Monarchy guaranteed, prompted the church to reject modernization, liberalism and mass mobilization. Only in the 1860s did it become possible to speak of an association between nationalism and Conservative-Catholicism. This development was favoured by the war in Africa, which the church was able to interpret as a new crusade against the Moor, thereby fusing the modern idea of imperialism with the old idea of Catholicism. Thereafter, the Conservatives created a new discourse around the idea of the popular resistance to Napoleon's troops as a crusade, this time against modern enlightened Jacobin atheism.

Like Liberals, Conservatives also reinterpreted ancient and modern history in accordance with their discourse. In this conservative tradition, Visigoth

Spain was the first important national myth. The Visigoth kings were considered the first Spanish kings, since they had converted Spain to Catholicism. The 'Reconquest' was presented simply as a war, lasting eight centuries, in which 'Spaniards' acted together against the Islamic invasion, inspired by the idea of recovering Visigoth-Christian Spain. The Catholic Kings Ferdinand and Isabella represented the culmination of this process as unifiers of the fatherland. A problematic feature of this discourse was that it appealed to people not as Spaniards, but simply as Catholics.

Pessimism has been another distinctive component of Spanish nationalist discourses. This could already be appreciated at the end of the 16th century. Westphalia put an end to Habsburg plans for an international order based on dynastic and religious homogeneity. The successive military defeats of the Spanish Catholic Monarchy produced feelings of incredulity, failure, isolation, decadence and bitterness. This was a collective self-perception full of complexes and self-pity, based not only on an awareness of decline but also on a sense of incredulity in the face of this decadence; the only possible explanation was the existence of an evil conspiracy against Spain. This kind of pessimistic discourse rose to the fore after the Disaster of 1898. At a time when 'the possession of colonies was seen as the hallmark of a vigorous nation' (Balfour 1996: 107), and when fashionable theories of social Darwinism ranked nations into superior and inferior 'races', the loss of Spain's last overseas colonies was experienced as a devastating blow to the country's collective self-esteem.

Spain's Significant Others

As we highlighted in the introduction and as the very title of this chapter underscores, Europe has become Spain's most significant other. In order to understand why it is necessary, first, to note the relative lack of interest in the American empire in the nationalist idealization of Spain from the 16th to 18th centuries. History written in this period, with its strong bias towards military affairs, systematically put more emphasis on Spain's European victories than on the conquest and colonization of America. In the early 19th century Spain lost most of its American empire. At a time when most of the European powers were flaunting their expansionist nationalism and extending their empires, Spain had slumped to the status of a third division power (Álvarez Junco 1998). During the 20th century the Liberals tried to develop a form of 'pan-Americanism' but to little avail. The dictator Primo de Rivera would later develop a similar idea, although now endowed with a more imperialist sense based on the idea of 'Hispanizising' the world. Nonetheless, this was essentially a question of rhetoric.

Second, it should also be noted that Spain has no significant ethnic minorities that might be seen as the internal other. The forced expulsion and/or conversion of the Muslims and Jews during the modern era homogenized the country. Hence there has been no tradition of claiming or drawing ethnic differences. In fact, the political issues raised by present-day peripheral nationalisms largely involve questions of language or territory, and are not posed in ethnic or racial terms. Immigration, which could have served this purpose, is a much more recent phenomenon, is heavily concentrated in certain areas, and is still far less significant in numerical terms than in other EU countries. Spain's only significant ethnic minority consists of the Gypsies who are, in fact, the victims of social discrimination; 'But since the Gypsies have never claimed to be a national minority and are not clustered in any clearly defined territory, they have not become a major political problem' (Álvarez Junco 2000: 209).

The Conflict between European Modernization and Catholic Traditionalism from the War of Independence to the Civil War

By the end of the eighteenth century, the desirability of adapting Spanish institutions to those of the rest of Europe had already become 'the stuff of national political controversy', in which the ideas of the Enlightenment were alternatively seen by the country's elites as a recipe for civilized progress (Liberals) or as a dangerous foreign heresy (Conservatives).

The impassioned dispute between *europeísmo* (European modernization) and *casticismo* (Hispanic traditionalism) became particularly intense in the aftermath of the Disaster of 1898. The project of *europeización* ('Europeanization') was fervently promoted by the influential intellectual Joaquín Costa as the most effective remedy to cure the national disease. Costa, the leading proponent of the current of thought known as *regeneracionismo* ('regenerationism'), was convinced that Spain would only be cured of its deteriorating condition if it assimilated Europe's rational mentality. 'Europe', in Costa's mind, was essentially the land of science, education, technology, and progress. In his view, this was the only medicine that would allow Spain to survive in the global struggle of rival national 'races'.

Not all intellectuals, however, agreed with this invocation of 'European modernity' as the ideal solution for Spanish decadence, since many saw the adoption of 'foreign' or 'alien' ideas as a dangerous threat to the unique traditions, and above all the Catholic spirituality, of the 'national spirit'. The diplomat and essayist Angel Ganivet, for instance, was repelled by the irreligious, egoistic materialism of 'European modernity'. In his view, 'European civilization' was characterized by 'anti-human', 'anti-natural', and 'pitiless mercantilism', while Spain was a morally superior land of spirituality, generosity, and idealism (cited in Beneyto 1999: 83). Hence, according to Ganivet, the resurrection of Spain could only come from within, by looking for the truth and the strength that lay hidden in the depths of the national soul.

One can see, therefore, the way in which during this difficult period of collective anxiety and uncertainty, 'Europe' was seen by some Spanish intellectuals as an inspiring other, an ideal model which should be imitated to save the nation by modernizing it, while others viewed it as a threatening other, a terrible danger which should be avoided at all costs to preserve the purity of the nation's Catholic soul. Indeed, this opposition between European modernization and Hispanic traditionalism led to a notorious public confrontation between the two most famous and influential philosophers of early twentieth century Spain, Miguel de Unamuno and José Ortega y Gasset. Both of these thinkers were fully 'Europeanized' Spaniards, in the sense that they spoke several European languages and were very familiar with the intellectual currents of thought on the other side of the Pyrenees. However, while Unamuno ultimately developed a rather hostile attitude to the modernizing project of 'Europeanization', Ortega fully embraced it with passionate conviction.

The discursive battle between Unamuno and Ortega was not, of course, a purely academic debate. On the contrary, these two intellectuals were very well-known public figures, and the issues they were debating with regard to the 'problem of Spain', and whether or not 'Europe' was the best solution, were at the heart of the political conflicts of the time. This was reflected, for instance, in the rival visions of national history promoted in school textbooks by Right and Left. Some historians have illustrated this point by referring to the conflict of the 'two Spains', 'a contest between the Spain of progress and free thought which looked to Europe and the inward-looking Spain of traditionalist Catholic values' (Carr 1980: 12).

Franco's Defence of 'Christian Europe' against the Threat of Liberal 'Europeanizers'

Not surprisingly, Franco himself originally defined his military uprising in 1936 as a 'national crusade' to protect the Catholic values of *la patria* from what he called the 'bastardized, Frenchified, Europeanizing' doctrines of modern liberalism. Indeed, throughout his life-long rule, the fundamental threatening others of Francoist discourse were Communist 'reds' and liberal-minded 'Europeanizers', as well as Basque and Catalan nationalists.

However, it would be inaccurate to define Francoist discourse as 'anti-European'. In fact, from his own particular standpoint, *el Generalísimo* actually claimed to be fighting for the authentic values of the 'true Europe'. Essentially, the crusade of 'national Catholicism' represented by his forces was located within the larger context of a continental struggle for the preservation of 'Europe's Christian civilization', threatened by the 'evil forces' of liberalism and communism. In this way, Francoist discourse constructed a symbolic representation of the 'real Europe' which was said to coincide with the spirit of the 'real Spain'.

Although Spain remained formally non belligerent throughout the Second World War, Franco did not conceal his moral identification with the kind of 'European order' envisioned by Hitler and Mussolini. The Allied victory, however, radically altered Franco's plans of renewed glory for the Spanish *patria*. Rather, his regime's collaboration with the defeated totalitarian powers led to a harsh period of international ostracism and economic penury. After an initial isolation, the US's strategic priorities in the Cold War ultimately provided Franco with a new vital source of money, prestige, and moral legitimacy. Franco, however, was much less fortunate in his attempt to gain an additional source of moral legitimacy by seeking admission into the European Economic Community (EEC). The Spanish request to join the EEC was not ultimately granted to an old ally of Hitler and Mussolini (Pollack and Hunter 1987: 134).

However, in opposition to this official 'European vocation' which the regime tried to promote, many Spaniards who rejected Francoism began to unify under the symbolic banner of a very different 'Europeanism', which stood for the full modernization and democratization of their country (Tusell 1977). Over the course of time, the legitimacy of Franco's version of Spanish 'patriotism' began to dwindle, and the rival national project of a modern, democratic, and hence 'European' Spain eventually gained the upper hand (Carr and Fusi 1981; Gilmour 1985). By the 1970s, Spain had been transformed into a fully industrialized, better-educated society by Franco's own regime. At this point, students, intellectuals, workers, Basque and Catalan nationalists, and even many representatives of the Catholic church were publicly rejecting the official discourse of the regime. A new national project was increasingly spreading, which sought the recovery of collective self-esteem through the achievement of the kind of 'freedom' and 'liberty' enjoyed in 'normal' European countries. Although the regime itself had repeatedly made the promise that it would satisfy the country's 'European vocation', the most it achieved was a purely economic trade agreement with the EEC in 1970. Association, least full membership, however, was never granted to Franco's Spain, and 'Europe' therefore remained an unfulfilled aspiration throughout the dictatorship.

'Europe' as a Unifying Symbol of Democratization during the Transition

After Franco's death, a new political discourse emerged in the Spanish public sphere that identified 'freedom' and 'democracy' with the desire to achieve a 'modern' and 'European' status. The leading politicians of the transition, such as the first democratically-elected prime minister, Adolfo Suárez, often associated Spain's modernization and democratization with the idealized concept of 'becoming European' (Armero 1989). Indeed, the aspiration to become a full member of the EEC was one of the fundamental issues on which there was a broad consensus in Spain amongst the political forces that made the negotiated transition to democracy possible. The concept of 'Europeanness' had become not so much something a country could *be* through mere geographical location, history, or culture, but rather something that had to be *achieved* through the accomplishment of certain moral and political conditions. One could say that 'Europe' was the mythical aspiration of the future which the majority of Spaniards desired to realize, as well as the means to secure those future achievements. In opposition to the radical, extremist, violent 'two Spains' of the past, the symbolic ideal that was promoted in the dominant political discourse of this period was the notion of a 'third Spain' characterized by moderation, tolerance, and dialogue. Only by respecting such values of mutual respect could the aspiration to 'European modernity' finally become possible. The successful transition to democracy therefore was, and continues to be, regarded by Spanish citizens as an accomplishment to be proud of. Being democratic allowed Spaniards to feel closer to Europe than ever before (Aguilar Fernández and Humlebaek 2002: 151). At the same time, being part of the EU was also a means to secure the transition to the new democratic regime. It is for this reason that Spain's ultimately successful accession into the EEC in 1986 could be celebrated as the culmination of the struggle for the widely cherished, quasi-mythical ideals of the transition: freedom, modernity, and democracy.

Relations with the European Union

As revealed throughout this chapter, Spain has always seen and measured itself mainly against Europe. The Spanish Monarchy was, and was consensus of being, one of the great European powers during the modern era. After losing its European and American territories in the 19th century, Spain still aspired to demonstrate to its European neighbours that it was a great power. We have also commented extensively on the role that Europe played in the various strands of nationalist ideologies (whether liberal or conservative, authoritarian or democratic). We will focus now on the present-day relations between Spain and the European Union (EU).

After Franco's death, the 'Europeanism' which for decades had been a unifying slogan of the opposition movements to the regime now became the officially sanctioned national project defended by the leading political figures of the transition period. Spain is the only country, of all those which have joined the EU after 1957, whose political parties, including the Communist Party, were all in complete agreement on this issue (Álvarez Miranda 1996: 1). From the beginning, the aspiration to 'enter Europe' was presented in the discourse of the leading figures of the Suárez government not only as a question of economic interest, but also of Spain's moral commitment to the 'European' values of democratic pluralism and human rights (Armero 1989: 81). Nevertheless, Spaniards still had to wait almost ten years before their European dream became a reality. After a prolonged period of complex negotiations, Spain finally gained accession into the EEC in 1986, under the leadership of the Socialist government of Felipe González. This was an achievement which was celebrated as a great national triumph that symbolized the nation's democratic consolidation and its recovery of a respectable status on the international stage.

The legacy of this historical trajectory has clearly been reflected in the dominant discourses on the EU that have prevailed in Spain until the present day (see Álvarez Miranda 1996). For the most part, there has been a widespread political consensus in Spain with regard to the crucial importance of EU membership for the country's economic prosperity and international influence, both during the period of Socialist rule under González, as well as under the conservative governments of José María Aznar between 1996 and 2004. As Moreno (2001: 167) puts it, in contemporary Spain 'there is no national project which is not directly linked to the recuperation of its European vocation'. Indeed, one could say that it is a taken-for-granted commonplace of Spanish political culture that only through the EU can Spain guarantee its future economic progress, as well as its capacity to maintain a significant degree of influence in the international arena (Torreblanca 2001). For a country with a history of military intervention in internal politics, the development of a European Common Foreign and Security Policy has also been seen in Spain as a new respectable outlet for the country's modernized armed forces. Furthermore, the creation of a common European security space has been welcomed as a fundamental weapon to combat the continuing threat of ETA terrorism.

Mirroring the elites' discourses, the results from recent Eurobarometer surveys clearly suggest that the majority of Spaniards do not perceive a clash between their national identity and their membership of the European Union. On the contrary, as Table 4.1 shows, throughout the past eight years, the per centage of those who see themselves as both national and European has consistently remained higher than those who define themselves as exclusively Spanish. At the same time, the degree of compatibility between national and European identification is considerably higher in Spain than the EU average.

Table 4.1 Evolution of national and European identities among Spanish people (percentage of respondents, EU 15 average in parenthesis)

In the near future, do you see yourself as...?

Year	European only	European and Nationality	Nationality and European	Nationality only
1996	5 (5)	5 (6)	44 (40)	43 (46)
1997	6 (5)	3 (6)	43 (40)	44 (45)
1998	4 (4)	6 (7)	53 (43)	34 (43)
1999	4 (4)	6 (6)	53 (42)	31 (45)
2000	4 (4)	7 (7)	65 (49)	20 (38)
2001	3(3)	4(6)	52(44)	38(44)
2002	4(3)	5(7)	56(40)	29(38)
2003	4(3)	6(7)	59(47)	29(40)

Source: Eurobarometer Reports no. 46, 47, 50, 52 ,54, 56, 58 and 60.

In the Eurobarometer of Autumn 2000, it is noteworthy that Spain ranked first among all the EU member states in terms of the total percentage of people who felt 'European'. This high degree of identification with Europe cannot be explained in reference to the length of time Spain has belonged to the EC/EU, given that it has only been a member since 1986. Nor can it be explained by the widespread perception of a common European culture, since Spaniards rank well below the EU average (coming in 13th place) when asked whether they agree or disagree that Europeans share a common cultural identity.[4] Hence, considering the particular historical trajectory which we have traced here, the most plausible explanation for the attachment that most Spaniards feel towards Europe is that EU membership has been closely identified with their country's achievement of modernization and democratization, as well as with the recovery of its international

---

[4] Eurobarometer 52 (Autumn 1999).

prestige. Indeed, it is noteworthy that in the Eurobarometer survey, 78 per cent of Spaniards stated that they are proud of their country (compared to an EU average of 69 per cent), and 59 per cent referred to 'being European' as a source of national pride (compared to an EU average of 33 per cent).[5] Therefore, the majority of Spaniards currently display a relatively high degree of national pride, and a significant dimension of this sentiment of collective self-esteem can be linked to their status as 'Europeans'. Recent surveys of levels of support for EU membership also suggest that Spain is marked by a relatively high level of enthusiasm for the process of European integration. The idea that EU membership is a 'good thing', as well as the belief that Spain benefits from the EU, has consistently been more widespread than the EU average.

Concluding Remarks

Spain's historical trajectory represents a fascinating illustration of how national sentiments may become smoothly combined with the incorporation of a European identity. It is also a fundamental example of how the European integration process can contribute to strengthen national identities and nation-states themselves.

As we have argued, it is precisely the notion of *una España europea* (a European Spain) which played a crucial symbolic role in the construction of a cohesive national identity in the aftermath of the Franco dictatorship. Since the notion of Europeanization became synonymous in Spain with the values of modernity, democracy, tolerance, and dialogue, this ideal became a key component of the national self-image that helped to heal the polarized oppositions of the past between the 'two Spains' that clashed in the Civil War. Hence, the historical self-understanding which predominates in current representations of Spanish nationhood typically depicts the country's entry into 'Europe' in 1986 as the climax of a democratic transition process that allowed Spain to regain a significant, respectable status on the international stage.

The emergence in Spain of an emotionally charged Europeanist discourse illustrates how national identities have not only a cognitive, but also a crucial affective dimension. They not only classify individuals as members of nations, vis-à-vis other nations, but they can also fuel sentiments of superiority and inferiority, or pride and shame, in response to national successes and failures. One can see how in Spain the achievement of 'becoming European' was viewed as representing great promotion or a step up in the world's pyramid of international prestige. Entry into Europe, therefore, became a crucial source of national pride, not only in the sense of acquiring greater political influence and economic prosperity, but also of recovering a sense of moral respectability in the international arena. To be accepted by 'Europe' was viewed as a just reward for the 'peaceful', 'civilized'

---

[5] These are net results for national pride (percentage of 'very proud' plus 'fairly proud') minus percentage of 'not very proud' plus 'not at all proud', Eurobarometer 54, Autumn 2000.

way in which the Spanish people had managed to become a 'modern democracy' in which human rights were respected. This historical experience crucially determined the relative smoothness with which national sentiments have been combined with EU membership in Spain, and it also underlies the considerable sympathy that exists amongst Spaniards towards the Eastern European countries that today similarly hope to stabilize their democracies by 'returning to Europe'.

The case of Spain therefore reflects a historical trajectory in which a dominant vision of Spanish nationhood that stressed ethnic, cultural-linguistic, and religious dimensions (the 'national Catholicism' and Castilian homogeneity promoted by Francoism) was replaced during the transition period by a civic ideal of Spain as a plural modern democracy in which basic political freedoms had been re-established and the linguistic diversity of the country's 'nationalities and regions' was recognized. It was within this framework that, as we have argued, 'Europe' became the inspiring other of a Spanish national project committed to overcoming the backwardness and isolation of the past, fundamentally through participating in and contributing to the project of European integration.

Ultimately, both Spain's exemplary transition to democracy and its successful integration in the EU have contributed to re-elaborate Spanish nationalism and to reinforce Spaniards' self-esteem. Twenty five years after the democratic constitution was approved (1978), Spain can claim to have a stable democracy, a growing economy, a leading role in the EU, and a status of middle range power in the international scene.

Throughout history Spaniards have had to deal with five major historical problems concerning their collective project. These have been: first, the privileged role of the Catholic church; second, the problematic civic-military relations; third, its diminished international status and frequent isolation; fourth, the persistence of social inequalities and the resulting class divisions; and fifth, the articulation of Spanish nationalism and Basque and Catalan national identities. It is today evident that of all these problems, the last one lacks a least than satisfactory solution for all parties. Also, the legacies of national-Catholicism and the authoritarian past mean that Spaniards will continue having trouble with identifying themselves with typical symbols of nationhood, such as the flag, the anthem and the coat of arms which had been inherited practically untouched from the dictatorship. At the same time, the liberal and progressive elites lack an alternative vision regarding how to articulate these elements in their civic project for the Spanish nation.

References

Aguilar Fernández, P. (1996), *Memoria y Olvido de la Guerra Civil*, Madrid: Alianza.

Aguilar Fernández, P. and Humlebaek, C. (2002), 'Collective Memory and National Identity in the Spanish Democracy. The Legacies of Francoism and the Civil War', *History and Memory*, 14, pp. 121-164.

Álvarez Junco, J. (1996), 'The Nation-building Process in Nineteenth Century Spain', in C. Mar-Molinero and A. Smith (eds), *Nationalism and the Nation in the Iberian Peninsula: Competing and Conflicting Identities*, Oxford: Berg, pp. 89-106.

Álvarez Junco, J. (1997), 'El Nacionalismo Español como Mito Movilizador: Cuatro Guerras', in R. Cruz and M. Pérez Ledesma (eds), *Cultura y Movilización en la España Contemporánea*, Madrid: Alianza, pp. 35-68.

Álvarez Junco, J. (1998), 'La Nación en Duda', in J. Pan-Montojo (ed.), *Más se Perdió en Cuba: España, 1898 y la Crisis de Fin de Siglo*, Madrid: Alianza, pp. 405-476.

Álvarez Junco, J. (2000), 'Spain: A Product of Incomplete Nation-building', in L. Hagendoorn and others (eds), *European Nations and Nationalism, Theoretical and Historical Perspectives*, Aldershot: Ashgate, pp. 183-215.

Álvarez Junco, J. (2001), *Mater Dolorosa. La Idea de España en el Siglo XIX*, Madrid: Taurus.

Armero, J.M. (1989), *La Política Exterior de España en Democracia*, Espasa, Madrid: CIS.

Balfour, S. (1996), 'The Lion and the Pig: Nationalism and National Identity in Fin-de Siécle Spain', in C. Mar-Molinero, and A. Smith (eds), *Nationalism and the Nation in the Iberian Peninsula: Competing and Conflicting Identities*, Oxford: Berg, pp. 107-118.

Beneyto, J.M. (1999), *Tragedia y Razón. Europa en el Pensamiento Español del Siglo XX*, Madrid: Taurus.

Blas Guerrero, A. de. (1991), *Tradición Republicana y Nacionalismo Español*, Madrid: Tecnos.

Blas Guerrero, A. de. (ed.) (1997), *Enciclopedia del Nacionalismo*, Madrid: Tecnos.

Carr, R. (1980), *Modern Spain: 1875-1980*, Oxford: Oxford University Press.

Carr, R. and Fusi, J.P. (1981), *Spain: Dictatorship to Democracy*, London: George, Allen, & Unwin.

Fusi, J.P. (2000), *España: La Evolución de la Identidad Nacional*, Madrid: Temas de Hoy.

Gilmour, D. (1985), *The Transformation of Spain. From Franco to the Constitutional Monarchy*, London: Quartet Books.

Linz, J. (1973), 'Early State-building and Late Peripheral Nationalisms against the State', in S.N. Eisenstadt and S. Rokkan (eds), *Building States and Nations*, London: Sage, vol. 2, pp. 32-116.

Núñez Seixas, X.M. (1999), *Los Nacionalismos en la España Contemporánea (siglos XIX y XX)*, Barcelona: Hipótesis.

Pollack, B. and Hunter, G. (1987), *The Paradox of Spanish Foreign Policy: Spain's Relations from Franco to Democracy*, London: Pinter Publishers.

Saz Campos, I. (2003), *España contra España*, Madrid: Marcial Pons.

Torreblanca, J.I. (2001), 'Ideas, Interest and Institutions: Explaining the Europeanization of Spain's Foreign Policy', Arena Workings Papers No. 01/26.

Tusell, X. (1977), *La Oposición Democrática al Franquismo*, Barcelona: Planeta.

Chapter 5

Italy and Europe: Internal Others and External Challenges to National Identity

Anna Triandafyllidou

Introduction

Contemporary Italian society is faced with conflicting tendencies. On the one hand, it is characterized by a strong European orientation and modern profile as an industrial force. On the other hand, inefficient governance, corruption, undocumented immigration and regional protest challenge this view and put Italian democracy to the test. The country is under constant pressure to keep pace with economic and social development in the EU while facing, together with the other member states, the prospect and process of incorporation of Central and Eastern European countries into the Union. These developments raise a number of social, political and economic issues, not least in relation to citizens' identification with the nation/Italy and/or the EU/Europe, as well as the representations of these entities in the media, political party and lay people discourse.

This chapter explores the historical and relational factors that have conditioned the (trans)formation of Italian national identity. My aim is to illustrate how the historical background and contemporary internal and external challenges to the Italian nation shape the country's relationship with the European Union, with particular reference to the link between national identity and the feeling of belonging to Europe. In the following sections, I discuss critically the dominant discourses of nationhood and the role of Significant Others in shaping the definition of the national Self, taking into account the historical background of Italian nationalism. Particular attention is paid to the relationship between Italy and the European Union both in policy and identity terms. In conclusion, I discuss what lessons we can learn from the Italian case concerning the entanglement, change and ambivalence of national and European identities today.

Dominant Discourses of Nationhood

Analytically speaking, nations are distinguished with reference to their primarily ethnic or civic character (Smith, 1986; 1991). The main elements constitutive of an ethnic nation are the belief that its members are ancestrally related, a common set of cultural traditions, collective memories and a link to a specific historical territory, the nation's homeland. Civic nations in contrast are based on a common political culture and a legal system that assigns equal rights and duties to all members, a common economy with a single division of labour, and a territory that is the geo-political basis of the community. Each national identity includes both ethnic and civic features (Smith, 1991: 13). Therefore, the distinction is better understood as a continuum. I shall define ethnic nations as those in which ethnic features are prevalent and civic ones as those in which civic and territorial elements play the most important part in defining who belongs to the community and who is a foreigner.

Italian identity may be seen as a blend of civic and ethnic elements. The notion of 'Italianness'[1] initially developed in the Renaissance period as a cultural concept. Only in the nineteenth century was it transformed into a political project, which became reality with the unification of Italy in 1860. Of course, in Italy just as elsewhere, there are competing discourses and conceptions of the nation. My aim here is to discuss the main elements involved in the formation of the Italian identity – including both its unifying forces and its centrifugal tendencies – and to thus highlight the predominant conception of the Italian nation.

Ever since the creation of the independent Italian state, the nation has been conceptualized as a community of people living in a territory and sharing a common set of political and cultural traditions. Thus, the national community has been primarily defined with reference to a specific territory and a particular political culture (Rusconi, 1993). The idea of its historical continuity has been formulated through the integration of the Roman tradition, the *Risorgimento* – the movement of national revival in the first half of the nineteenth century – and the fascist legacy, into a common national past. The blending of these traditions and historical memories has, however, been characterized by internal contradictions that played an important role in impeding the consolidation of a national identity (Brierley and Giacometti, 1996: 172-6).

The formation of the Italian nation was compromised not only by the cosmopolitan heritage of the Roman empire and the Catholic church but also by the failure of the emerging Italian bourgeoisie to incorporate within it the intellectual and literary elites (Gramsci, 1985). These last remained idealist and cosmopolitan in their attitudes and promoted the *Risorgimento* movement as a counter-reform – re-discovering tradition through change, linking revolution with restoration, and avoiding radical ruptures with the past (Veneziani, 1994: 8-10) – preventing, thus, the development of a strong national bourgeois class and the spreading of a secular and scientific ideology, as happened in the rest of western Europe.

Moreover, this division between the producing class and the intellectuals perpetuated the existence of two cultures, a *high* culture of the literary strata and a variety of *low*, popular cultures and their respective dialects among the peasants and workers. This duality impeded the spreading of a common Italian vernacular, which would allow for the linguistic and cultural homogenization of the rural population. Gramsci (1979: 16) points to the gap between the literary and the popular strata and

---

[1] For a detailed review of the process of nation formation in Italy see Duggan (1994) and Doumanis (2001).

the absence of a romantic nationalist movement in Italy in the nineteenth century. Eventually, Italianness remained a legal, idealist concept that failed to penetrate the popular culture and identity.

The intellectual movement of the *Risorgimento* sought to integrate 'from above', as part of the nation, the artisan and peasant populations. The high, humanist culture created through the exaltation of the rural ethic in the works of Alessandro Manzoni, the reconstruction of the history of the Italian Republics, and the denial of the imperial tradition were thus re-interpreted as the core elements of Italianness. In reality, the idealization of life in the countryside was a strategy for opposing the advent of industrialism (Bollati, 1983: 101; Duggan, 1994). Italy's economic backwardness by comparison to other European states was masked and implicitly justified by a discourse on the country's aesthetic superiority. The beauty of the landscape, the rich artistic and cultural heritage and the beauty of its people were seen as intrinsic national characteristics, emphasized as emblems of the nation's superiority (Gundle, 2000: 127-9). This discourse has been reproduced throughout the nineteenth and twentieth century until nowadays. The term '*bel paese*' (literally 'beautiful country') is still used in common parlance and by the media as synonymous to Italy. The recent development of Italy's fashion and design industry has only corroborated this view. However, this aesthetic conception of the nation has often been intertwined – especially during the Fascist regime but also by liberal politicians like D'Annunzio in the early twentieth century – with authoritarian, imperialist and racialized views concerning the inherent superiority of Italians towards other peoples and civilizations (Gundle, 2000).

Furthermore, the myth of a presumed Italian 'national character', i.e. a specific constellation of personality features that characterizes people belonging to the same nation, was built on the basis of the aforementioned rural ethic and beauty discourses. This myth, which is still evoked nowadays, depicts Italians as inherently 'kind people' (*brava gente*) and emphasizes the cult of virtue and beauty and the Catholic tradition of solidarity as the essential elements of Italian culture and identity.

Religion and language, although usually identified as two fundamental elements intertwined with national identity, in the case of Italy play a contradictory role. The universalistic dogma of the Catholic church, which is by definition in contrast with any nationalist ideology, and the standard Italian language, that has never been able to completely override local dialects, tend to weaken rather than reinforce the national identity.

Another important element that characterizes Italy is regionalism both as a political-administrative reality and as a civic tradition including cultural and linguistic traits. As a matter of fact, Italy is constituted by a plurality of territorial units with their own separate histories. The division between North and South is not a mere matter of geography that can be attributed to environmental differences or to supposed ethnobiological features, which distinguish northern from southern Italians. The origins of this division lie in the past, in the different economic, social and political experiences that each region has had (Putnam, 1993) but also in the discourse on the South's 'alterity' that has been dominant in Italian society and politics ever since the Unification (Schneider, 1998a).

The importance of regionalism for the concept of Italianness is obvious if one considers that more than a century after the unification of the country, regional identities and socio-economic realities continue to threaten the national unity, as the success of *Lega Nord* has demonstrated. The key to understanding this problem lies, first, in the relatively late formation of the Italian nation-state and, second, in the fact that the unification was imposed by a small elite rather than the masses (Bollati, 1983; Duggan, 1994). The unification process was experienced by a large part of the population, mainly the southern peasants, as a civil war, or as a war for the conquest of the central and southern parts of Italy by the Piedmont region. It was certainly not a fight for national liberation (Duggan, 1994: 133). Moreover, the policies of the new state were not successful in inculcating a feeling of belonging to the nation amongst the rural populations of either the North or the South. The opposite interests of the northern bourgeoisie and the southern landowners prevented the new state from tackling effectively its main social problems – such as low level of literacy, poor transport and communications and land reform – and creating a national consciousness among the masses (Brierley and Giacometti, 1996: 174). Nonetheless a 'historical block' (*blocco storico*) was formed between the northern bourgeoisie and the southern landowners soon after the unification, which served the interests of both classes but seriously hampered the South's economic and industrial development (Davis, 1998; Schneider, 1998b).

The failure of integrating regional diversity into the nation-state may also be attributed to the fact that territorial identities have been neglected for a long time. The creation of a centralized state left little room for local or regional politics. The state administration and institutions introduced after the unification succumbed to the pre-existing traditions and socio-economic realities, instead of fostering the homogenisation of the regional politics (Putnam, 1993: 145). Thus, *campanilismo*[2] and clientelistic politics prevailed instead of a modern bureaucracy that would have supported national integration.

The conception of the Italian nation has also been influenced by the fascist legacy. A strong nationalist sentiment was generated only during the fascist era, though again for a short time. According to Biocca (1997: 229-31), support for the fascist regime was relatively widespread in both the North and the South of the country and remained so even after the approval of anti-Semitic legislation in 1938. The collapse of the regime in 1943, the subsequent occupation of Italy from the Nazi forces and eventually the double defeat of the country – within its own alliance and from the allied anti-Nazi forces – marked Italy's post-war re-birth. The need to rehabilitate the idea of the nation and the nation-state as a territorial and cultural community, to dissociate it from the racial overtones of Fascism and Nazism and to thus provide a basis for the rebuilding of a democratic society and political system led to the rejection of the fascist past. Any earlier popular support of the Mussolini regime was drawn into question and reconsidered (Biocca, *ibid.*). The complete rejection of and dissociation from Fascism, however, led to a somewhat paradoxical effect. Instead

---

[2] The term comes from the word *campanile* (the church's tower bell), which symbolises the strong affiliation with one's family, friends, village and local patron who are one's group of reference and allegiance, and through which one pursues and protects one's interests.

of elaborating the fascist experience and integrating into the national history, the Mussolini years were simply silenced and if not literally at least symbolically 'hidden'. This lack of critical inquiry has in fact obscured cruel 'details' of the Fascist policies such as the Italian concentration camps where the Slav populations of the northeastern regions and Dalmatia were interned in 1943 and, in general, the Fascist policies against ethnic minorities in that region (Walston, 1997). Masking Fascism behind the 'brava gente' national self-stereotype has also prevented a critical analysis of the continuities that exist between earlier conceptions of Italian national identity and Fascist ideology and policies. Indeed, the Fascist representation of the Slav population as a threatening internal Other was built on pre-existing stereotypical images of the Slavs as *allogeni* (literally 'of another kind'), culturally inferior to Italians and a 'problem' for the nation-state (Sluga, 2000).

The foundation myth of the new Italian Republic has been based on the movement of Resistance against the Fascists and the German occupation (1943-45). Nonetheless, the symbolic value of the Resistance as a national liberation struggle has been contested by many. The movement was divided into minority groupings which claimed to fight for national liberation but who fought also with a view to imposing their own socio-economic model for the reconstruction of the new Italian state (Dunnage, 2000; Rusconi, 1993). Thus, the Resistance was from its very beginning intertwined with party politics and failed to provide for the symbol of national unity. More recently, historians (De Felice, *cit.in* Biocca, 1997: 228) have questioned the size, spread and strength of the Italian resistance movement. Resistance appears to have been more a doubtful unifying myth than a historical reality or indeed the main tenet of Italian post war national identity.

Many scholars argue (Biocca, 1997; Galli della Loggia, 1996) that both the military and the civilian elites failed to respond to the acute social, political and economic problems that the country faced during and immediately after the war. Traditional institutions like the monarchy or the church did no better than the elites. Nevertheless, a small 'Italian miracle' took place in the second half of the twentieth century. The country experienced remarkable economic growth and social development and managed to establish a democratic if unstable political system. These changes however did not help overcome the fundamental weakness of Italian nationhood. Distrust towards state authorities, regional diversity and disparity, and the lack of strong national symbols and historical memories that would resonate with the feelings of Italian citizens across the peninsula, all made national identity fragile.

The most recent developments of the 1980s and 1990s, notably the crisis of the party system and economic elites, the reform of institutions in favour of de-centralisation, and the consistent support for Italy's full (political and economic) participation into the European integration process have generated both centripetal and centrifugal tensions within Italian nationhood. Integration into the European Union, for instance, has been perceived as a remedy for national ills and a source of national pride (for 'having made it' to be part of Europe and the Euro zone). Similarly, the pattern of crisis and reform of the political and institutional system was seen as an expression of Italy's non-existent national identity and at the same time as a desire to re-affirm national unity albeit within a decentralized, regional system of government.

The national currency (the Italian lira) was at the same time a national economic symbol and a source of worry and shame for its constant fluctuation in the 1990s.

In sum, post-war Italy bears with it the signs of its national past. On the one hand, national identity has been consolidated through democratic politics, the granting of autonomy to the regions, and the integration through national politics, the media and consumerism of local or regional identities as sub-cultures within a common national culture (Brierley and Giacometti, *ibid.*). On the other hand, however, it still has not come to terms with regional diversity and autonomy, nor has it succeeded in creating a common national myth.[3]

A number of scholars (Diamanti, 1999; Nevola, 1999; Rusconi, 1994) have argued that Italian national identity is predominantly a civic territorial concept that for some is weak and problematic (Galli della Loggia, 1996; 1998) and for others stable and flexible (Diamanti, 1999). Although I have strong reservations about the prevalence of a civic conception of nationhood in Italy today, I agree that from a historical point of view only a civic territorial concept of nationhood appears possible in Italy. The lack of nationalist elites, the uneven development of the country after unification, the pre-existing regional social, cultural, political and economic differences and, last but not least, the universalist tendency of the Catholic church have created a fragmented concept of nationhood and a divided national reality. In this context, common historical experience mainly after – but also before – national unification in sharing the national territory and a civic conception of community appear to be the tenets on which the Italian nation rests.

Nonetheless, the rise and crisis of the Italian Republic in the post war era and the persistent distrust between citizens and the state suggest that even these civic foundations of national identity are weak. According to Galli della Loggia (1998) and in agreement with Eurobarometer results (Eurobarometer, November 1998, *cit.in* Diamanti, 1999: 304), integration into the European Union provides for a necessary and much desired support for the construction of a civic Italian nationhood. This view is also indirectly supported by survey results (Cinnirella, 1997: 26) that show Italians to be proud of their cultural heritage and artistic achievements but not of their democratic institutions. A more recent survey (Ceccarini and Diamanti, 1999; Diamanti, 1999) suggests that Italian identity is weak because of, or rather thanks to its strong adaptation capacity. National identity, according to this survey, is based on a civic conception of nationhood that focuses on citizenship and legality and rejects ethnic origin as a criterion for national belonging or exclusion.

---

[3] Scholars and politicians tend to disagree on this matter. Opinions vary between those who view Italian identity as a feeling of belonging to a civic-territorial community (Rusconi, 1993) and those who, like Bocca (1990) or Umberto Bossi, the leader of the Northern League, are quite sceptical as to whether an Italian identity exists at all. Nonetheless, debate is fervent over the meaning of 'Italianness,' the historical roots of the nation and, most importantly, its future. One of the most prestigious Italian publishing houses, *Il Mulino*, has launched a book series entitled *'L'identità italiana'* (the Italian identity), whose purpose is 'to re-discover the Italian national identity' (*Panorama* weekly magazine, 28.04.1998, pp. 150-4).

Contrary to these findings, my own research as well as that of other scholars[4] suggests that when confronted with the question of immigration, Italian national identity, as expressed in the media, political but also lay people discourse, takes up an ethnic connotation *in addition* to its civic dimension. Emphasis is put on the ethnic origin of the immigrants, their being 'foreigners' in 'our' country and also on the existence of a 'national character', namely a stable psychological predisposition that supposedly characterizes each nation (including Italians).

This ethnic component of the nation has in fact been cherished and preserved in the context of nationality law. The evolution of Italian nationality law has largely been characterized (until its recent reform with law no. 91/1992) by the desire to keep and strengthen the links of Italian emigrants abroad with their mother country (Bianchi 1998; Pastore 2001). The role of nationality legislation has been both symbolic and practical in promoting national unity and, more recently, in preventing the integration of non-EU immigrants that reside in Italy. Italian citizenship is predominantly ethnic in character because it is related to kinship by blood or through marriage. The law allows for foreign permanent residents to apply for naturalization and does not require cultural assimilation. However, the bureaucratic procedure established for the naturalization is so complex, and time and effort-consuming that it effectively acts as a deterrent to potential applicants. Thus, while the law adheres to a conception of the nation as a civic community and not only an ethno-cultural one, it does so only in form but not in substance.

In conclusion, contemporary Italian nationhood emerges as a force of opposition, in contrast to political corruption and to immigrants, and as an identification with a complex and diversified community of people that are bound together by a varying combination of ethnic, cultural, territorial and civic ties. These last appear to have been reinforced in recent times through European integration. It is not clear yet however if the trust in and support for a united Europe as a means to redeem the civic values of the nation will further strengthen or weaken national identity.

Italy's Significant Others

In order to achieve an in-depth understanding of the Italian national identity and of its entanglement with images of Europe and the European Union, it is worth examining more closely the nation's Significant Others and how these have shaped the former's identity.

Quite surprisingly, Italy's Significant Other *par excellence* since the national unification, is its fragmented national Self and, more specifically, 'the South'. Indeed, the 'Southern question' and the dominant image of a country divided in two opposite poles, 'the North' and 'the South', is an element that

---

[4] Xenophobic and racist attitudes or behaviour have been documented in sociological (Campani 1993, among others), social psychological (Sniderman *et al.* 2001), anthropological (Cole 1996), media and political discourse studies (ter Wal 1996; 2000; Triandafyllidou 2001; 2002).

permeates and characterizes Italian society and politics. Rather than debating on the variety of regional Others that potentially exist in the Italian peninsula, the national discourse has concentrated on the North vs. South opposition, which has been largely reified and has absorbed into it the plurality of regional identities and realities that actually exist in the country.

Analyzing critically and to the full either the Southern question or the debate around it goes beyond the scope of this chapter. It is worth noting however how this construction of the South as the negative Other has helped justify the incomplete realization of the national Self, creating a paradoxical situation in which national unity is defined in contrast to an Other that is part of the ingroup and, at the same time, its very source of division. As Schneider (1998b) points out, the South's pejorative image has not been constructed only by northerners or outsiders but also by southerners themselves. Such views were later supported and indeed complemented by official statistics of the young Italian nation, which gave 'scientific' backing to the South's alterity. This orientalizing discourse was confronted with Gramsci's alternative and critical work on the question of the *Mezzogiorno*. For Gramsci, 'the Southern question was a national question, in so far it was a question of lack of communication between the social classes of the South and between the North and the South' (Urbinati, 1998: 137).

A line of critical sociological inquiry on the Southern question was developed more recently by sociologists like Alessandro Pizzorno (1971) and Sidney Tarrow (1996) who criticized Banfield's (1958) and Putnam's (1993) work. Recent economic and sociological studies have documented in depth the economic diversity of the regions that constitute the South and the unpredictable, unstable and disruptive nature of economic change in these regions (see Davis, 1998 for an overview). These studies have attempted at creating a new discourse on the 'Southern question'. However, this discourse has not yet managed to displace the dominant political, media, and to a certain extent scholarly, representations of the South as Italy's 'Other within' and as the main impediment to national integration and development. Cultural essentialist and racialist explanations of the South's supposedly unchanging backwardness and the Southerners' negative personality traits continue to permeate public stereotypes, at least in the North (Sniderman *et al.* 2000: 86-7). The Northern League's propaganda against the central government is based on an essentialized and polarized distinction between a hard-working and civic-minded North and a chaotic and corrupt South. Thus, the South is represented as the cause of national disunity.

By contrast to the 'Southern question', ethnic and linguistic minorities that have historically existed at border areas, like the French-speaking minority of Val d' Aosta, the German-speaking population of Trentino-Alto Adige or the Slav population of Venezia Giulia, occupy a marginal position in the Italian public and political debate as Significant Others. With the exception of Apih (1966) and Rusinow (1969), there has been very little research on the role that minorities in border regions played in the formation of the Italian national identity. Despite the initial conflict and divided national allegiances that have characterized their incorporation into Italy and their oppression by the Fascist regime, these regions have gradually been integrated into the Italian national state, partly also thanks to the special statutes of autonomy conceded to them.

The Northern League has not been framed as one of Italy's Significant Others, either. Its extremist actions and discourse, including for instance the proclamation of a Padanian Republic in the autumn of 1996, the subsequent creation of a Padanian parliament and a Padanian civil guard, have attracted relatively mild reactions from the central state. While anti-Italian sentiment is one of the main features of identification with Padania and the League (Diamanti, 1998; Ceccarini and Gardani, 1998) – in short, Italy is Padania's Significant Other – the League's secessionist movements have not been perceived as the Italian nation's Significant Other. Rather the League's discourse has been interpreted as another manifestation of the national *malaise* that has its roots in the North-South divide and the inefficiency of the central government.

A new Other has emerged for Italy in the past two decades: non-EU immigrants who have followed both legal and unlawful paths to enter Italy and find employment there. The rising immigrant population in the country – about 5per cent of the total population in 2003, in its largest part legal after successive regularisation programmes – has attracted the attention of the media, the government and, naturally, the public.

A recent study of parliamentary debates on immigration (ter Wal, 2000) points to the different discourses developed by the then (in 1997) incumbent left-wing forces and the right-wing opposition. Either side organized its discourse in terms of an ingroup (the host society, Italians) – outgroup (the immigrants) contrast. All parties recognized the problem of crime and the need for ensuring citizens' security. However, while the right wing forces, *Alleanza Nazionale, Lega Nord* and partly *Forza Italia*, attributed agency to immigrants involved in deviant or criminal activities, the left-wing government pointed to the legitimate motives of immigration adopting the perspective of the hopes and needs of the immigrant outgroup. The only party which engaged in an overtly racist discourse Othering the immigrants through concentrating on cultural differences as a problem and, in particular, on Islam as a 'threat' was the *Lega Nord*.

My own study (Triandafyllidou, 2001) based on the analysis of the weekly press discourse in the period 1990-95 and on interviews with social and political actors conducted in 1996, has yielded similar results. Overall, civic values provided a marker for distinguishing between insiders and outsiders: immigrants were excluded because they were 'illegal' – that is, undocumented. Nonetheless, the press appealed to the civic consciousness of the domestic population and placed emphasis on the values of solidarity and tolerance: immigrants could be accepted if they abided by the law, and the national boundary was thus permeable. Among the social actors (trade unions, ministry employees and NGOs) interviewed, the boundary between Us and Them regarded ethnic origin, culture and civic values. Cultural difference was rarely seen as a good thing and immigrants were expected to assimilate to the host society's culture.

The ambivalent views towards immigrants that permeate Italian society have been documented in anthropological research conducted in Sicily (Cole, 1996). Cole argues that very few Palermitans viewed immigrants as a specific racial group with unalterable and undesirable qualities that constituted a threat to Sicilians. Their view on immigrants was situated in a network of power relations between working class natives, the Mafia, employers and the Italian state, the three last seen to exploit native workers as well as immigrants. The interviewees constructed a positive identity partly in relation to their (presumed) superiority over the 'Turks' [immigrants].

A recent survey study conducted by the Italian journal *LiMes* (see Ceccarini and Diamanti, 1999) has explored the views of Italian citizens concerning immigrant integration. Diamanti's analysis of the survey findings (Diamanti, 1999: 308-17) concludes that even though immigration is a source of worry for Italians and indeed perceived as something undesirable or threatening by some, a civic conception of citizenship is largely prevalent. According to his analysis, the results of the study show that Italian citizenship is based on a set of civic values including the respect of the law and a feeling of territorial belonging (expressed as stability of residence) that potentially open the way for immigrant acceptance and integration. In other words, Diamanti points to the relative absence of cultural and ethnic closure and of perceived links between nationality and genealogical descent. In my view, in the light of the qualitative studies presented above, the *LiMes* survey largely corroborates the finding that legality and a supposedly strong (but in reality rather weak) civic culture are used as a shifting inclusion/exclusion barrier and a strategy for strengthening national identity. Indeed, the acceptance of cultural and religious diversity within the Italian society is still a contested matter (Triandafyllidou, 2002b).

Relations with Europe: Interests and Identity

Italy was one of the founding states of the European Economic Communities. It was a co-signatory of the Treaty of Rome in 1957 and has ever since played an important albeit ambivalent role as the third (after France and Germany) and later the fourth (when the UK joined the EEC) largest country participating in the Community.

The end of World War II and the fascist regime left the Italian economy destroyed and the Italian state discredited in the eyes of its European neighbours. The will of the Italian government to support the project of European economic (and possibly later political) integration was a clear expression of its will to put the fascist past aside, confirm its peaceful and democratic vocation, and follow a path of socio-economic development in collaboration with the rest of western Europe. Italy's participation to the EEC may be seen as a participation 'against the odds': Italy was the only Mediterranean country among the EEC founders, it had a weak industrial sector, important regional disparities in its economy and an unstable political system after two decades of Fascism and the turbulent years immediately after the war in which the Communists were bitterly confronted with the Conservative forces.

From an economic point of view, Italy benefited enormously from its early participation in the Common Market. As Duggan argues (1994: 263), northern Italian industry was sufficiently developed in the late 1950s to take advantage of the free trade conditions created by the Treaty of Rome. Italian exports towards other EEC countries doubled between 1958 and 1963. The boom of the Italian industry in the late 1950s and 1960s was a combination of a number of forces, including the availability of cheap labour from the South, the construction of communication and transport infrastructures by the state, the benefit of new energy sources available at low prices, and a developing steel industry thanks mainly to government investment (Duggan, *ibid.*). However, this growth potential found its full realization within the European Common Market.

The southern regions remained outside this small economic 'miracle'. Not only were they less economically developed than their northern counterparts, but they were also further disadvantaged by the Common Agricultural Policy decided by their fellow EEC partners. Its limited political influence within the EEC prevented Italy from successfully defending the interests of its farmers whose Mediterranean crops (fruits and vegetables) differed largely from those of France and Germany (wheat and cattle). Moreover, it has been argued (Sbragia, 1992: 81) that the Italian delegation failed to negotiate favourable conditions for the national agriculture at the Treaty of Rome because of internal disagreement. When later Italian governments tried to rectify the situation, they realized that gains in negotiations were hard to achieve.

The unfavourable conditions of the southern Italian economy became a further matter of contention between Italy and the other EEC countries as the former put pressure on the latter for measures and funds (like the European Social Fund and the Structural Funds) that would assist the socio-economic development of the *Mezzogiorno* and combat unemployment. According to Sbragia (1992: 84), Italy played a crucial role in setting the foundations of the structural and regional policies in the Treaty of Rome already. It pushed for the creation of the European Investment Bank, the European Social Fund and the Guidance Section of the European Guidance and Guarantee Fund of the Common Agricultural Policy (CAP) which constituted the main instruments to combat regional underdevelopment before the establishment of the European Regional Development Fund in 1975.

Somewhat paradoxically this marginal position of Italy with its 'peculiar' regional problems may be seen also as its point of strength, as these very issues that were dear to Italian governments, namely combating regional underdevelopment and promoting certain sectors of the CAP, became central concerns for Community policy as successive waves of enlargement brought into the club Ireland, Greece, Spain and Portugal. It may thus be argued that Italy's institutional and policy contribution to the EEC/EU has been important. It anticipated the development of the Community and is still pertinent in the wake of the Union's enlargement to the East.

In discussing Italy's contribution to the institutional design and political decision-making in the EEC/EU, two elements must be taken into account. First and foremost, the relative incapacity of the Italian administration – which to a certain extent persists until nowadays – to deal with the breadth and complexity of Community issues (Wallace, 1973: 25). Both the lack of administrative skill and internal divisions (Padoa Schioppa, 2001: 19) concerning the definition of a common national interest prevented Italy from handling Community affairs effectively and influencing the decisions taken in the EEC.

Italy has been also famous for its enthusiastically pro-European attitude and support for deeper and larger integration and its low record of compliance with Community directives. However, this paradoxical situation can also be read inversely, as Padoa Schioppa (2001: 35) suggests. The country's political elites have alternated periods of non-compliance with moments of exceptional effort and stamina in pursuing large scale reforms of the national financial and administrative system in order to bring it into line with EU policies. Thus, regular non-compliance, which in any case has been receding in the more recent years, should be considered also in relation to the breadth and depth of the reforms undertaken in some cases.

The second element to be considered is Italy's role and capacity as mediator between its fellow member states. Italy played a difficult part as the cushion between France and Germany in the early years of the EEC and later as the fourth largest power in the club of the big three, France, Germany and the UK. However, the positions supported by Italian governments have been consistently pro-European, favouring compromise rather than conflict. The influence of Italian politicians and thinkers who, like Luigi Einaudi, Altiero Spinelli and Mario Albertini, got actively involved into EEC affairs and promoted European integration alongside the more famous French thinkers and politicians like Jean Monnet and more recently Jacques Delors, has generally been underestimated.

Moreover, the Italian 'crafts' of building consensus and forging compromise, which are often deplored in the domestic political arena, proved useful at the European level where the achievement of consensus is a *sine qua non* for decision making. Typical Italian devices such as delaying decisions when an agreement was hard to reach, searching for support from the opposition, aiming at compromise decisions acceptable to all participants in a coalition, proved to be useful techniques for bargain and accommodation at the EU level (Padoa Schioppa, 2001: 27).

In sum, the relations between Italy and the EEC/EU are both complex and ambivalent. Economic gains from early participation into the EEC have been significant albeit concentrated on specific sectors of the economy (industry and small and medium enterprises) while other sectors paid the price for integration (agriculture). From a political point of view, Italy has gained from the political stability of the EEC/EU environment but at the same time has also made an important contribution to the Union as a mediator and negotiator. The poor performance of the national administration in complying with EU norms has been to a certain extent counter-balanced by the intensity of effort and the pro-European enthusiasm of Italian governments and voters (see also the following section concerning public attitudes on the EU).

More recently, after the public corruption scandals of the 1990s, Italian citizens seem to have turned to Europe hoping that it will constrain their domestic elites and literally impose an efficient and transparent system of governance in the country. In fact, the political and social crisis caused by and manifested in the

Tangentopoli affair may be considered to have marked a turning point in the relationship between Italy and the EU. The shock of the revelation of widespread corruption amongst even the most high-ranking figures in the business world (senior managers of Fiat, for instance) began a wide-ranging debate in the media and the political parties on the foundations of the Italian polity and, most importantly, on its position among EU member states. The purging of the corrupt politicians and the rationalization of the public finance came to symbolize the European orientation of Italy. The extent to which a set of civic values identified with EU governance can provide for a link between an emerging European identity and a feeling of belonging to the Italian nation is a question for research. It is however a matter of fact that Italy's pro-European policy and public opinion have persisted and guided the country into the first round of the Euro zone implementation, despite gloomy predictions.

My own study (Triandafyllidou, 2002a: 85-110) of the press discourse on the EU during the last fifteen years offers some interesting insights into the representation of the relationship between Italy and the EEC/EU in the Italian public and political discourse. Two competing discourses were identified in the two major national newspapers (*Corriere della Sera* and *La Repubblica*). On one hand, an *EU primacy discourse* subordinated Italy's position and role to that of the EU as a supranational political and economic entity and recognized the primacy and expertise of the EU over both domestic (Italian) and international affairs. On the other, a *national interest discourse* emphasized the independent political will and socio-economic interests of the country. This does not necessarily imply that European integration was viewed negatively. Italy was seen as an independent national actor that had to protect and negotiate its interests with the EU, which was also subject to the influence of the other member states. Both discourses developed around political as well as economic issues. Thus, in the EU primacy discourse, the debate over the national economy and Italy's compliance with the preconditions for integration was developed as a self-criticism, while the EU's competence and legitimacy to check the country's economic development and decide over its performance was recognized. In this discourse, Italy's interest was represented as identical to EU integration and EU interests. Acquiring a decent position in the united Europe was seen as the main national goal, and the country's political and economic elites were criticized by the press for failing to face up to the challenge. The nation was seen as an integral part of Europe, and national pride or shame was expressed in relation to its 'Europeanness'. This discourse prevailed in the press in 1989 and 1993, while it appeared weaker in 1999.

The national interest discourse, in contrast, discussed Italy's participation in the EEC/EU in critical terms. Competing interests between national currencies and member state central banks were emphasized, and the need to protect the Italian lira and safeguard the country's interests was underscored. This discourse was not critical of European integration as such but rather pointed to the fact that Italy had to protect its own, national, interests from EU regulation, harmonization and competing member state interests. This type of discourse first appeared in 1993 but was further reinforced in 1999. The shift was not from a pro- to an anti-

European discourse, but rather from a European representation of Italy to an Italian representation of Europe.

Even though both discourses were present in all four periods studied, there was a change in the representation of Italy and the EEC/EU and the definition of the ingroup and outgroup across time. The EU was overall integrated into the Italian identity as one of its constitutive elements. It was however perceived as one element to be striven for. In 1993, Italy's Europeanness was more secure in terms of identity, despite the country's poor economic performance and severe political crisis. Thus, the identification of Italy with the united Europe was dominant while, at the same time, the specific mode of integration was criticized. Most recently, in 1999, when EU integration was a reality, Italy seemed to rediscover its national distinctiveness, not against Europe but within it. Interests and policies were nationally defined, while the EU was recognized as an integral part of the nation/country and as a unitary actor in relation to third countries, under which Italian interests were subsumed. Italy, together with other member states, was seen as part of a common decision-making process concerning the social and political guidelines for European integration.

The lack of polarity between Italian and European identity is striking, albeit not surprising. In recent times, integration into the European Union has fulfilled a double function with regard to Italian identity. On one hand, it has been perceived as the model of civic community that is absent from national politics. Thus, a European identity somewhat paradoxically may have reinforced national identity. Identifying with Europe was seen to provide the common civic basis necessary to consolidate the nation's unity. On the other hand, the economic welfare and political power (perceived to be) involved in the European integration project have provided a means for achieving a positive identity within the international community. Italy's all too common political crises during the post-war period, the country's relative poverty (by Western European standards) until the 1970s, and the more recent monetary and public finance crises provided a weak basis for achieving a positive national identity in the increasingly competitive international scene. Integration into the European Union has been seen as a powerful remedy to such past illnesses.

The ambivalence, however, between the two discourses suggests that one should be cautious about inferring that European integration is an element that may provide for the civic cultural basis of Italian national identity. The press expressed concerns regarding the kind of civic and social values inherent in the EU project. The two discourses reflect varying views concerning 'the state of the nation' which lie between the two extremes of seeing Europe as 'the saviour' of Italy and being attached to 'the beautiful country' (*il bel paese*) and taking pride mainly in national accomplishments. Eventually, this is also a discourse about the priority of social vs. economic principles in defining a 'good', 'modern', 'developed' society. The Italian press saw the EEC/EU to privilege economic welfare and efficient government while an Italian representation of Europe was concerned more with social welfare and democracy. For instance, the eagerness in the 1993 press discourse to ratify the Maastricht Treaty expressed this concern over the democratic deficit and (perceived) lack of a strong political vision in the EU.

Conclusions

Italy as a nation and as an EU member state presents a number of particularities that are worth noting for comparative purposes. Nation formation has remained incomplete, unifying national symbols are even nowadays hard to find and the nation appears fragmented and even divided within. The revival of regionalism in the late 1980s and 1990s and the continuing dominance of an orientalizing discourse towards the South pose serious challenges to national unity. The EU, in this context, acts both as a resource for national identity, providing for the civic dimension that the former is lacking, and, by contrast, as a centrifugal force because it opens new levels of governance accessible to regions, independently from the nation state.

Participation in the Common Market and later the EU has brought many advantages to the Italian economy and industry. These have initially accentuated and even indirectly fostered larger regional disparities between the North and the South. Nonetheless, in the last two decades of the twentieth century Community funds have been used for the restructuring of the *Mezzogiorno*. Italy has played an important part in the institutional development of the structural and regional policies of the EU, paving the way for assistance to the more recent southern European member-states like Greece, Spain and Portugal.

Immigration further complicates Italy's relations with the EU and the related representations of EU nations and citizens as opposed to '*extracomunitari*'. The country's recent transformation to a host has opened a debate on migration policy and also on culture and identity issues. This debate may take a different twist when in a few years time a number of non-EU immigrants (both regular and undocumented) originating from accession countries (like Poland), will become EU citizens.

Last but not least the divergent views on the relationship between Italy and the EU manifested in the national press discourse reveal interesting combinations of national and European loyalties and the ways in which the two can be intertwined.

References

Apih, E. (1966), *Italia, Fascismo e Anti-Fascismo Nella Venezia Giulia 1918-1943*, Rome: Laterza.

Banfield, Edward C. (1958), *The Moral Basis of a Backward Society*, Chicago: The Free Press.

Bedani, G. (2000), 'The Christian Democrats and national identity' in G. Bedani, B. Haddock (eds), *The Politics of Italian National Identity*, Cardiff: University of Wales Press, pp. 214-38.

Bianchi, Andrea (1998), 'Alla ricerca degli oriundi perduti', *LiMes*, 1, pp. 21-31.

Biocca, D. (1997), 'Has the nation died – the debate over Italian identity', *Daedalus*, 126(3), pp. 223-39.

Brierley, W. and Giacometti, L. (1996), 'Italian national identity and the failure of regionalism' in B. Jenkins and S. Sofos (eds), *Nation and Identity in Contemporary Europe*, London: Routledge, pp. 172-97.

Campani, Giovanna (1993), 'Immigration and racism in southern Europe: the Italian case', *Ethnic and Racial Studies*, 16(3), pp. 507-35.

Ceccarini, Luigi and Diamanti, Ilvo (1999), 'Il vantaggio di essere italiani', *LiMes*, 1, pp. 239-58.

Ceccarini, Luigi and Gardani, Ludovico (1998), 'Dieci, cento, mille Zermeghedo', *LiMes*, 1, pp. 163-72.

Cinnirella, M. (1997), 'Towards a European identity – interactions between the national and European social identities manifested by University students in Britain and Italy', *British Journal of Social Psychology*, 36, pp. 19-31.

Cole, J. (1996), 'Working class reactions to the new immigration in Palermo', *Critique of Anthropology*, 16(2), pp. 199-220.

Connor, W. (1978) 'A nation is a nation, is a state, is an ethnic group, is a...', *Ethnic and Racial Studies*, 1(4), pp. 377-400.

Davis, John (1998), 'Casting Off the "Southern Problem": Or the Peculiarities of the South Reconsidered' in J. Schneider (ed.), *Italy's "Southern Question": Orientalism in One Country*, Oxford: Berg, pp. 205-24.

Diamanti, Ilvo (1998), 'La tentazione del Nord: meno Italia e meno Europa', *LiMes*, 1, pp. 151-163.

—— (1999), 'Ha senso ancora discutere della nazione?', *Rassegna Italiana di Sociologia*, XL(2), pp. 293-321.

Doumanis, Nicholas (2001), *Italy. Inventing the Nation*, London: Arnold.

Duggan, C. (1994). *A Concise History of Italy,* Cambridge: Cambridge University Press.

Dunnage, J. (2000), 'Making better Italians: issues of national identity in the Italian Social Republic and the Resistance' in G. Bedani, B. Haddock (eds), *The Politics of Italian National Identity*, Cardiff: University of Wales Press, pp. 191-213.

Galli della Loggia, Ernesto (1996), *La morte della patria*, Bari: Laterza.

—— (1998), *L'identità italiana*, Bologna: Il Mulino.

Gramsci, Antonio (1979), *Letters from prison*. Selected, translated and introduced by Lynne Lawler, London: Quartet Books.

—— (1985), *Selections from Cultural Writings*, edited by David Forgacs and Geoffrey Nowell-Smith, London: Lawrence and Wishart.

Gundle, S. (2000) '*Il bel paese*: art, beauty and the cult of appearance' in G. Bedani, B. Haddock (eds), *The Politics of Italian National Identity*, Cardiff: University of Wales Press, pp. 124-141.

McCarthy, P. (2000), 'The Italian Communists and Italian national identity: the question of difference', in G. Bedani, B. Haddock (eds), *The Politics of Italian National Identity*, Cardiff: University of Wales Press, pp. 239-58.

Nevola, Gaspare (1999), 'Nazione-Italia', *Rassegna Italiana di Sociologia*, XL(3), pp. 435-60.

Padoa Schioppa, Tommaso (2001), 'Italy and Europe: A Fruitful Interaction', *Daedalus*, Italy: Resilient and Vulnerable, volume I, The European Challenge, 130(2), pp. 13-44.

Pastore, Ferruccio (2001), 'Nationality Law and International Migration: The Italian Case', in R. Hansen and P. Weil (eds), *Towards a European Nationality*, New York: Palgrave, pp. 95-117.

Pizzorno, Alessandro (1971), 'Amoral Familism and Historical Marginality', in M. Dogan and R. Rose (eds), *European Politics: A Reader*, Boston: Little Brown.

Putnam, Robert with R. Leonardi and R. Nanetti (1993), *Making Democracy Work: Civic Traditions in Modern Italy*, Princeton: Princeton University Press.

Rusconi, G. E. (1993), *Se cessiamo di essere una nazione*, Bologna: Il Mulino.

—— (1994) 'Razionalità politica, virtù civica e identità nazionale', *Rivista Italiana di Scienza Politica*, Vol. 1.

Rusinow, D. (1969), *Italy's Austrian Heritage, 1919-1946*, Oxford: Clarendon Press.

Sbragia, Alberta (1992), 'Italia/CEE Un partner sottovalutato', *Relazioni Internazionali*, 2, pp. 78-86.

Schneider, Jane (1998a) (ed.), *Italy's "Southern Question": Orientalism in One Country*, Oxford: Berg.

—— (1998b), 'The Dynamics of Neo-orientalism in Italy (1848-1995)', in J. Schneider (ed.), *Italy's "Southern Question": Orientalism in One Country*, Oxford: Berg, pp.1-26.

Sluga, G. (2000) 'Italian national identity and Fascism: aliens, allogenes and assimilation on Italy's north-eastern border' in G. Bedani, B. Haddock (eds), *The Politics of Italian National Identity*, Cardiff: University of Wales Press, pp. 163-89.

Smith, A. D. (1986), *The Ethnic Origins of Nations*, Oxford: Blackwell.

—— (1991), *National Identity,* London: Penguin Books.

Sniderman, P. Peri, P. de Figueiredo Rui, J. Jr. and Piazza, T. (2001), *The Outsider: Prejudice and Politics in Italy*, Princeton: Princeton University Press.

Tarrow, Sidney (1996) 'Making Social Science Work Across Space and Time: A Critical Reflection on Robert Putnam's *Making Democracy Work*', *American Political Science Review*, 90, pp. 389-97.

ter Wal, J. (1996), 'The social representation of immigrants: the *Pantanella* issue in the pages of *La Repubblica*', *New Community*, 22(1), pp. 39-66.

—— (2000) 'Italy: *Sicurezza e Solidarietá*', in R. Wodak and T. van Dijk (eds), *Racism at the Top. Parliamentary Discourse on Ethnic Issues in Six European States*, Vienna: Austrian Federal Ministry of Education, Science and Culture, pp. 311-53.

Triandafyllidou, Anna (2001), *Immigrants and National Identity in Europe*, London: Routledge.

—— (2002a), *Negotiating Nationhood in a Changing Europe: Views from the Press*, Wales and Washington D. C.: Edwin Mellen Press.

—— (2002b), 'Religious Diversity and Multiculturalism in Southern Europe: The Italian Mosque Debate', *Sociological Research Online*, 7(1), www.socresonline.org.uk/7/1/ triandafyllidou.html.

Urbinati, Nadia (1998), 'The Souths of Antonio Gramsci and the Concept of Hegemony' in J. Schneider (ed.), *Italy's "Southern Question"*, Oxford: Berg, pp. 135-56.

Veneziani, Marcello (1994), *La rivoluzione conservatrice in Italia: genesi e sviluppo della ideologia italiana fino ai nostri giorni*, Sugarco, Varese, 2nd edition, (1st edition 1987).

Walston, J. (1997), 'History and memory of the Italian concentration camps', *Historical Journal*, 40, pp. 169-83.

Wallace, Helen (1973), *National Governments and the European Communities*, London: Chatham House.

Chapter 6

Modern Greece:
A Profile of a Strained Identity

Nikos Kokosalakis
and
Iordanis Psimmenos

Introduction

The long history of Greece, from pre-classical antiquity to the present, makes the question of its identity in modern times a particularly complex and debated issue. Having produced, in ancient, classical and Hellenistic times, a great civilization of its own upon which a substantial part of modern European civilization rests, Greece has the rightful claim to be and feel quintessentially European. Yet, modern Greece is also heir to the Christian Byzantine civilization which, for the greater part of the middle ages and up to the present day has been in tension with western, Latin Christianity. Thus Hellenism and Orthodox Christianity combined and in synthesis or in conflict and in tension, according to the historical socio-economic and political circumstances, constitute the basis of modern Greek identity and have often divided it.

In the turbulent political history of modern Greece, from its establishment in the 1830s as a nation state to the present day, this long and complex cultural heritage, in the context of its dialectic with modernity and the West, has constituted an arena of debate and tension over Greek ethnic identity. The debate at times looked inconsistent and contradictory as modern Greece has been trying to transform a long historical cultural identity into a political one (Tsaoussis 1983: 21). The classical image of Greece, which was constructed in Europe, placed a particular burden on the socio-economically very weak Greek society. Thus the tensions involved have been largely generated by complex internal and external political and socio-economic interests and by the country's aspirations to modernization.

This circumstance – in the context of an ambiguous cultural fusion of Hellenism and Orthodoxy on the one hand and 'Europe' and/or 'the West' on the other – set the framework for a turbulent political process of nation building, riddled with cleavages, tensions and contradictions. The initial institutions of the Greek state were intended to function on the basis of western ideas and the

Enlightenment. These were congruent with – indeed based on – the classical Greek spirit and culture and were espoused by many intellectuals and the urban and commercial Greek middle class, inside and outside the country. Yet the whole policy of the nation from the 1840s to the early 1920s operated in the context of an unrealistic and utopian vision of irredentism (*Megali Idea*), aiming at repossessing what were once Greek Byzantine lands.

In all this the Greek Orthodox church played an important role as a central institution of Modern Greek society tied to the state. As the church represents and carries forward the continuity of Byzantine culture, it has also functioned as the basic institution which embodies the representation of ethnic identity as inseparable from Orthodoxy. But the church has been used by the state for political and even political party ends very frequently. This has placed the church in an invidious position vis-à-vis the modernization and democratization of Greek society (Kokosalakis 1987).

The rise of a liberal middle class and the forces for democratization, reflected in the liberal party of Venizelos from about 1910, clashed with the policies of the Monarchy during and after the First World War. This, and the large influx of Greek refugees from Asia Minor in 1922, led to a deep long-lasting division (*dichasmos*) in the country between the social and political forces of the centre and the left and the reactionary forces of the right. With the prevalence of the right, in the mid-war and post Second World-War period, the division took a severe ethnic character, which led to the civil war (1947-1949) and then to the dictatorship of the Colonels (1967-1974). All this obstructed and significantly delayed the democratization and modernization of Greek society and produced tensions, which at times took an ambivalent and even schizophrenic character towards the West and towards Europe.

Yet it should be stressed that the tensions within Greek identity have not obstructed the country's accession and membership of the EU. All major political parties and the great majority of the Greek people are well disposed towards Europe and the EU. Certainly there is no evidence of incompatibility between the European and the Greek identity, although there have been heightened nationalist feelings in the country due to events in the Balkans during the 1990s and because of recent geopolitical developments. Also, emphasis on the symbolic aspects of Greek identity remains high, but this is in accord with a conception of a pluralist, multicultural Europe.

The Cultural, Discursive Elements of Greek

A union between the Greek classical and Hellenistic culture on the one hand and Christianity on the other is believed to have taken place during the first four centuries B.C. This union between Christianity and Hellenism was strengthened, indeed, consolidated in 330 when the Emperor Constantine transferred the capital of the Roman Empire from Rome to Constantinople. Christianity then became not only *religio licita* but also the official religion of the state. The connections between classical philosophy and Christianity were worked out by the early Christian fathers, of whom St. Basil, St. Chrysostom and S. Gregory the theologian have become patrons of letters and education in modern Greece.

The cultural importance of these connections is recognized by all Greeks, although there are varying, and sometimes diametrically opposed interpretations of their value and significance for modern Greek identity and society. Many Greeks, especially clergymen, some academics and certain politicians, believe and argue that there is a bond between Hellenism and Greek Orthodoxy which together with the Greek language constitute the basis of both Greek ethnic identity and the unity of the Greek nation. Others, some intellectuals in particular and politicians of the left, maintain that this is only a historical relic but it has been often used as a tool for political control and has served as an obstacle to modernization of Greek society. However, polarities apart, religion always had and continues to have important functions in Greek society, especially at the juncture of culture and politics. So Greek Orthodoxy, the Hellenic heritage, along with the Greek language, have been basic discursive elements in the shaping of modern Greek identity.

Specific historical events have sometimes strengthened the Hellenic and sometimes the Christian dimension but have never separated them completely. Rather, external forces have contributed to strengthen and consolidate the fusion between the religious and the ethnic factor. Because of the conflict between the Eastern and Western church, which was also a conflict about political power between the papacy and the Byzantines, after the schism in 1054 the Greeks of Byzantium, especially the intellectuals, started calling themselves *Hellenes*. Before that, and especially during the early centuries A.D, the term *Hellene* and the term *ethnos* carried negative connotations and were attributed to non-Christians, to idolaters (*ethnikoi*) (Campbell and Sherrard, 1968: 20-21). Thus, the 11th century in Byzantium marks both the beginning of the modern Greek ethnic consciousness and a historical landmark for the consolidation of the cultural and political distance and mistrust between the Greek Orthodox East and the Latin Catholic West. During the late centuries of Byzantium, especially during the dynasty of Palaiologoi, the idea of a distinctive Greek consciousness developed and a link with the classical Greek heritage was attempted. The so called 'hellenizing' movement, mainly by intellectuals led by George Gemistos Pletho, claimed a direct continuity of Byzantium with Hellenic classical antiquity (Svoronos 1975: 21). This movement was interrupted by the fall of Constantinople to the Ottomans (1453), but the idea and the image of the nation (to genos) as a heritage and a dream of aspirations for freedom and independence, grew and became the moving force for the Greek revolution (1821). Throughout the period of Ottoman rule the Orthodox church, led by the Ecumenical Patriarchate, was the institution which carried the ethno-religious identity of the Greeks and became a cultural symbol and a bridge between Byzantium and modern Greece.

Yet the representation of Greek ethnic identity at the point of the establishment of the Greek nation state was ambiguous to say the least. Although the unity of the nation became well formed during the period of the Ottoman rule and the Greeks fought the war of independence with a strong Greek consciousness (Svoronos 1975), that consciousness was strained and consisted of complex cultural and historical strands. Following the establishment of the Greek state, the ambiguity of what constitutes *Hellenicity* was enhanced and often has amounted to a crisis which has permeated modern Greek society throughout its history (Tsaoussis 1983: 17). The main reason was that a long and glorious cultural heritage had to be accommodated into weak and problematic social and political institutions and, initially, an elementary subsistence economy.

As a result the state became dominant over society from the beginning. Indeed, an imagined idea of the nation and of what constituted 'the national interest' was at each particular time largely constructed by the political elite. Nationalism, of course, was basically an imagined construction everywhere (Anderson 1991) but for Greece, especially unique configurations of cultural with socio-economic and political factors determined the process of nation building and established the dominance of state over society. Consequently, politics in modern Greece have become the dominant feature of social and cultural life.

The Background to the Formation of Modern Greece

Along with 25 March 1821 – the date of the launching of the Greek War of Independence – 29 May 1453 are the most important dates of modern Greek history, which every school child has to memorize. The Conquest of Constantinople by Mahmout B' meant not just the end of the Byzantine Empire but the beginning of a dream for the birth of a new Greek nation. Soon after the fall of the 'Polis', with its magnificent Byzantine churches (especially that of St. Sophia), popular songs expressed the aspirations of the Greeks: '*Pali me chronia me kairous, pali dika mas thane*' (Again with years to come, again they will be ours). A myth thus developed that a new Greek Orthodox Christian Commonwealth could arise, like the Phoenix, out of the ashes of Byzantium.

After the conquest the Ecumenical Patriarchate took up not only the religious and spiritual care over the *Orthodox Millet*, but also exercised over it all ethnic and civic functions. Also, a fundamental preoccupation of the Greek Orthodox church as a whole, throughout the period of occupation, was the protection of Orthodoxy from the threat of Islam as well as from western propaganda. The defence mechanisms of ethnic identity and the national idea strengthened even further the already strong fusion between popular culture, official religion and the political fortunes of the enslaved Greeks. So, from the 15th to the 19th centuries the church was the sole cultural and political agent of the nation.

Although the role of the church during the Greek uprising has been at times exaggerated the fact remains that, by its very institutional position, its contribution was outstanding. This was not because the church was or is a revolutionary or progressive institution but because she was and continues to be tied to the ethnic identity of the Greeks. At the dawn of Greece as a nation state the church was the basic institution which embodied the national dream in a new social and political setting.

But there was another vision substantially or drastically different from it. As mentioned earlier, already before Independence the ideas of the Enlightenment were widespread amongst Greek intellectuals (some of them clergy), who questioned the cultural hegemony of the Patriarchate. For many of them in fact Byzantium meant a period of obscurantism, religious dogmatism, superstition, and corruption; the very antithesis of the values of the Enlightenment. A secular, Hellenic rationalist spirit had been cultivated for some time by some eminent Greeks. The most prominent amongst them, by common acknowledgement, has been Adamandios Koraes (1743-1833), the son of a merchant from Smyrna who studied in Europe and settled in Paris. He, along with many others, visualized the rebirth of Greece and its identity in the modern world not on the basis of the Byzantine religious culture but in the context of a secular civil society guided by the old Hellenic spirit and rational, humanistic and philosophical values. He was not an atheist but was a strong advocate of modernity.

Such modern tendencies amongst intellectual circles were strong if we judge from the large number of publications of a secular character, which appeared in Greek during the first two decades of the 19th century. According to Clogg (1979: 36) 1,300 Greek books were published during that period and some editions ran to several thousands. There were also many translations of the French Encyclopaedists and other philosophers and scientists. Some sections of the small but vibrant Greek middle class, which was spread throughout the Balkans and Europe, were imbued with new liberal ideas and read the classics. These tendencies, which emphasized the secular and rational strand of classical Greek culture, were congruent with the ideas of the Enlightenment and the subsequent secularization and modernization of European societies. They were also congruent with the ideas of modernity and the general revival of neo-classicism, which was then sweeping Europe (Jenkyns 1980).

It should be strongly emphasized, however, that this image of classical Greece was constructed in Europe and was imported to the newborn Greek state (Tsoukalas 2002). Modern ideas touched the general Greek population only marginally, if at all. There were substantive sociological reasons for this. Economically, politically and culturally Greek society, before and after the Revolution, was unable to adopt rationalist modernizing ideas and programmes. Such ideas were utopian in the face of Greek social reality, as philhellenes such as Byron and others discovered. The mass of Greek people were illiterate and landless peasants who were steeped in popular religious culture and the superstitions of rural society. Over 60 per cent of the population was rural and 80 per cent of these had no property at all. The rest owned small holdings between ½ and 1 acre in the mountainous areas and the richer ones between 5 and 20 acres in the fertile planes (Svoronos 1975: 79). Both in the time of Kapodistria (1827-1831), the first Governor of the new-born Greece, and King Otto (1833-1862), land distribution and reform remained the crucial problem. Up to 1856, out of 721,000 acres of national arable lands only 28,00 were distributed to the peasantry and even those went to the stronger ones (Svoronos 1975: 79-80).

Apart from a small middle class, the general population was largely uneducated, and even in the lower clergy only one per cent could write their names (Frazee 1969: 101). Also, socio-cultural developments in the newborn nation, throughout the 19th century were influenced by a multiplicity of conflicting interests both internal and foreign. Certainly what determined modernization and the formation of national identity were not the ideas of the Enlightenment and of modernity but harsh and conflicting political, ideological and economic realities and interests.

After the assassination of Kapodistria (1831) there was anarchy for some time and then Greece was governed by an imported young monarch, Prince Frederic Otto of Wittelsbach, the seventeen year old son of King Ludwig of Bavaria. This was a cultural and political anomaly, for not only was the young king a Catholic and a foreigner invited to rule over an Orthodox nation, but besides this, the three man regency council which was in fact to rule was also Bavarian and Protestant. What came to be called 'the Protecting Powers' exercised such an influence on the newly-born state that the first political parties were named appropriately 'the English party', 'the French party', and 'the Russian party'. Supporters of these parties represented nascent class structures in Greek society but above all these parties represented corresponding foreign influences and interests.

The foreign administrators had no understanding of the indigenous culture. As they attempted to adapt western legal and cultural norms to Greek society their original aims of modernizing it were compromised and failed (Legg and Roberts 1997: 29). The conflicting interests of the protecting powers over Greece, and the policies of the Bavarian administration along with the activities of various Protestant Biblical societies, invoked a revival of the Orthodox ethos amongst the people, which is well described in the memoirs of General Makriyannis (1996).

Greek Irredentism and Nation Building 1844-1922

The ideology of the Greek revolution, albeit well underpinned by the ideas of the French Revolution and the Enlightenment, also had a nationalist irredentist character from the beginning. The *Philiki Etairia* (the secret friendly society which prepared the Revolution), consisted of people from various walks of life and envisioned a free Greece to include all enslaved Greeks. Against this ambition the initial Greek kingdom included only the Peloponese, the provinces south of Thessaly and some of the islands of the Aegean. By 1840 it was obvious that Greece was unlikely to develop along the cultural patterns of modernization prevalent in Western Europe. Greek nationalism was evolving along a specific, idiosyncratic pattern. Industrialization was virtually absent and the whole structure of the economy was clearly pre-capitalist. The whole political edifice was underdeveloped and functioned in the context of personalized clientilistic politics which expressed the web of powerful family relations and interests. The political parties which existed, as already mentioned, reflected the interests and the antagonisms of foreign powers (Petropoulos 1968). Both Kapodistria and the King's administration intended Greece to develop along the European prototype; but the regency especially, being conservative and oligarchic, proved entirely inept as they attempted to impose changes from above without sensitivity to the problems of the infrastructure of society.

One of the major problems in the new state was its strained relations with the Ecumenical Patriarchate because the Church of Greece was severed unilaterally from it (Frazee 1969). In his efforts to modernize the country, Maurer (the head of the Regency Council) closed down most of the monasteries (412 out of 593) and confiscated their property. The King, after severe pressure from the grass roots and the intervention of the army (3 September 1843) was forced to concede a constitution. Yet the oligarchic policies of the King continued to function, and the rift between the Church of Greece and the Patriarchate was not mended until 1850 when the *autocephalous* status of the former was recognized by the latter.

Apart from the fact that the socio-economic and political structure of the country was not brought to develop along western paths (Mouzelis 1978), the ideological and cultural development also pointed to a different direction from that which Koraes and other intellectuals had envisaged. Instead, a romantic, utopian nationalism was born, underpinned on the one hand by the Byzantine religious culture and on the other by a nostalgic vision of ancient Greece. The Greeks seemed able to combine those two strands of identity and culture ever since. The *Megali Idea* (the Great Idea) to expand the Kingdom eastwards and redeem all enslaved Greeks formed an essential policy of the state well up to 1922. As a vision it was supported by almost all Greeks at that time, and Otto himself became an enthusiastic advocate of it. In reality, however, this utopian, irredentist idea served as a smoke screen for corruption and the severe socio-economic problems faced by the government and as an excuse for the even greater blatant intervention of the Great Powers in Greek affairs (Clogg 1979: 76-79).

There were failures, tragedies and disappointments as well as some successes in trying to implement the 'Great Idea', but there is insufficient space here to deal with these. Suffice to say that the vision revived the historical connections between Orthodoxy and Hellenism and constituted a fusion which became, in varying intensity and form, the basic discourse for modern Greek identity. This was during the time when nations in the Balkans and in Europe at large were seeking to consolidate their cultural and historical roots. For a new, small and weak state like Greece it was imperative that the continuity of its cultural heritage, going back to classical and ancient times, should not be doubted. Yet the cultural historian Fallmerayer put forward theories to question precisely that. The reaction inside and outside Greece was very strong. Historians like Paparigopoulos and ethnographers or folklorists like Politis undertook the tremendous task to prove the long historical continuity of Hellenism. Later at the turn of the century the linguistic problem, that is the problem of the use of archaic (*katharevousa*) or the demotic language, also revived the problems and the debates over the continuity of Greek civilization; and all, of course, was linked back to the problems and discourses over Greek identity and nationalism and its relation to Europe.

On the political plane Otto's rule was becoming increasingly discredited and after the Crimean War the forces of the opposition rallied together demanding liberalization and western style parliamentary polity. In October 1862 Otto was dethroned and left Greece, but the protecting powers, England in particular, found a new King in the person of William-George Glyxbourg of Denmark, who took the throne under the title *George A' King of the Hellenes* (Svoronos 1975: 96). England, as a goodwill gesture, ceded to Greece the Ionian Islands in 1864, which Greece held as a protector since 1815, and all this fitted well with the policy of *Megali Idea*. There was a new democratic Constitution (1864), which limited the powers of the King, and in 1875 Charilaos Trikoupis introduced the system of crowned parliamentary democracy. There followed substantial socio-economic development, with the Greeks of the diaspora contributing significantly to it.

Throughout the second half of the 19th century and up to the first World War, the policies and aspirations of the emerging Balkan states, the problems of the disintegrating Ottoman Empire; and the interests of the Great Powers in the region were combined to constitute what has been called 'the Eastern Question' (*to anatoliko zitima*). It should be stressed that that the interests between these parties were mostly in conflict and all together presented a problem of great complexity. Certainly, the interests of the Balkan states were in conflict not just with Turkey but also with each other. Thus, along with frequent warfare, a substantial amount of horse trading had to take place between the interested parties for any part of the Ottoman empire which was ceded to any Balkan state. Following the Treaty of St. Stefano (1878) and the Congress of Berlin (1878), Greece and Turkey signed a treaty in Constantinople (1881) by which Greece was acquiring the province of Thessaly and the county of Arta from Epirus. In 1897 the policy of *Megali Idea* faced a substantial set back by the defeat of Greece in a short war with Turkey. The great complexity of interests in the region led to the Balkan Wars of 1912-13, which were followed by the First World War.

The outcome of these developments was congruent with the aspirations of *Megali Idea*. After successive treaties, (London 1913; Bucharest 1913), Greece acquired much of Macedonia, Epirus, Crete and the north-eastern islands of the Aegean. Greek land increased by 70 per cent and the population almost doubled from 2,800,000 to 4,800,000, some of whom were Slavs and Turks. Venizelos, the young liberal politician, had contributed to this expansion with his shrewd diplomacy and exceptional political capacity. After the assassination by a madman of King George I, Prince Constantine took the throne. In the excitement at the time about the Greek victories, many hailed the new king as the successor of Constantine XI Palaiologos, for as the prophecy had it another Constantine would recapture Constantinople (Clogg 1979: 104). Yet, in reality, it was largely due to the type of nationalism of this King and his clash with Venizelos over the policy on the First World War that Greece was to enter a long period of bitter division, the consequences of which have been plaguing Greek society to the present day.

The problem, which came to be known as '*Ethinicos Dichasmos*' (national schism), started with the different attitude between the King and his Prime-minister Venizelos towards the powers of the *Entente* (Britain, France and Russia). The King insisted on neutrality whereas Venizelos opted for alliance with the Entente at the outbreak of the war. The clash over the issue of neutrality was such that Venizelos had to resign (March 1915). The real cause, however, lay in the fundamentally different politics of the two men. The politics of the King and of his supporters were deeply conservative whereas the politics of Venizelos were liberal and reformist. At bottom the issue was about democratic politics and a clash and deep division on this between royalists and Venizelists. After internal political turmoil and pressure from the Entente, the King without abdicating went into exile (1917); but he came back to the throne in 1920 after the defeat of Venizelos in the national elections of a nation exhausted after eight years of wars.

In the spring of 1921 the Greek Army, under the command of the King himself, undertook a major expedition in Asia Minor aiming eventually at Istanbul itself. The expedition, however, was ill-fated – as in August 1922 the Turkish Army under Mustafa Kemal in a counter-offensive forced the Greek troops out of Asia Minor altogether and looted and burned Smyrna, which was virtually a Greek city. About 1,100,000 refugees fled to Greece from Asia Minor. The King abdicated and a revolutionary government came to power. In January 1923 there was an agreement of exchange of populations between Greece and Turkey, and this had a decisive impact on the socio-economic life of the country throughout the twentieth century. 'The catastrophe', put an end to Greek irredentism, and Greek nationalism itself took a different orientation. With the treaty of Lausanne (24 July 1923) Greece had to abandon any claims to Asia Minor and limit its border west of the river Evros in Thrace. The question whether Greece was going to be a Monarchy or a republic became crucial, and the division between Venizelists and royalists was to dominate Greek political life throughout the mid-war period.

The Crisis of Politics and Identity 1922-1974

The year 1922 marked a new era because the whole socio-economic, ideological and political life of the country took a new turn. The shock of the Greek defeat in Asia Minor meant a deep soul searching for Greek nationalism and a deep appraisal of the relationship of Greece and the West. Visions for a greater Greece had to be abandoned and the modernization of the country towards a European model had to be taken seriously. The issue whether Greece could really follow a policy of isolation from the Great Powers was thus an issue dividing royalists and Venizelists.

In 1928 the Greek population had risen to 6,204,674 from 5,016,589 in 1920. The large influx of the refugees had set in motion a significant labour movement in the urban centres and an acute problem of agrarian reform in the countryside. There was a large anti-royalist feeling which resulted in the establishment of the first republic which, with intermittent military interventions, lasted from 1924 to 1936. Throughout that period there was a struggle to shift from an ethnic nationalism as it was expressed in *Megali Idea*, to a civic nationalism which would be based on modern political institutions. Yet the democratic forces were weak and unable to function due to a weak economy and deep ideological and political divisions.

In 1935, after the intervention of army officers and a plebiscite with a 'patently rigged result' (Clogg 1978: 129), the monarchy was restored. Following political unrest General Metaxas, appointed Prime Minister by the King, suspended the Constitution in August 1936. Metaxas' dictatorship divided even deeper an already divided country. His ideology of the 'Third Hellenic Civilization' (akin to the Italian and Nazist fascism), claimed to be a combination of the virtues of classical Greece and Byzantium, but in practice it suppressed any democratic idea and even banned some classical anti-authoritarian texts.

The German occupation of 1941-1944 provoked a substantial resistance at the grassroots of Greek society and provided an opportunity for the political forces of the left to organize themselves for the first time. Heroic acts of resistance and sabotage by the *National Liberation Front* (EAM), the major organization of the left and the communists (Ekdotike Athinon 2000) became frequent from the beginning. By 1942 EAM also had a military organization, the *National Popular Liberation Army* (E.L.A.S) pronounced as Ellas, the name of the country itself. The great majority of the people were against communism but were very sympathetic to EAM and many, including many women, joined it not only as an act of defiance against the fascist occupation but also in order to participate in social life from which they had always felt excluded. According to Clogg (1979: 150) 'by the end of the occupation the membership of EAM has been variously estimated at between a million and two million'.

If the end of the first World War found the Greek nation deeply divided, the end of the second World War triggered the beginning of a devastating civil war fought on the pretext of who was patriot and who was a traitor. Many royalists and populists (in addition to others) during the war expressed German sympathies or even co-operated with the enemy. For most Greek people these were traitors (*prodotes*) or *dosilogoi* (Ekdotike Athinon 2000: 43-47). On the other hand, the fear of a communist take over after the war, enhanced by the intervention of the British and later of the Americans, contributed greatly to present all the communists and a large part of left sympathizers as *enemies of Greece*. With the defeat of the 'democratic army' of the left at the end of the civil war in 1949 *communism* and *communist* became dirty words and *ethnikofrosyne* (loyalty to the nation) was elevated onto highest virtue, indispensable for every citizen. The communists were not just outlawed but exiled and enclosed in concentration camps, unless they confessed and denounced their 'horrendous ideology'. The literature on this is so large that there is no room or need to be mentioned here.

What has been called the *Kingship of the Right* (Svoronos 1975: 144-148) meant 'a new nationalism, fanatic and self-complacent, which resembled that previous one of the 19th century. In contrast to that, however, the new nationalism was not embedded in a general holistic irredentist programme, but was defensive, reactionary and inward looking' (Tsoukalas 1986: 36). From about 1946 to 1974, Greek citizens had to produce a certificate of social thinking (*pistopoiitiko koinonikon fronimaton*) not just to exercise a citizen's right or get a job but even to enter a hospital. During this period although the polity was ostensibly democratic, in reality 'the parliament never, or almost never, was entrusted and a status quo of liberties never developed. Sometimes the will to retain power, sometimes fear, always the excuse of difficulties and conspiratorial threats, marked, maimed and finally killed democracy in Greece' (G.Vedel in preface to Alivizatos 1983: 16).

The shift of Greek nationalism to the right culminated in the dictatorship of the Colonels 1967-1974. This was not simply a shift towards an extreme right, nationalist ideology; it was also a blow to civic nationalism and an affront to the idea and practice of democracy. The basic political ideology of the dictators was, as with previous dictatorships, a specific mythologization of Greek history. Again the term 'Helleno-christian' was installed to the core of Greek identity and the official ideology of the state. In fact this was a barbaric totalitarianism that was not only a distortion but also an affront to both the values of classical Greece and those of the Christian Orthodox religion. Greece, of course, became isolated in Europe and in the world during that period – although the US Cold War foreign policy seemed to favour the Colonels access to and retaining power. But this regime, apart from being inefficient, was so hated by the people and thus could not last. Its collapse (July 1974) opened for Greece a new period of political, economic and social presence in Europe with access to the EU as a member state.

Greece's New and Formal Relation to Europe

The period from 1974 to the present clearly constitutes a new period of modern Greek history and a transformation of Greek identity in its relation to Europe. Over the last thirty years or so the historically ambivalent position of Greece towards Europe is clarified and settled. In the words of the first Prime Minister of that period and then President, K. Karamanlis, 'we now belong to the West'. The traditional asymmetrical and dependent relationship between Greece and North-western Europe is transformed steadily. With Greece's accession to the EU in fact the relation becomes one of parity and symmetrical in institutional, legal and normative terms. Thus, old syndromes of inferiority/superiority of Greek identity towards Europe recede and gradually atrophy or disappear. Europe itself, of course, having been torn apart with two world wars, which it generated itself, has opened a totally new page in its history with the vision and dream of European unification, which with difficulties, various setbacks, problems and tensions, seems, nevertheless, to progress steadily.

Because of fundamental national interests but also because of its close dialectical relationship to Europe, which we have sketched, Greece could not remain outside the procedures of European unification. Already from 1962 Greece had signed bilateral agreements with the then EEC. These were shelved during the dictatorship 1967-1974 but in 1975 the government of K. Karamanlis made an official application of accession. After negotiations Greece became a member of the EC in January 1981. The country's socio-economic position has been improving and after the collapse of the socialist block, Greece has been exercising a special influence in the Balkans. Being a member of the EU, of NATO and the Western European Union Greece has been in a unique diplomatic position as a mediator between the West and the problems in former Yugoslavia (Ekdotiki Athinon 2000: 413-417; Kokosalakis 1999). Economically too Greece has been an important agent in introducing the rules and institutions of the free market in the region. These developments contributed to increased tension between Greece and Turkey in the mid-ninenties but recently relations between the two countries have improved remarkably as Greece now is an active supporter of the European orientation of Turkey.

While Greece has advanced significantly in socio-economic terms over the last thirty years or so, there is still a general perception that the country still lags behind other western countries in terms of civil society and socio-economic development. There is thus a substantial sector of politicians and academics who believe and argue that Greece needs to modernize itself towards western standards. (Verelis et al. 2000; Mouzelis 1995). The socialist party (PASOK), which was in government for over twenty years, pursued a policy of modernization which involved an effort to improve the civil services, to rationalize and improve the productivity of the economy, and to combat bureaucracy at all levels. Its success in this area, however, has been modest and its policies lately met with substantial disapproval. The party was thus voted out of power in the elections of March 2004.

A substantial number of politicians and academics believe that Greece is a place where tradition and modernity can coexist side by side and in fusion. They argue that the way ahead lies not in the dichotomy between traditional and modern cultures but rather in their creative synthesis (Babiniotis 1995: 228). According to the above argument after the cold war and Greece's full membership to the EU, the bipolar dichotomies of East/West, traditional/modern, Greek/European no longer make sense and should be surpassed.

This view is supported also by the fact that the cornerstone of the project of European unification and integration is respect for the different cultures of the member states. Indeed, it is crucial to stress that for the first time ever the common is built mainly through the different. Thus, it is through dialogue, negotiation, compromise and respect for the autonomy of the *other* that the process of European unification proceeds. So, respect for the different cultures, languages, traditions and religious background are essential elements in European membership and for national identities like the Greek one, where these elements are crucial and indispensable.

The actual tangible benefits for Greece's membership in the EU have been largely recognized by most political parties and by the great majority of the Greek people. Such benefits have been in the socio-economic and political sphere and concern the area of development, the improvement of civil society, the consolidation of democratic principles, the external security and defense of the nation, and the increase and strengthening of the international image and position of the country in the Balkans, and in the EU (Ioakeimides 2001: 148-158).

The historically specific relationship between Greek identity and Europe, of course, remains. Indeed, Greek national identity, for various geopolitical reasons and because of membership with the EU, has been strengthened lately. This in no way implies incompatibility between Greek national and European identity but it does imply a concern of Greek citizens about the procedures of European unification and above all the substantial democratic deficit they perceive and their non participation in these procedures. This was also confirmed by the great show of abstention of the European citizens generally in the last elections for the European Parliament.

Conclusions

The profile of modern Greek identity and its relation to Europe which has been presented above shows that both concepts are fluid and ambiguous, but both of them have been at the heart of modern Greek history and development. Ethnic identity for the Greeks thus remains a crucial yet strained notion which links the present with the past as well as with the future. The concept of identity, in the human social context generally, is not static but open and dynamic. It is a process rather than a structure. In the Greek case it is more so as it has been always characterized by severe tensions and even contradictions without ever disintegrating or losing its historical continuity.

Historically and especially after the establishment of the Greek nation state in the 19th century there has been a close dialectical relationship with Europe. This relationship has been very specific, asymmetrical and one of dependence, and was often characterized by tensions and contradictory tendencies. In the Greek identity the relationship was often expressed by syndromes and feelings of inferiority/superiority. The specificity is located in the indigenous, in many ways self conflicting, cultural characteristics on the one hand and on the other in the fact that an ideal image of classical Greece was constructed in Europe – an image to which the weak modern Greek state had to aspire.

Thus, since the early nineteenth century, the basic problem of modern Greece has been that its long cultural heritage could not be turned into a political identity in the confines of a weak and dependent modern nation state. Yet, this has been exactly the effort, indeed the struggle, of modern Greece, and this according, to most analysts, has produced severe tensions and contradictions in the life of the country. Nevertheless, despite this, modern Greek identity seems to flourish and is taking on its stride both tradition and modernity.

With Greece's membership in the EU their historically asymmetrical relationship changes radically and becomes symmetrical and one of partnership at least legally, institutionally and normatively. Now the fate of Greece seems inseparable from the fate of Europe. Paradoxically, far from entailing the weakening of Greek identity, this seems to be fostering its strengthening. Certainly it entails its transformation in a new European context.

References

Alivizatos, N. (1983), *The Political Institutions in Crisis 1922-1974: Aspects of the Greek Experience*, Athens: Themelio (in Greek).

Anderson, B. (1991), *Imagined Communities: Reflections on the Origins and Spread of Nationalism*, 2nd edn, London: Verso.

Babiniotis, G. (1995), 'The blending of tradition and innovation in modern Greek culture', in Constans, D. and Stavrou, Th. (eds) *Greece Prepares for the Twenty-first Century*, Washington D. C. : Woodrow Press.

Campbell, J. and Sherrard, P.(1968), *Modern Greece*, Washington D.C. : Praeger.

Clogg, R. (1979), *A Short History of Modern Greece*, Cambridge: Cambridge University Press.

Ekdotiki Athenon, (2000), *History of the Greek Nation: Contemporary Hellenism from 1941 to the End of the Century*, Vol. 16, Athens: Ekdotiki Athinon. (in Greek).

Frazee, A. (1969), *The Orthodox Church and Independent Greece 1821-1852*, Cambridge: Cambridge University Press.

Ioakeimides, P. (2001), *The Treaty of Nice and the Future of Europe*, Athens: Themelio (in Greek).

Jenkyns, O. (1980), *The Victorians and Ancient Greece*, Oxford: Blackwell.

Kokosalakis, N. (1999), 'Balkan States', *Encyclopedia of Politics and Religion*, Vol.I, Washington D.C. : Congresssional Quartely Inc.

Legg, K. and Roberts, J. (1997), *Modern Greece: A Civilization in the Periphery*, Oxford: Westview Press.

Makriyannis, J. (1996), *The Memoirs of General Makriyannis*, ed. and tr. By H.A. Lidderdale, Oxford: Oxford University Press.

Mouzelis, N. (1978), *Modern Greece: Facets of Underdevelopment*, Basingstoke: Macmillan.

Svoronos, N. (1975), *Review of Modern Greek History*, Athens: Themelio (in Greek).

Tsaoussis, D. G. (1983), *Hellenism and Hellenicity: The Problem of Modern Greek Identity*, Athens: Estia (in Greek).

Tsoukalas, (1986), *State, Society, Work in Post-war Greece*, Athens: Themelio (in Greek).

-------- (2001), 'The Irony of Reciprocities: The Greek meaning of Europe as a historical inversion of the European meaning of Greece', in Malmborg M. and Strath B. (eds) *The Meaning of Europe*, Oxford: Berg.

Verelis, Ch. Et al (2000), *Questions of Modernization*, Athens: Kastaniotis (in Greek).

Chapter 7

Nation, State and National Identity in Modern Hungary

Paszkál Kiss
and
György Hunyady

For long periods of its history Hungary was an almost indistinguishable part of great empires that dominated its land, integrated its national institutions to a greater or smaller extent, or exported their political-ideological system to the country. In recent times, if the country was remembered in the world, it was for the Hungarian revolution in 1956, an important sign of cleavage within the Soviet block, and a heroic but failing attempt to establish national independence. (Others may remember its famous soccer team *almost* winning the World Cup in 1953.) In a closer look it is clear that struggles for lost national independence and heroic defeats are the most luminous, celebrated times in Hungarian national remembrance since the middle ages. An empathic analyst of the Hungarian national identity, George Schöpflin (2000), finds it important to emphasize that today Hungary is a 'kin-state' with sizeable numbers of co-ethnics just across the border living as citizens of neighbouring states. Similarly, another recent analysis (Haynes 1995) starts from an argument that Hungarian national identity resembles to that of the mid-war German national identity.[1] Thus, from a comparative-regional perspective one of the most important issues is the great number (over tow million) of minority Hungarians in neighbouring countries, and the necessary contemplation on the historic chain of events that ended in this situation. From inside (as attribution theory points out in social psychology) it is the situation, the accommodation to the changing international context and the integration of different social impulses, that is at the forefront.

In this chapter we will try to give an overview of the most important elements and some social processes of Hungarian national self-reflections. This account will not be exhaustive due to the limitations of space and the great breath of the topic. Apart from presenting the 'Hungarian case', we also present some general points about national identity.

---

[1] Although more similarity can be seen in dilemmas about the nation than in proposed answers or consequences. Despite the completely different international context, Hungarian nationalism is not as tough-minded (or aggressive) and not expansionist as German ideology was in the mid-war period.

1. Hungarian national identity is a good example for considerable changes over time, reflecting new historic-political situations and reacting to them. An important example of such a change is the relation between nation and state. Hungarian national identity had been based primarily on the (historic) state before the Trianon treaty;[2] this shifted naturally into a kind of a cultural/ethnic nationalism[3] after the peace agreement. Another example is the issue of Hungarian minorities in neighbouring countries which triggered a mixture of irredentism and propagation of ethnic majority principle first in the mid-war period, a complete denial of the problem during the communist era, and an emphasis on regional autonomy and European integration after the democratic changes.

2. It follows from the above examples that Hungarian national identity is hard to be classified as essentially and eternally *ethnic* (or civic). Theorists of nationalism (e.g. Brubaker 1999) have pointed out that it is hard to deal with the vague categories of *ethnic* and *civic* nationalism, and it is not easy to avoid the implicit qualifications associated to this distinction. Thus we try to avoid such essentialization and oversimplified classification; instead we show 'how they [civic/ethnic elements] are mixed in different manners and proportion' (Brubaker 1999: 58) in different times.[4]

3. We argue that *adaptation* has been a fundamental aspect of Hungarian national identity. The people of a relatively small country at the crossroad of imperial interests were not free in evolving their separate national identity. Imperial domination of many kinds seriously constrained the development of national identity, while inspirations from the West motivated national development (to take two examples).

4. Thus, the European integration is not the first time when Hungarians face an inspiring and binding outside influence. This had been more the rule than the exception before. The novelty is in the process itself; as it is based on mutual agreement and negotiations rather then mere geopolitical dominance. Apart from that, there has never been contradiction between national identity and European attachments for the vast majority of Hungarians in most of Hungarian history.

We shall sketch the historic aspect of Hungarian national identity built around collective memory and lay people's history. Thus, we chose a 'bottom-up' strategy in giving an impression of the thousand years of Hungarian history. Starting from some empirical results regarding the content of public memory of the national past, we build a mainly chronologically structured representation around these bits.

---

[2] A peace treaty signed by the Hungarians after the First World War, where Hungary lost two-thirds of its historic territory and one-third of ethnic Hungarians became citizens of neighbouring states.

[3] The term 'nationalism' refers here to a common sense understanding of national interest, not necessarily an explicit ideology.

[4] Thus we would disagree on this point with some interpretations of Hungarian national identity (e.g. Csepeli 1992) labelling it schematically as *ethnic*.

Then we try to show two instances of how the elite played a constitutive role in shaping national identity. In the last part of this chapter we raise some of the most important issues for Hungary in the accession to the European Union.

Hungarian National History in the Public

Remembering a common past, and the cultivation of its values and the lessons learnt from the past are essential conditions for, and content of, national identity. A nation as a collective actor can be unfolded, created, and shown from its historical 'deeds', struggles, and achievements. Past strategic dilemmas orient present efforts, and recruit the strength to realize common aims. They motivate people to think over historical antecedents repeatedly, and to search for inspiring examples and critical lessons. Regarding Hungarian national identity, some scholars have already shown (e.g. Thuval 1997) that it is structured into differentiated cycles that correspond to changes in geopolitical context, and the mission of the nation was constantly renewed by new geopolitical situations.

At the millennium of the Hungarian state, a public opinion research (Gallup Hungary 2000) asked a representative sample of adult Hungarians about their image of Hungary, about their attitudes and values attached to their national identity. Most of them agreed that this country has a bright past. As an indicator for the common views of history, most of the Hungarians evaluated the time of the renaissance king, Mátyás Hunyadi, as the peak of Hungarian history. They also appreciated the reign of István I., the founder of the Hungarian state in 1000 AD. More than half of the sample evaluated positively the period from the 1960s to the 1980s in Hungarian history. The darkest past times were judged to be the Turkish dominance in the 16th and 17th centuries, the hard-line communism of the 1950s, and the Horthy area in the mid-war period. The time of democratic transition was evaluated moderately positively. Concerning temporal changes in history, the majority saw a positive change in the availability of goods, they experienced a a closer relationship to Europe, found free exercise of religion easier, faith and religion more widespread, and improving reputation of the nation. More than half of the Hungarians saw freedom of speech, unconstrained achievement, independence of the country, opportunities for participating in local public matters, and democracy as being more pronounced with time. Negative changes were perceived in public safety, in existential security, in climate of opinion, and in social care.

Earlier empirical studies on people's factual historical knowledge (Hunyady 1998; Csepeli 1992) had also supported mainly that Hungarians saw the course of history through a web of historic events: foundation of the medieval state (1000 A.D) and the rule for István I.; the rule of King Mátyás; 150 year dominance of the Ottoman Empire; 1848 revolution and freedom-fights; Trianon Peace Treaty; 1956 revolution. Historians themselves also emphasize these events in reviewing the critical points in the course of Hungarian history (Hanák 1994; Kósa 2003).

General Time and Space Aspects of Hungarian Collective Remembering

Early history on the origins It is an often recalled basic element of national consciousness that Hungarians came to the Carpathian Basin from Asia in the 9th century.[5] Comparative linguistic analysis of the language lists Hungarians among the Finno-Ugric ethnic groups, but there are also many signs of living together with Turkish people for long periods. The first Hungarian king, István I, adopted Christianity at the end of the 10th century and founded the Hungarian state, at the same time as the Scandinavians and Slavic nations in the northern and eastern parts of Europe did. Despite temptations, the country followed western Catholicity, which brought a sharp boundary between Hungary and the southern and eastern Slavs. The establishment of Christian religion set the country into a system of cultural and political relationships. The foundation of the state itself is generally attributed to an act of (forced or creative) adaptation to more developed West European models.

Between East and West Another often recited, fundamental aspect of Hungarians' self-reflections is that the nation stands alone in Europe (indeed in the world) in linguistic isolation (see e.g. Thuval 1997; Szűcs 1997). A number of historical analyses bear the title referring to the intermediate position of Hungary in between East and West (e.g. Kiss 2000; Romsics 1998). The predominance of the East-West dimension is not new in Hungarian intellectual life. Seen from the periphery, economic, political and cultural changes in the modern history of Europe were considered as models and challenges motivating social and cultural movements. The attitude of 'facing westwards' has been a characteristic of the mentality of Hungarian elites. The title of a representative exhibition organized by the Hungarian National Museum in 1994 'Hungarians in the midst of East and West – National symbols and legends' itself reinforces the importance of this dimension (Hofer 1996). The East-West dimension has been not only a major orientation for Hungarian élites, it also represented a division or schism within the Hungarian culture. Hungary was referred to as a 'ferry-country' by one of its greatest poets, Endre Ady (a prestigious author of the literary periodical 'Nyugat'[West]). In this poetic symbolism the experiences of dividedness and the decisive role of outside forces is condensed where Hungary is driven ashore once in the East then in the West.

Small country in the shadow of empires Hungary was many times under the threat or domination of outside powers, multi-national empires. As early as in the 13th century the Mongol horde swept through its land, but the Hungarian feudal state of the time survived this eastern invasion, became stronger, and grew to be a regional power under the economically prosperous and Renaissance-spirited rule of the House of Anjou and then of Mátyás Hunyadi. Some centuries later, Europe as a whole was threatened from the south-east by the Muslim Turkish Empire.

---

[5] Interestingly, distant Asian nations also consider Hungarians as their relatives who were swept to Europe by the tide of history.

Hungarians remember vividly that the country served as 'the bastion of Christianity' at the time.[6] Hungarians are not alone in forming such symbolism about their crucial role in fighting the Ottoman Empire; the Poles, Croats, Slovaks, Romanians, Greeks are also proud of being a shield for Europe against the Turks. By the beginning of the 16th century, however, Hungary could no longer resist the expansion of the Turkish empire: Hungary suffered a crushing defeat in 1526, and as a result, a considerable part of the country lay under Turkish rule for as much as the next 150 years.

Not much later the strong Reformist movements interpreted the defeat as God's punishment for the sins of Hungarians. This interpretation not only gave a supranational (thus unquestionable) explanation of the traumatic event but oriented people to the future and criticized political weaknesses (e.g. dissent) together with general moral transgressions. As many explanations, this had a self-esteem-increasing component too: the analogy between the Jews of the Old Testament and the Hungarians as chosen people. This explanation of past sins was so generally held that it became part of Kölcsey's *Himnusz*, the official Hymn of Hungary written in the 19th century.

After the Turks had been driven out, the Hungarian kingdom became a province of the Austrian empire. There were several waves of Hungarian fights for freedom against the Austrian rule; the most famous ones are linked to the name of Rákóczi and Kossuth. They both hoped that the enemies of the German-Austrian Empire would help them, but they did not get genuine help neither in the 18th, nor in the 19th century. Nevertheless, the search for relations and emigration as a consequence of the later subdued movements did create a distant relationship and interest in the direction of Europe beyond the German land.

Crucial Times and Changes in Hungarian History

1848 – the birth of modern Hungary The early 19th century is called the era of reforms in Hungarian historiography. This was the time when the Hungarian language was modernized; romantic artists, poets and literary men painted an animated picture of modern Hungarian national identity. It is commemorated as a time when modern Hungary (in political, economical, and cultural terms) was grounded. It is worth mentioning that this cultural change was accompanied by attempts for the technical and social renewal of the agricultural-feudal country. A protagonist of this change, István Szécheny, saw facilitating examples during an extended stay in England. Széchenyi and others considered Hungary in an international context; they were conscious about its set-backs and desperate in changing the economic, infrastructural and cultural backwardness for the better. At this time the concept of then nation (1) was connected to the notions of liberty; (2) was open and receptive and tolerant towards difference; and (3) was closer to the rationalistic French conception than to the romantic German ethnic conception of

---

[6] This is commemorated by the cultural historical fact (less well known abroad) that the Pope introduced the noonday bell in honour of the Hungarians' resistance to the Turks.

the nation.[7] (4) This generation accused itself for the adversities (Hanák, 1994). As a seminal expression of these principles, the 1848 Hungarian revolution and the later evolving war of independence erased the feudal rights and gave new civic rights to everybody regardless of nationality (ethnicity).

Before and after Trianon After the defeat of the 1848 War of Independence, a sequence of more ambivalently evaluated periods came to Hungary. Austria – having been excluded from Germany – accepted a compromise with Hungary in 1867. This period of the dual Austro–Hungarian Monarchy is appreciated for having brought economic prosperity to the nation; but it is also considered to have caught the political elites in a mindset that prevented them from searching new solutions to the deepening social and ethnic conflicts. After the First World War, the Trianon Peace Treaty failed to create national states, but truncated the Hungarian institutions and brought one-third of the population outside the national border. An anti-Hungarian co-operation of the newly established neighbouring countries also became established within the Little Entente system of alliance. The kingdom was formally re-established, but without a king: Miklós Horthy was appointed regent. This period is generally regarded as conserving feudalistic power structure in the newly established independent state. Political pressure was exerted on labour movements, liberal forces and the Jews (it was at this point that the 'numerus clausus' was passed, the first law which discriminated against Jews by limiting their educational opportunities). The national system that emerged was a complex one: it maintained the feudal symbols of the past, and large estates survived within the restricted borders of the country; but a multi-party parliament operated, and the Jewish plutocracy also preserved the positions it had achieved under the dual monarchy. The authoritarian political system was used in the attempt to control the social conflicts which, inevitably, began to emerge. It mixed this policy with conservatism, established in the name of anti-Bolshevism. Thus this mid-war period may be seen essentially as times of cleavages and tensions.

Haynes (1995) notes that: 'The events of the twentieth century have profoundly weakened the mythological and intellectual underpinnings that gave Hungarian identity its coherence before the First World War. The Treaty of Trianon destroyed the sense of Hungarian mission to govern the nationalities of the Danube basin' (Haynes 1995: 100). She argues that this is similar to what happened at the same time in Germany. Despite the obvious similarities, we would emphasize that size does matter even in this case. Hungary was much more dependent on the international context than Germany. It would have been unable to start a war by itself even if it had wanted to, and on the contrary it was very much kept in subjection by Germany when it started its expansions. Even conservative leaders of the time saw clearly the dangers of binding Hungarian aspirations to German expansionist answers.

---

[7] Thus Brubaker rightly recognizes that these national movements were closer to concepts of a *Staats* nation than to that of a *Kultur* nation.

Communism and national issues After the Second World War, a multi-party 'coalition government' existed between 1945 and 1948. The revolutionary change started by this government did have considerable social support. A swift social change was refreshing, but because it involved the most nationalistic sector of society, it tended to work against communists international ideals and ideology which were to take over. In 1948, one-party 'dictatorship of the proletariat' was instituted in Hungary as in other countries of Soviet domination. It is was especially clear at this early stage of strong dictatorship that the communist regimes destroyed all kinds of identities (e.g. national, religious) to establish an identity of obedience to the Party (Gereben 2003).

The dramatic events of 1956 left two unforgettable memories with all those who lived them through in Hungary. The *first* was the feeling of unprecedented national unity on 23 October. A wide national and democratic resistance developed in response to the Soviet military intervention. At this point, the *second* fundamental truth of 1956 emerged, one which was to become the determining political experience of a whole generation: the loneliness and defencelessness of a country, being entirely on its own, and the knowledge that despite their reassurances, declarations of solidarity, and real humanitarian intentions, not one other country was prepared to help Hungary in its armed fight with the Soviet army. By this outside intervention, János Kádár became the head of a new puppet government to stay in power for an entire generation. Despite being successful in establishing a modus vivendi during his lifelong stay in power, he probably could never forget his personal responsibility for the bloody retaliation; neither could the latent public opinion of the country.

In its international relations the Soviet policy was to use the nationalisms of the so called 'peoples' republics' in East Central Europe (Kiss 2000). They permitted the cultivation of anti-German traditions, but in the meantime demanded the submission to Soviet supremacy. They wished to separate the satellite states from each other. Czechoslovakia and Poland could keep their national herald; for Romania and Hungary a new one was fabricated that was surrounded by a corn-ear coronary taken from the Soviet herald. This discrimination was similar to that of the Hungarian leaders, who drew upon the compunctious labels of the 'last satellite' (of Germany) and 'sinful nation'. National holidays were changed in all dominated countries; the major ones were remembrances of the anti-German victory in the Second World War. National uprisings starting with the Hungarian revolution of 1956 would have been jarring for the Soviet leadership; accordingly, the role of national traditions was re-evaluated. The communist party used the 'progressive' elements of national history; national heritage or patriotism were used to a greater extent. But a black and white perception of ideologies dominated historiography and public debates over national history (Szűcs 1997).

In the 1960s and 1970s the communist totalitarianism was engaged with national traditions. Thus, nationalism itself appeared even before the democratic changes in East Europe. Part of this nationalist turn was the revival of 19th century mythology, the upgrading of the importance of independent statehood, and the undervaluation of neighbouring nations and minorities (even the use of the totalitarian means to extinguish these minorities). In literature, the historic novel and essay became popular; historic monuments were built; journalism referred to national pride; and national prejudices and anti-Semitism appeared. Only one taboo remained: relations towards the Soviet Union were not disputable. But as a sort of an opposition to these nationalist moves of the communist authorities, 15 March[8] even became an occasion to express reservations toward the existing regime in Hungary. Although discussing the problems of the Hungarian minorities in the neighbouring countries remained a non-issue for decades, it was as a form of resistance the intellectuals expressed solidarity towards them in personal relations and in the semi-public circles that were characteristic of the time – not acknowledged but tolerated by the authorities.

Re-emerging national symbols after 1989 The democratic changes after the fall of communism in East Central Europe naturally gave birth, or rebirth to the national principle. The questions arose and the national differences grew regarding how this shift from a quasi colonial status to an autonomous national policy had happened. An important factor in shaping public opinion was Hungarians' collective memories about the once existed civil middle class and the system of parliamentary democracy until 1949. These memories, briefly revived in 1956, had survived for more than half a century; dim and fragmentary as they were, they still served as a kind of cultural breeding ground for the change of the political system. This factor also distinguishes the Czech Republic and Poland from other countries in the region; there too, it may have had a significant effect on the direction and speed of social transformation.

A gradual re-establishment of public elements of national consciousness was detectable in social-political changes during the transition. During this period, the values of independence were stressed, and traditional national values were revitalized in the re-establishment of national symbols. Regarding national days, the foundation the Hungarian state and the revolutions of 1948 and 1956 have become publicly celebrated in expressing historical continuity. The emergence of the national principle triggered fears and opposition too. The 1990s were full with heated political and intellectual debates over the essence and extent of a modern and democratic Hungarian national identity.

Elite Reflections on History

It is not necessary to argue against any pre-modern root of modern nations if one acknowledges that the development of nations is not completely spontaneous and is not done without self-reflections. And self-reflection is not meant to be a disguise for building a nation 'by design' (Smith 1999), but models a process through which intellectuals and public thought shape national identity. As one author of a widely read, classic volume on Hungarian national character László Ravasz (1939), a celebrated bishop in the reformist church drew an analogy

---

[8] The day for remembering the civic revolution of 1848 that was not an officially held holiday in the communist era.

between romantic love and patriotic feelings: self-reflections can bring disappointment in both cases, but may also lead to greater understanding of the self and the other.

Hungarian Character and Historical Blind Alleys for Hungary – the Question of Internal Others

The study of national characters was fashionable at the turn of 19th and 20th centuries not only in Hungary. After the national romanticism it was a new and widely accepted approach of the time to regard the history of the nation as one course of interconnected events to shape distinguishable features of a nation. This side of studying national character seems to be merely a sign of national consciousness. But it is true that the nation was also a key ideological concept in Hungary between the two world wars. It was used as a tool for self-assurance and rationalization for the political system after Trianon, but it was also a target of self-criticism. Szekfű (1939), a distinguished historian and ideologist of the epoch, followed the European scientific discourse of the time, and analyzed the Hungarian national character together with many scholars in the representative volume. In his analysis he discarded any reference to genetic attributes; he assessed instead the impact of history on the present characteristics of the Hungarians. The character that was extracted from the flow of history received less attention in the debate than did questions regarding the expanse of the nation, and who belongs to the nation (see also Németh, 1992). The debate itself became a sign of opposition against the expansionist political moves and racist ideology of the Nazi Germany. A celebrated writer, Mihály Babits (1939) aimed high in this often heated discourse: 'I would not be afraid of the dilemma that we become either Jews or Germans. Still, I think that Jews and Germans will become true Hungarians among us' (p. 571).

    After 1945, following the second collapse of the nation in the 20th century, István Bibó (1986) presented a line of thought that followed Szekfű in its style, but debated his arguments. He also analyzed the course of Hungarian history to explain historic downfalls of his time. Instead of external corrupting influences, he blamed the social structure and the counterselection of the elite alienated and divided from the people. He put the emphasis on the diverse possibilities for a political elite to answer historic challenges. His explanations, tinted with mass psychology, accused the blind alleys of Hungarian history of creating hysteric feelings and wishful thinking that resulted in blurred sight of Hungarian elites and erroneous answers to historic-geopolitical challenges. He blamed the Habsburg Empire for mixing up the paths to nation formation. He could see three major problems the historic Hungarian state and nation faced at the beginning of the 20th century: (a) there was a historic state that was not entirely Hungarian speaking; (b) after the defeat of the war of independence in 1849, a fear cemented the Hungarian elite, that taking all the consequences of democratization would lead to the loss of territories dominated by national minorities; and (c) the shock caused by the Trianon Peace Treaty obscured existing differences (e.g. in the proportions of ethnic Hungarian inhabitants) between detached territories.

After some decades in a completely changed political climate the official communist ideology blamed the previous – anti-German – nationalism in searching for the causes of the revolution of 1956. The peak achievement of the emerging scholarly debate was Jenő Szűcs's (1984) analytic work devoted to the historical development of the concept of nation and to the social constraints of national characteristics. He pointed out that national character is not eternal, but is a consequence of a given historical development. It does not explain anything in a nation's history, but national character itself needs (historic) explanation.

These contemplations about the past and the future of Hungary have been themselves re-visited later (e.g. Hanák 1994; Kósa 2003) in scholarly or public debates, but they did not reach their goal in influencing political decisions of their time.[9] In sum, we might agree with Haynes (1995) in his conclusion that this contemplative nature in Hungarian self-consciousness reflects that 'Hungarian national identity is constantly open to redefinition […] may be associated alternatively with democratic values and with exclusive and intolerant varieties of nationalism' (p. 87). But this instability is not only about democratic or authoritarian solutions. Rather, it shows more: Hungarian national identity has a certain inner dynamic or ambivalence which animates debate and oppositions. A nation without a state, between East and West, dominating ethnic minorities and being dominated by others, has necessarily developed a complex, sometimes contradicting national consciousness that has left much space for ingroup dynamics – ever changing instances of deepening or bridging existing schisms within the nation. This instability may give impetus to national aspirations, or it may ruin them completely, leaving nothing but paralyzed public and a flood of self-pity.

Old Dilemmas and New Challenges after the Fall of Communism

Despite the lack of a necessary historic perspective, a look at the contemporary elite discourses might be needed here as a footnote to the dilemmas at the beginning and the mid-twentieth century. Many scholars took the above mentioned thoughts as starting points for contemporary analyses of the challenges Hungary is facing (e.g. Hanák 1994). Some emphasize the lack of such general, deep and far-sighted analyses of the messages of history (Kósa 2003). Others hesitate over their usefulness and historiographic value (Gerő 2001). Opinion leading elites in the early 1990s revitalized the opposition between urbane and rural attitudes of the mid-war period, instead of reflecting systematically on the effects of the communist era that passed after. Several reasons might have led to this lack of general and future-oriented reflections. Péter Hanák (1994) was one of the few scholars, who systematically reanalyzed Hungarian history based on Bibó's original diagnosis, and extrapolated it up until the end of the 20th century. He concludes that although many would think that Hungarians have rolled out from

---

[9] Indeed these explanations themselves were much more luminous and of a better quality than many of the political decisions in the recurring situations with severe delimitations for Hungarian administrations. Intellectuals can receive great public attention because the political élite cannot formulate and give voice to its answers to the same dilemmas.

the blind alleys of history and that western orientation is the realpolitik for Hungarians, doubts might be raised as to whether the mentality of the present (political) elite is in harmony with the necessary accommodation[10] to the West. He finds the absence of autonomous thinking and acting citizens the most important problem in this respect.

Another thorough analysis (Granasztói 2000) was elicited explicitly by the European integration of Hungary. Granasztói uses dilemmas concerning the relations between moral obligations and power motivations in politics to dig deeper in a social-historical analysis of the situation triggered by European integration. Granasztói denies the premise that history forms a monolithic (linear) structure. His argument is based instead on a conception of the past in which different mentalities, cultural traditions (i.e. different realities) may exist side by side and even integrated, enriching each other. He draws an analogy between the birth of the European Union and the democratic changes in Hungary after communism. He takes both as moments of truth (in a state of grace), when moral principles and political decisions were born relatively rapidly to provide a basis for the following slower times (depending on the qualities of the actors involved). He considers the European Union to be born from the wish to rebuild Europe after 1945. For this, he emphasizes three principles: (1) the rejection of extremities and barbarism that led to the holocaust; (2) the perception that new Europe should not be based on the dominance of the triumphants over the defeated; and (3) the reconciliation between the French and the German.

The Hungarian democratic change missed such clear guiding principles according to Granasztói. Hungarians lived through the times of democratic change as a silent, hardly comprehensible conversion, not as a morally renewing catharsis. There were no clear norms and horizons. Ruptures divided the relations of different groups within the society. This ended in alienation and mechanistic interpretations of actions resulting in a moral deficit and the intransparency of neither-nor. In this case he regards religious faith as an important possible source of norms constricting violence and politics and legitimating them in the mean time in a peculiar balance. But he extends the need for norms outside the spiritual sphere and reminds us of the need for refinement of European moral obligations after Bosnia, Kosovo and Rwanda.[11] Many of these changes were closely followed in Hungary in the minds and actions of its peoples. He concludes that through these experiences (e.g. the support of the allies in the Kosovar conflict) Hungarians have accumulated the necessary emotions and experiences for the country's European integration. He demonstrates that reflections on Hungarian political changes and recent history are strongly tied to experiences of European integration.

---

[10] Using Bibó's term of accommodation, he refers to a clear and realistic view of chances and challenges present in the political-historical context. This is not an uncritical acceptance and opportunistic application of answers provided by the West.

[11] He pays a special attention to minority conflicts and crisis as strong forms of moral conflicts leading to the re-interpretation of the concept of *autonomy* (personal, territorial, cultural) and *community* (membership not mutually exclusive).

Thus it is a lively tradition in the Hungarian elites to reflect upon the national past, and to form psychologically and sociologically based abstractions of history to answer present challenges. Although the original forms of these self-reflections invoking a stable national character are generally questioned today, the role that they played in the early 20th century seems to be an important one and occasionally acted upon even after a century.

Hungary and European Integration

There is truth in contemporary analysis which is critical regarding the Hungarian adaptation to new challenges. Instead of clear values and sound moral basis for political strategy, we find confusion and instability after 1989. From the time of democratic changes there are only a few consensual goals to guide national politics. One is the aspiration to join the Euro-Atlantic community through memberships in NATO and EU. From a historic perspective, (West) European orientation is not new to the Hungarian public and elite. It was there well before the actual accession to the EU. This may have made it easier for the Hungarian public and political parties to accept almost immediately, and without serious doubts, that there was no real alternative to joining the EU after the democratic changes. There has been an overall consensus ever since in this matter. Aspirations of the elite and the public coincided here, despite a small minority having explicitly negative attitudes to accession.

The main difference in the Hungarian public thought of 1990 and 2004 (the year that Hungary joined the EU) would be in representation rather than in attitudes. The 'West' has always formed an ideal for the Hungarians, including lots of wishes and illusions. During the age of communism it was filled more with hopes and illusions and less with knowledge and experience.[12] Open borders and everyday encounters have contributed to more elaborate and complex knowledge about west European ways of life. The decade-long political process of accession to the European and Trans-Atlantic organizations also provided lots of experience for the Hungarian public. The prolonged process of Eastern enlargement has been a useful time of orientations. East Central European people could discount much of their illusory view about the West, about the free world of democracy and market economy. European norms on the other hand infiltrated gradually the political discourse and even everyday life.

In these years there might have been more hesitations within EU member states: e.g., fears of migrations, and of the estimated costs of integrating a less developed and a precarious region. However, former communist countries became more distinguishable and common stereotypes could have been confronted with more personal, first hand experience as the domestic conditions of these countries were explored more by the West European public.

---

[12] Travels outside the socialist block were restricted administratively by the communist regime, even if these restrictions were eased especially in the late 1980s. These experiences, despite their lack of uniformity, might have contributed to public discontent.

Hungarians Representing Europe, Public Opinion about Accession

The concept of Europe gained new political significance in the 1990s in the opinion of Hungarians (Hunyady 1998). To the question of which area or continent differed definitely from Europe, respondents of a representative sample chose Africa the most often, followed by Asia (in the latter case a much greater number of countries were specifically mentioned, almost 3 per cent said China). These answers constituted about one third of the sample; only a quarter of the sample mentioned the American continent in one way or another (half of them definitely pointed at the United States). There appeared a (non-extreme) Euro-American connection and delimitation in the overall subjective image, while differences at the other 'pole' of the world, between Asia and Africa, were expressed (although in a rather dull form).

In a study on random French, German, Austrian, and Slovene samples (Gallup Hungary 2000), the French and Hungarians had slightly more positive attitudes to the EU than others. About half of the respondents thought that Hungary might offer much to the European Union. Most of them thought that their nation would profit more than lose by Hungarian membership. There was a general consensus among all nations that 'the more members the EU has the more secure peace is'; 'the more members EU will have the more important role it will play in the world'; 'with more member states, the European Union will be richer'. Concerning Hungary they thought that: 'Hungary's membership in the EU is both historically and geographically reasonable'; 'the EU membership could help the Hungarian economy'; 'with the enlargement, Hungary would gain importance in Europe'; 'Hungarian leaders do what is necessary for Hungary to be a member of the EU in the near future'. A general conclusion of the research is that chances for Hungarian integration were perceived quite positively, most of the people of these nations knew that Hungary is applying for EU membership, and it is generally supported in these countries. But the mutually positive public attitude lacked a firm ground of factual knowledge or opinions in Hungary. While citizens of European countries had a more or less developed system of arguments concerning the enlargement process, consisting both pros and cons, these were missing in the Hungarian public, probably due to the lack of public debates about economic, cultural and political gains or losses of joining the EU.

A small country in the EU Nevertheless, there are some topical elements of the Hungarian public discourse about the country's accession to the European Union. At least from the Trianon Treaty, Hungarians have emphasized their country as being small – with all of its brighter (less responsibility and visibility in world politics) and darker (greater interdependence, greater need for accommodating outside influences) sides. The aims and results of a small country's integration may be different from those of great powers: Its dependence on outside influences is more pronounced; its main interest lies more in commerce than in geopolitics, in a more intensive international exchange than in separation. Small countries might be more oriented toward the status quo, and have stronger regional ties to or dependencies on greater powers. Thus the best milieu for a small country is a functioning power balance. Experiences in recent years have reinforced that the country's economic prosperity and policies were already strong under outside influence. Thus an important argument to distinguish EU integration from earlier, imperial dominance is that here the loss of sovereignty is vastly outweighed by the gains in international competences and possible influence.

Central European co-operation and the EU Another aspect of Hungarian integration is that Hungary (together with its neighbours) has had to resolve certain national conflicts within the region. These small nations have been in historic rivalry for a long time. Even communist leaders appealed to nationalistic emotions and sentiments in the old regime. Building a realistic co-operation has not been easy in this region as these countries seemed to forget about each other in orienting themselves to the West. The process of EU accession has helped to find common interest even if a strong co-operation did not appear among these countries. It is a remarkable fact that Hungarians did not see a real alternative to European integration, except that of standing alone, which is regarded as outdated and 'expensive'. Another side of neighbourly relations in the region is that the EU and other European institutions encouraged these countries to resolve debated issues and ease fears in formal bilateral agreements. Thus, taking earlier experience of non-cooperation into account, we may risk saying that wider European identifications have reinforced regional connections among small states in Eastern Central Europe more than the 'brotherly' connections during the Soviet rule. But these relations still depend very much on long-term and down-to-earth collaboration than on formal agreements and momentous coalitions of interest.

Minorities and the EU Although until recently the political-economical scenarios and their impact on Hungary were the issues of accession that received greater attention, gradually, minority and nationality problems have received more attention (Gergely, 1998). A change in the attitude of European institutions towards national minorities helped in this respect. The status of minority groups became more important in judging democratic achievements of a country. Consequently, minority status has ceased to be stigmatised extensively in East Central European states – although many states, irrespective of their ethnic composition, would still be built on the ideas of 19th century nationalism.

In the 1990s minorities have gradually begun to participate in local politics more and more extensively in East Central Europe. The minority issue has two important sides in Hungary. One is the question of Hungarian minority in the neighbouring countries. The other is minorities within the borders; most importantly, the problems of the Roma population. Minority policies towards the Roma emphasize social aspects and positive discrimination in education. Efforts in providing more opportunities to them were magnified in recent years. Hungarians pay a special attention to the issues of their national minorities (e.g. Germans, Croats, Serbs, Romanians, Slovaks) too, despite their small number in the country. In the case of Hungarian minorities outside Hungary, cultural and regional autonomy is seen to be a solution.

Even if Hungarian political or even scientific approaches are often too idealistic in respect of regionalism and autonomy as solutions for the problems of minority Hungarians, a valuable aspect of these political goals is that they fit well into the course of changes in the EU and that they refer to a brighter side of Hungarian minority politics by emphasizing political and cultural means instead of using power. But regionalism as a solution to minority problems is not without problems. Firstly, it is a solution only for rather great, homogenous groups of minority Hungarians. Secondly, these goals reach further than what is consensually accepted in Europe at present, and are not especially welcome by the majority in all neighbouring countries. Thus even if one is optimistic about the final results, the long period of transition itself may cause many problems. The most important among such problems is the steadily decreasing population of these minority groups. Minority Hungarians are not only facing with forces of assimilation to the majority but also tempted to migrate from their homeland to Hungary.

In sum, integration to the EU offers as many advantages as challenges with regards to the minority issue in Hungary. Mainstream political and cultural movements nevertheless regard the integration of all neighbouring countries to the EU within the close future as a main step ahead in resolving these problems. Then dividing borders would not separate Hungarians from each other. But in the near future, challenges might also come in this respect, such as in the introduction of Schengen rules towards Serbia and Ukraine, for example.

Nation-State and European Integration

We cannot avoid the question about the survival of nation-states in the analysis of the European integration. A growing body of empirical results and expert analyses show that national identity matches European identification very well. There are no signs of tensions between these two loyalties. Europe seems to be regarded as a second, greater homeland for European peoples. We saw in previous sections that European orientation was a characteristic of Hungarian national development at virtually any time since the founding of the medieval state.

Kosáry (2001) in his historical analysis firstly draws our attention to the fact that the changing role of nation-states is not a global phenomenon, but mainly a characteristic of the European development.[13] He considers that further globalization of the economy (which has never been solely national) will not create a radically new situation for nation-states; and it is the European political integration that influences them predominantly. He notes that capitalism and nation-states were both born in Europe, and the latter has now arrived at the crossroad of historic alternatives. It would pay, according to him, if we found a place for nation-states in the European integration by discounting for some of their sovereignty. They would be able to reserve and enrich their positive attributes in this way. He contrasts this with another alternative that is to renew the wrong traditions of nationalism by keeping the absolute nationalist demands, which

---

[13] Thus it is not necessarily applicable to contemporary changes in the USA, among other examples.

endanger severely the environment and ultimately the nations themselves. According to Kosáry, European and essential national interests are not in opposition, but both are opposed to a contemporary revival of the erroneously interpreted nation-state concept of the 19th century. He argues for adjusting and humanizing the concept of the nation instead of for its elimination. Even if integrated, Europe will not become one state and one nation, as it consists of many nations now, and will contain greater diversity with its enlargement. Another senior Hungarian historian, Péter Hanák (1994) argued for a similar synthesis. We should not regress, according to him, to a classic liberal conception of nation-states which were conquering and assimilating. That conception of nation-state did not acknowledge collective rights but was based instead exclusively on individual's rights. He finds a solution neither in the liberal nor in the conservative understandings of nation-state, but in the autonomy and federation of ethno-regional units into which the European realpolitik is evolving.

Conclusions

We presented the Hungarian case starting from the point that collective memory and historiography have primary importance in national identity and that they are especially in the focus of Hungarian national identity. Throughout the chapter we tried to illustrate the uses of national past in shaping national identity and tried to follow the main stages in the history of Hungarian national identity. Based on these examples, we also argued for a general conceptualization of national identity. Adaptation to political and historic changes emerged as one of the most important concepts in understanding Hungarian national history. The future of a relatively small country overshadowed occasionally by empires of all sorts has been dependent upon its capacities in adapting to the changing international context. Throughout its history Hungary seemed to be always open more or less to European influences and its national development was inspired by European examples. We understood nations as communities of collective remembering in which specialized elite groups have a fundamental role. Elites interpreted the past not only as a luminous background for the present, but as a source of self-reflections and explanations for their time and for future goals. The counterselection of elites was shown to lead to problems in this adaptation. In contemporary analyses of Hungarian national history, European integration itself seemed to provide an important outside point of reference in shaping national consciousness after the democratic changes.

Some key issues emerged in the process of accession for Hungary. The European Union has been represented as part of the West even though increasingly distinguished from the USA. For Hungarians, the loss of sovereignty has been seemingly counterbalanced with the increased possible influence of a small state through the EU. European integration has proved to be a facilitator in resolving conflicts with neighbouring nations. Common goals and interests in the process of accession turned contradictions to co-operation with other East Central European countries. The minority issue has appeared as a challenge for the future of

Hungarian national identity. European norms and values have provided a basis for resolving these problems in the long run. The future of nations is not interpreted as contradicting with further European integration. Rather, the European Union may help European nations to overcome some dangerous components of nationalism (e.g. exclusivism and rejection of multiple identifications) while keeping national identity as an important form of social identification.

References

Babits, M. (1939), 'A magyar jellemről', in Gy. Szekfű (ed.) *Mi a magyar?*, Budapest: Magyar Szemle Társaság, pp. 37-86.

Bibó, I. (1986), *Válogatott tanulmányok*, Budapest: Magvető Kiadó.

Brubaker, R. (1999), 'The Manichean Myth: Rethinking the Distinction Between "Civic" and "Ethnic" Nationalism', in H. Kriesi et al. (eds) *Nation and National Identity: The European Experience in Perspective*, Chur: Ruegger, pp. 55-69.

Csepeli, Gy. (1992), *Nemzet által homályosan*, Budapest: Századvég Kiadó.

Gallup Hungary (2000), *www.gallup.hu*.

Gereben, F. (2003), 'Vallási és nemzeti identitás Közép-Európában', in B. Ábrahám, F. Gereben, and R. Stekovics (eds), *Nemzeti és regionális identitás Közép-Európában*, Piliscsaba: Pázmány Péter Katolikus Egyetem Bölcsészettudományi Kar, pp. 61-75.

Gergely, A. (1998), 'Kisebbségek és integráció', in K. Kulcsár (ed.), *Az integráció: történelmi kihívások és válaszkísérletek*, Budapest: MTA Politikai Tudományok Intézete, pp. 125-183.

Gerő, A. (2001), 'A fogalmak foglya. Bibó István a XIX. sz. második felének magyar történelméről', *Beszélő*, 6(10), pp. 94-104.

Granasztói, Gy. (2000), 'Erkölcs és politika európai csatlakozásunk küszöbén', *Magyar Szemle*, 9(9-10), pp. 5-24.

Hanák, P. (1994), 'Alkat és történelem. Egy Bibó-tanulmány továbbgondolása', *Világosság*, 5-6, pp. 3-37.

Haynes, R.A. (1995), 'Hungarian National Identity: Definition and redefinition', in. P. Latawski (ed.), *Contemporary Nationalism in East Central Europe*, New York: Palgrave, pp. 87-104.

Hofer, T. (1996), *Magyarok Kelet és Nyugat közt. A nemzettudat változó jelképei*, Budapest: Balassi Kiadó.

Hunyady, Gy. (1998), *Stereotypes in the Decline and Fall of Communism*, London: Routledge.

Kiss, Gy.Cs. (2000), *Nyugaton innen, keleten túl*, Miskolc: Felsőmagyarországi Kiadó.

Kosáry, D. (2001), *A magyar és európai politika történetéből*, Budapest: Osiris Kiadó.

Kósa, L. (2003), 'A magyar nemzettudat változásai', in B. Ábrahám, F. Gereben, and R. Stekovics (eds), *Nemzeti és regionális identitás Közép-Európában*, Piliscsaba: Pázmány Péter Katolikus Egyetem Bölcsészettudományi Kar, pp. 61-75.

Németh, L. (1992), *A minőség forradalma*, Budapest: Püski Kiadó.

Ravasz, L. (1939), 'A magyarság', in. Szekfű Gy. (ed.), *Mi a magyar?*, Budapest: Magyar Szemle Társaság, pp. 13-36.

Romsics, I. (1998), *Nemzet, nemzetiség és állam Kelet-Közép-Európában a 19. és 20. században*, Budapest: Napvilág Kiadó.

Schöpflin, G. (2000), *Nations, Identity, Power*, London: C. Hurst and Co.

Smith, A. (1999), *Nationalism and Modernism*, London: Routledge.

Szekfű, Gy. (1939), *Mi a magyar?*, Budapest: Magyar Szemle Társaság.

Szűcs, J. (1984), *Nemzet és történelem*, Budapest: Gondolat Kiadó.

Szűcs, J. (1997), *A magyar nemzeti tudat kialakulása*, Budapest: Balassi Kiadó – JATE – Osiris Kiadó.

Thuval, F. (1997), 'Geopolitika és magyar identitás', *Magyar Szemle*, 6(7/8), pp. 77-84.

Chapter 8

Czech Republic: Nation Formation and Europe

Karel Kubiš, Vlasta Kubišová, Karolína Růžičková and Michael Voříšek

This chapter presents a brief overview of the historical development of the Czech statehood based on a national principle. It characterizes the perceptions of significant others in contemporary Czech society and, most of all, it provides a survey of a basic discourse on perceptions of Czech national identity in relation to Europe and the European Union.

The Czech nation in a modern shape has been formed as a peripheral ethnic group since the end of the 18th century within the territory of a large multi-national state (the Habsburg monarchy) with one reigning nation. Czech nationalism thus belongs to the group of Eastern European nations that developed from the bottom – the underprivileged groups of newly formed middle class and emancipated rural folks were the driving force of Czech national emancipation. Finally, the Czech national identity was very heavily influenced by the presence of the strong German minority that has been living in the territory of the present day Czech Republic since the 13th century. The relations with the large nations surrounding the small Czech nation have been the omnipresent essence of Czech national identity discourse.

1. Historical Overview of the Czech Nationhood

'Why are the Czechs a small nation?' (Seibt 1996: 27). Today's Czech citizen has to come to terms with the fact that he is a member of a small nation. The interpretation of Czech history has been constantly confronted with the presence of large nations (the Germans, Russians, to some extent most recently, the European Union and the large nations within the EU). These pressures can threaten Czech independence or the existence of Czech culture, which is the main attribute of Czech nationalism.

As Ernest Gellner noted, the Czech nation followed similar paths of nation building as other Central-Eastern European states. Various national groups were going through a process of modernization and national emancipation but without a strictly defined territory. Moreover, the movement was driven by the underprivileged, not the political elites as it was the case for the Western European nations. National emancipation thus occurred hand in hand with the process of democratization and a struggle for equal political representation. Such nationalism of periphery groups did not occur in a historical vacuum. Simultaneously, the ruling elites were nationalized and identified with the idea of the Pan German State (Gellner 1997: 100-101). The Czech nation also detached itself from its own Czech aristocratic elite more distinctly than the rest of Central Europe (Seibt 1996: 10). This elite had much closer ties with the Austrian and/ or German nationalism and did not see Czech nationalism as its chance to gain political equality.

The national movement proceeded within the framework of the land unity of Bohemia and Moravia respectively. The Czech Republic lies within the borders of the Czech kingdom that emerged in the 13th century. Due to the geography, i.e. that the Czech borders are clearly defined by a range of mountains and rivers, the task of marking the territory for the modern Czech nation was not debated. These borders were not drawn along ethnic lines. The Czech national movement had the richest and most complex social structure. The process was driven by limited intelligence both sacred and secular. The Czech patriots' aims were based on the language as a basic identifying hallmark of the Czech ethnic group, and the Czech national movement's aim was to re-establish the autonomous position of the formerly independent Czech state. The first phase of national agitation came several decades after the serfdom had been abolished. It turned into a mass national movement after the revolution of 1848 when the feudal dependence of peasantry was abolished and a political emancipation of formerly subdued social groups began (Hroch 1986: 251). A prominent historian and politician at that time, Frantisek Palacky, could not imagine a further existence of the Czech nation outside of the Habsburgs' empire. In the second half of the 19th century, a full political emancipation did not occur however, for those who identified themselves as Czechs.

A significant shift in the perception of Czech national identity occurred among the Czech elites during World War I. The political and economic crisis of Austria-Hungary made Czechs realize that there is no hope for their national emancipation within the current Habsburg monarchy. The Habsburg elites failed to offer a viable civil ideology that fulfilled the aspirations of all the social groups within the monarchy. It lacked any of the significant features of identification (language, unifying historical interpretation) that a modern nation state possesses. Instead, the Austrian elites defended their particular interests and turned to German nationalism, thus excluding a large number of ethnic minorities that began to seek their fulfillment of national aspirations outside of Austria-Hungary (Suda 1997: 107). The international circumstances were also more favourable for the creation of an independent Czech state as the Allies took a positive approach towards the Central European and Balkan national movements, particularly after the Russian revolution of February 1917.

The modern Czechoslovak state was formed on 28 October 1918 with the union of the historical Czech lands forming the centre of the state, together with eastern Slovakia. Carpathian Ruthenia was incorporated in the summer of 1919. Three million Germans and a half million Hungarians remained inside the borders of the Czechoslovak Republic. The largely multinational state was struggling for its survival during the turbulent inter-war period. The idea of one Czechoslovak nation offered an attractive option for the Slavic population within the new state, or so the founders of Czechoslovakia thought.

During the 1920s, the relations between individual ethnic groups were stabilized. As hostile regimes emerged over the Czechoslovak border in Germany, Hungary, Poland and Austria, the peaceful coexistence of the ethnic minorities in Czechoslovakia came to an end. Thanks to Hitler's nationalistic propaganda, the German minority in Bohemia and Moravia began to disintegrate the state from within. The western powers failed to react appropriately to the most aggressive actions which Hitler was using to test their resolve. Their policy of appeasement put heavy pressure on Czechoslovak politicians to resolve the situation, thus resulting in the Munich agreement. Munich left its imprint on the nation, causing an ingrained distrust of the Allies and a deep, long-term depression over Czechoslovakia's own weakness. In March 1939 Hitler announced the formation of the Protectorate of Bohemia and Moravia. This protectorate only ceased to exist at the end of WWII. At the same time, the Slovakian representation declared an independent Slovak state which was closely related to the Third Empire.

After 1945, Czechoslovakia was restored but with a significantly altered population structure. Through the decision made at the Potsdam conference, the transfer of German inhabitants from Bohemia and Moravia into defeated Germany was carried out successfully. The transfer of Hungarians from Slovakia, however, was not. The communist coup in February 1948 stopped any attempts to bring the remaining nations of Czechoslovakia to a just and peaceful coexistence and Czechoslovakia was drawn into Eastern Europe under the supervision of the Soviets. The 'Prague spring' in 1968 resulted in a short intermezzo of a revival. However, this was soon brought to a halt by the armed forces of the Warsaw Pact in August 1968. For the Slovaks there was a positive side as they demanded significant decentralization of power – Prague to national, i.e. Slovak administration. Their hopes were realized with the establishment of federal institutions. After the 'velvet revolution' in November 1989 the communist regime was peacefully destroyed. The process of democratization and economic transformation brought to the surface between many conflicts Czechs and Slovaks which had not been out in the open over the 50 years. The Czechs entered the new historical reality in a better economic state and with more optimistic attitudes than their Slovak counterparts. The increasing demands for Slovak national autonomy, connected with claims for greater financial assistance due to the deepening economic crisis in Slovakia, resulted in hostile reactions from the political elite in Prague. Thus a political conflict over the speed and intensity of the Czech economic transformation emerged which divided the population along ethnic borders. Such a different approach to transformation manifested itself in totally different political preferences among Czechs and Slovaks. Therefore, after the elections in 1992 when the political spectrum was clearly divided along the ethnic lines, the Czech and Slovak political representation chose to peacefully disintegrate Czechoslovakia into two separate autonomous and independent national states. Masaryk's dream of one democratic nation composed of two branches disappeared indefinitely.

2. Significant Others in the Czech Society

The Czech nation was formed in relation to approximately four ethnic groups which fundamentally influenced the process of creating the Czech national identity. First, the Germans living in Austria-Hungary were the most important group of so called 'significant others' from the beginning of the national movement until the formation of the independent state. As a group, the Czechs define them as being one that is principally different from their own national identity. After 1918, the Slovaks come to the fore and yet they played part of a related ethnic group. It was even desirable to create a common nation with them. In this case, the Czechs were in the opposite role of an ethnic group towards which the Slovaks defined themselves as an independent nation and which they finally rejected in their claim for their own state. Nowadays the Roma, who are almost the only ethnic minority living in the Czech Republic, play an important role. The Roma ethnic group asks for the right to self-determination and thus contributes to the redefinition of the Czech national identity. Last but not least, it is necessary to stress that the Czechs speak of national feeling increasingly in relation to the European Union, together with the contemporary and future members of the EU.

The Czech-German Relations

The process of the Czech national emancipation was defined in opposition to a strong German minority which had been living in the territory of the historical Bohemian Kingdom since the 13th century. The ethnic border between the Czech and German population constituted often a social division between a richer urban class and a poorer, mostly Czech rural population.

The Czech patriots' attitude was based on language as a fundamental identifying hallmark of the Czech ethnic group. National autonomy and the demand to use Czech as the mother tongue at schools and in administration, expressed the effort to balance social differences between the particular ethnic groups in the Austrian monarchy. The Czech national consciousness was only formed in opposition to German identity (Suda 1995: 107).

At the end of the 19th century, Thomas Garrigue Masaryk presented an alternative to the Czech nationalism that was only defined on a language base. Masaryk realized that the Czech question could not be defined only negatively in confrontation with the Germans. He outlined a positive program of Czech national emancipation based on the heritage of the Czech religious reformation. By identifying with the ideals of Protestantism, he connected Czech nationalism with the major national movement in Western Europe (the United Kingdom, the USA, Germany). However, the Czech inhabitants' negative identification towards the Germans prevailed thanks to the dramatic events in the inter-war development in Germany and particularly due to the experience with the German totalitarian regime during WWII, which resulted in the mass transfer of the Czech [Sudeten] Germans out of Czechoslovakia. Out of three million Germans, several thousands were allowed to stay. This meant a significant step towards the homogenization of the formerly multinational Czechoslovak State.

After 1989, the character of mutual Czech-German relations was distinctly influenced by voices of the Sudeten Germans and particularly the Sudeten German Landsmanschaft. The Sudeten Germans began to question the decrees of president Benes legalizing the collective transfer of Czech and Moravian Germans. They were calling for the right of returning to Sudeten and they required the re-evaluation of the Germans transfer, which they considered to be an unjust and illegal act of collective guilt. The Czech population understood the contemporary claims of the Sudeten Germans in the context of their historical experience as an act of calling into question the integrity of free Czechoslovakia.

Relations between the nations are not in an entirely normal state. The reason is that the historical memory of the nations has not yet been laid to rest. Reservations over the haphazard transfer (although entirely incommensurate in the light of the historical experience of the Czech nation during WWII) bear nevertheless a certain moral appeal as the transfer of the Sudeten Germans was based on the principle of collective guilt and was accompanied by excesses of uncontrolled violence (Musil, Suda 1998: 138). The negative German-Czech historical experience results in the ambivalent attitude of the Czechs to present day Germany. Nevertheless, Germany remains one of the most important political and economic partners of the Czech Republic. Meanwhile, the Czechs consider Germany as a potential danger (Kostelecký, Nedomová 1996: 25).

The Czech educational system has still been encumbered, with some exceptions, with stereotypical interpretations of the continuous expansion of the German neighbour to the east and of the consequent threat to the Czech nation.

Czech-Slovak Relations

The relationship between the Czechs and the Slovaks differs considerably from that between the Czechs and the Germans. At the end of the World War I, Czech representatives raised the idea of creating an independent state. T. G. Masaryk developed a national programme of a future state, which, in time would also embrace the Slovak nation. He saw the main motive for the enlargement of the national basis necessary in order to gain the majority over the three-million minority of the Czech Germans. By joining with Slovakia, and later also with Carpathian Ruthenia, the Slavonic population gained the majority and pushed the Germans to the position of that of a minority. Czechoslovakia had become the state of the single Czechoslovak nation. This artificially created nation was unique in that two ethnically different national movements appeared. This artificially created construct survived for more than seven decades and, although the uniform consciousness of the common Czechoslovak nation was not created, the majority of the Czechs and Slovaks considered the common state natural and functioning until its cessation.

In the Czech national consciousness the idea of Czechoslovakism was accepted naturally as the logical result of forming the Czech national identity. The Czechs accepted the new state as their own, because it offered them a political framework for a fully constituted Czech nation. They perceived the notion 'Czechoslovak' as more and more coinciding with the notion 'Czech' (Suda 1997:

118). The national feeling of the Czech ethnic community was so closely attached to the Czechoslovak identity that there was not much room for the specifically Slovak attachment. It would come as no surprise that the Slovaks did not figure in such an identity – Czechoslovak in its nominal meaning, but Czech in its factual meaning (Barša 1999: 258).

In 1939, Slovak separatists created an independent Slovak state under the auspices of Nazi Germany. The Czechoslovak representatives had to abandon the conception of one Czechoslovak nation and to accept the existence of the Slovak nation as an irreversible fact. After WWII the Slovak elites worked on establishing an autonomous administrative structure within communist Czechoslovakia. The power transfer facilitated Slovak emancipation after the unsuccessful attempt of democratization in 1968. The Soviet invasion and abolishment of the Czech reformist movement brought to power a new Slovak elite in the Communist party that succeeded in creating a federal regime within Czechoslovakia.

In connection with the split of Czechoslovakia in 1993, numerous social scientists asked why this had to happen. The idea of the Czechoslovak nation suffered a fatal defeat at the moment when it had to pass the first democratic test. When the elections in 1992 ended in a stalemate, both wining parties gave preference to the split and their own path to political and economic transformation.

The state was split without the approval of its citizens in any referendum. Nevertheless it seemed as though the Czechs regarded the split of Czechoslovakia as an unsentimental event. The dissolution of Czechoslovakia resulted in another step towards the creation of a homogenous, one-nation state. Between 1993 and 1999, 97 per cent of citizens living in the Czech Republic identified themselves as Czech. Although Slovaks make up the largest minority, their share of the total population is minimal – between 1.5 and 2 per cent (Ruzickova 2000: 65).

Czech-Russian relations

Relations with Russia played an important role in the period of the National Revival. The Russians performed the role of a big Slavonic brother who was to be on the side of the other more subdued Slavonic nations. In this interpretation, the Russians were characterized as peace-loving Slavs, looking after their smaller brother nations. The Germans, on the other hand, played a negative role in subduing the Slavs. This interpretation was based on Herder's thesis on the democratic nature of the Slavonic race, which was put in contrast with the feudal nature of the Germans. Such a picture of Russia was supported by part of the conservative wing of the national revivalists who paid no regard either to factual Russian aims – i.e. taking control over the Slavonic territories after the fall of Austria-Hungary (experience of the Poles under the Russian domination, very often more repressive than the Austria-Hungary domination, was not taken in regard), or to the underdeveloped political and social situation in Russia.

During the Second World War and in the period that followed, the Russians were again perceived as liberators and were contrasted with the Germans. Such relations towards the Russians continued until 1948 when the communists took power and Czechoslovakia officially found itself in the Eastern block under the direct domination of the Soviet Union. At that moment, the Russians changed into the foreign power restricting the freedom of the Czech nation. It should be added that the official policy significantly differed from the opinion of part of the population against the Russians; but holders of such opinions could not freely publicize their ideas. Direct aversion towards the Russians developed after the occupation in 1968. The Russian domination was put in direct contrast to the Czech national identity. The Russians were again perceived as oppressors, though the real power was held by the Czechs tributary to the normalization process. During the demonstrations at the end of the 1980s, the Russians were in the position of direct enemies of the Czech nation. It is not a coincidence that the negotiating opposition required the removal of Soviet troops from Czechoslovakia as the nation's main priority (Holy).

Czech-Romany relations

The Romanies, who are nearly ethnically homogenous, are the last distinct group that stayed in the territory of the Czech Republic. They form about 3 per cent of the Czech population, although this data is based on an estimate as most Romanies describe themselves as Czechs in population surveys.

The Romanies form a community that has historically been living on the Czech territory since the 15th century (Nečas 1995: 17). For many centuries, the Romany ethnic group, like the Jews, had to face pressure for assimilation within mainstream society. On the other hand, the Romanies were perceived as culturally different and non-Czech, even in the period of the Czechoslovak state (Nečas 1995: 33).

The assimilation policy was in place from the time of Maria Theresa until the communist era resulted in the destruction of the traditional way of life for the Romany. In the 1950s and 1960s, the forced settlement of the Romanies into flats among the Czech citizens broke strong family ties and worsened relations between the Romany community and the majority of society, who had to face the consequences of the bad adaptability of the Romany ethnic group to the new environment (Nečas 1995: 47).

After 1989, when the obligation of the entire employable population to work was discharged, social differences between the Romany and non-Romany society have deepened. Growing unemployment within the Romany ethnic group, which in 1997/1998 was estimated at 75 per cent (in some localities even 90 per cent) led to a rise in criminality.

Opinion polls to ascertain the attitude of the Czech population toward the Romanies show that the Czech population perceives the Romany ethnic group rather negatively. Opinions prevail that the Romanies are not true Czechs. Nevertheless, the Czech population does not seem to hold a fully derogatory approach to the Romany minority based on the racial theory of the inalterable temperament of a certain group. The majority of Czechs believe that capable and hardworking individuals exist among the Romany population; however, such an approach is still influenced by a long-standing tendency to accept the Romany ethnic group only if it becomes more thoroughly assimilated in the majority society.

The solution of the social problems of the Romany community is only one aspect of the complex of problems in the Czech-Romany co-existence. Nearly half of the society still insists on the opinion that the Romanies are quite a different ethnic group which does not constitute the integral part of Czech society. Negative, emotional and sometimes even racist opinions having been based on objective grounds for the conflict co-existence form a significant barrier to the full integration of the Romany population into Czech society.

3. Czech National Identity – Dominant Discourses of Nationhood

Forming Modern National Identity

The modern Czech identity has been formed since the end of the 18th century. Of the contemporary thought streams, the Enlightenment and romanticism had the strongest influence on this process. In the Czech lands it was particularly the philosophy of J. G. Herder and the ideas of early German nationalism which influenced Czech national identity formation. The nation has been perceived as a natural and autonomous cultural value and was defined through the mediation of language. The national movement was also inspired by older discourses related to the *Czech identity*. Firstly, the identity was defined by political values and representations connected with Czech statehood: constitutional unity of the Crown Lands of Bohemia, national saints as their symbolic representatives, the rights of estates guaranteed by country laws. Secondly, *Czech identity* was notably reflected, among from other ways, in religious controversies: the ethnic identity of the Czechs as advocates of the 'right' faith was important, (but not principal, see Šmahel 2000), for the Hussite movement in the 15th century. Representatives of the 'baroque nationalism' in the 17th and 18th centuries were, on the other hand, demonstrating that the Czechs do not have anything in common with Hussitism and other heresies any more.

During the first half of the 19th century, several concepts of national identity were competing for support from the mass population who began to exchange their religious and social identity (connected with relicts of the feudal system), for a modern concept of national identity. More or less real projects of national identity for the population of Czech lands were as follows: *Austrian identity*, *Pan-German identity*, *Slavic identity*, *Bohemian identity*, and *Czech identity* (Kořalka: 16-82). The success of Czech identity was determined by the fact that it won support from all of the strata including part of the nobility, the quickly evolving middle class and the recently emancipated rural class.

Austrian identity Identification with the state of Austria-Hungary and first of all with the reigning Habsburgs dynasty, won support from only a narrow elite directly involved in the government (officers, bureaucrats, part of the aristocracy). The *Pan-German identity* gradually succeeded with the German-speaking inhabitants of the Czech lands – the Czech-speaking population was (quite rightly) afraid of marginalization due to their rejection of German as their mother tongue. The *Slavic identity*, a Pan-Slavic identity, was more hypothetical than a real possibility (on its considerable symbolic value see below). *Bohemism* (from the word *böhmisch* derived from the toponym *Böhmen* in opposition to an ethnic *tschechisch*) was based on the identification with the state of the Czech lands regardless of the inhabitants' ethnicity. Its basis formed country patriotism of mostly the German-speaking nobility who often sympathized with and accepted the Czech cultural efforts. In the first quarter of the 19th century there was also an attempt to create a more modern, civic variation of the *Bohemian identity* (B. Bolzano). However, contesting with the Pan-German and Czech programmes it failed. Both Slavic and bohemian identity did not offer a viable set of values which the majority of the population could identify with and remained attractive only for a small group of the upper classes.

The *Czech identity* had succeeded with the majority of most population of the Czech lands. It was defined on ethnic lines (i.e. the language base). The country's patriotism became its inspiration and also a provisional strategic ally. Most representatives of the Czech national movement were searching for a mutually compatible compromise with *Austrian identity*, which was not often met with an obliged response from the other side.

Identity in the Czech National Movement

The Czech national movement was defined on a language base. It was particularly the image of the homeland – identified with the Crown Lands of Bohemia, and accompanied by the accent on its famous history or on its historical rights (Hroch 1999). A further feature of the national identity was the image of a plebeianship or a folk character of the nation originally responding to the social composition of the national movement participants. But that also remained at the time when even the 'own' social elite claimed to be followers of the nation. During the 19th century this identity grew stronger and the idea of the 'Czech State right' became a political demand. It insisted on historical Czech land's autonomy based on the ancient privileges of the estates.

Civic-Liberal and 'Slavic'-Ethnic Dimension of National Identity

For the Czech national movement, political democratization was a basic means to meet its demands. The ethnic and civic principles were in accord, and the national identity defined itself as democratic. Yet the attitude of the Czech identity to liberalism and citizenship gave rise to a conflict with Pan-Germanism. Regarding the German version it meant a liberal, whole-Austrian, Cisleithanian or Pan-German political system, with Czech lands' self-rule being paralyzed. The Czech version was a maximum political autonomy of the Czech lands with a system as democratic as possible. It was logical that since 1848 the Czechs had become opponents of the whole-Austrian or pan-German liberalism, while the Pan-Germans in the Czech lands diets defended against any liberalization. The Czech movement seemed to the Germans to be non-liberal and the Czech identity, non-civic. Rather than anti-liberalism, the political motive of the Czech movement was the effort to show that liberalism and civic principles become a weapon in the hands of German nationalists against the ethnic (and consequently also civic) rights of the Czech-speaking population.

'Slavic identity' played, unambiguously, an important part in the Czech national movement. It helped to stress the constituent difference from the dominating German culture and occasionally it was also a tactical political manoeuvre. Political fondness for tsar absolutism was in fact minimal among the Czechs and as *a small nation* the Czechs felt much closer to e.g. the Estonians or Latvians than to the Russians (Macura 1983: 178-197). The Czech considerations of Slavic identity remained deep-rooted in the Western Europe culture (Herder was their 'ideal'), and Slavic identity could be perceived as the original path of the Czech identity to European identity. The formation of the Czech ethnic identity was based on the primary orientation to European and civic values and on an effort to fill them under the conditions of its own existence, not because of an aversion to them. Czech national identity also included some non-liberal or anti-civic potential. But this came out much later under considerably different conditions.

Contests for the Form of National Identity

After forming the fundaments of the national movement, the efforts to modernize the national discourse became a dominant topic. In the so-called 'fight for the Manuscripts' at the end of the 19th century, the young scientific generation rejected the romantic fakes of the supposed historical old literary documents that should have boosted national self-confidence. Czech origin itself ceased to be an argument for the intellectual elite. This also found expression in the so-called 'dispute on meaning of the Czech history' at the turn of the century. Philosopher T. G. Masaryk tried to interpret the Czech history including the national movement as a vanguard of a historic process in which the ideas of modern humanism and democracy are filled. His opponents, particularly among historians, considered this interpretation to be unscientific; they preferred to incorporate the Czech development into the all-European context of peoples' formation which enabled them apart from other things to refuse Masaryk's anti-catholic attitude. However, both streams could be considered to be a search for the European dimension of the national identity.

The formation of the independent Czechoslovak Republic in 1918 generated an important impulse to re-form the national identity. The Czechs considered the state as a natural result of their emancipation efforts and they strongly identified themselves with it: the Czech national identity got etatist shapes. Masaryk and (more controversially) Beneš, the inter-war presidents, are still today strong identification symbols for several generations. The Czechs also quite ethnocentrically adopted the Slovaks into their own identity – Czechoslovak identity was created as an image of 'the Czechoslovak' nation, consisting of Czech and Slovak 'branches' but with an obvious superiority of the Czech element. The civic principle should have been united with the ethnic one in the Czechoslovak Republic. But the Czechs adopted the policy for which they had criticized the

German liberals before: to join a civic equality with an ethnic supremacy. Czechoslovakia as a national state of the Czechoslovaks guaranteed all political, cultural and civic rights to ethnic minorities. But the Republic uncompromisingly blocked any efforts of German ethnic enclaves to get a political territorial autonomy and made them adopt the role of the minority. Criticizing this arrogance (raised for example by philosopher Emanuel Rádl) was refused in the name of scientific-state ideology (Kilias 2000).

The Munich Agreement (1938) and the following decline of the Czechoslovak Republic in 1939 struck a severe blow to Czech self-confidence and brought about a serious disillusionment with the West. Most of the population felt betrayed and their identification with European liberalism was shattered. The Czech and German strategies of the 19th century, struggling for ethnic hegemony through the mediation of political dominance over mixed territory, ended in disaster; first, in the terror of the German administration (including the almost total extermination of the Jews and Roma) in the Protectorate (1939 - 1945), and then in the after-war forced transfer of the Germans from the Czechoslovak Republic. Now an extreme Slavic identity was stated to be a fundamental concept of the Czech identity – the concept that had so far been an ideal of some isolated personalities or a property of short-term political manoeuvres (Pfaff) or that was undergoing a remarkable discourse of 'Europenization' (Palacky, Masaryk). The unambiguous orientation towards the West was replaced with the image of a re-established Czechoslovakia as a 'bridge' between the East and the West. The direct leaning to the East and to the project of soviet socialism were perceived as the cause of an unravelling of the Czech Slavic identity. National history was consistently interpreted in an anti-German and Slavic spirit, and Czechoslovak identity was restored. The ideology of Czechoslovak communism added a stress on a social aspect to these motives, exploiting the element of plebeianship in the national movement. In the background of this development, the civic contents of the national identity were paralyzed after the Communists took power.

Main Elements of the National Identity Image

Even today the language, which defines affiliation to the nation, occupies a prominent place in the representations set. Other indexes, such as origin or race, have hardly asserted themselves. National *state* is a further important value. The image of a natural unity of the nation and state was strengthened by the post-war reality of the state territory that was in fact language-homogenous. The articulation of the national *raison d'etre* is usually represented by *history* or its interpretation created in accordance with the needs of a certain opinion stream. The national *cultural abundance* and the image of it as an asset for Europe are an important part of this historical image. Also the conviction that the Czech nation naturally belongs to the European West is an important part of the national identity. But this conviction could also acquire a dissident or aggrieved feature in the perspective that the nation was (or is being) sacrificed to mercenary interests of the West. For the Czechs, it appears that the West hypocritically ignores the principles of humanity.

Democratic tendencies or egalitarianism of an Enlightenment-plebeian character – often putting the Catholic variant of the national identity in the shade – is still a living motive. The Slavic identity has been successfully discredited by the communist regime, but *defining towards the Germans* (often based on the feeling of a threatened national existence) still remains as a strong motive.

The civic principle became one of the leitmotivs in the attempts to re-build the Czech national identity in 1989. It can be based on the Czech attraction to the West with the consequence of a spontaneous desire for 'getting back to Europe' after the revolution, and of the self-interpretation of the Czechs as a culturally European nation. The image of the democratic first republic and the traditional democratic-plebeian dimension of the Czech identity are a certain support. The state becomes an important element of national identity, which contributes to the redefinition of the civic principle. However, the Czech state has been so far defined ethnically – as the natural home of the Czech people. The co-existence of ethnic and civic principles (although both sincerely respected) has been in favour of the ethnic principles so far. A popular image of history justifies such a concept of the state for the time being, and the attempts to call it into question are difficult. The tendencies to feel bitterness towards the West have become another obstacle. It is probable that the further expansion of the civic principle could occur first of all at the expense of the currently predominant image of the Czech past and at the expense of national unity.

4. Relations with Integrating Europe

The relationship of the former Czechoslovak Socialist Republic (CSSR) with the countries participating in the process of European integration corresponded to the relations of that period between the East and the West of Europe in the conditions of the Cold War and its end.

The break-up of the communist block, the collapse of the communist regime in the CSSR (November 1989), and the end of the CMEA (28 June 1991) constituted a fresh impetus to co-operate between the EC and Czechoslovakia and gave such co-operation a new quality. (In April 1990 the CSSR became the Czech and Slovak Federal Republic, CSFR, and on 1 January 1993, after the dissolution of the Federation, the Czech Republic was established.)

The first (so-called federal) association agreement between the then CSFR and the EC was agreed as early as on 16 December 1991. In order to speed up the implementation of the trade parts of this *federal association agreement*, and so as not to hamper the creation of a joint free trade area, the so-called Interim Agreement was simultaneously worked out. The Council of the EC approved the *Interim Agreement* in February 1992 (the document came into effect on 1 March 1993).

The Czech Republic opened independent discussions on the timetable of negotiations for a new association agreement (the *Europe Agreement*) as early as 8 December 1992. In December 1994 the European Council adopted a pre-accession strategy based on four key elements: the performance of the *Europe Agreement*, the maintaining of a multilateral structured dialogue, preparations of central and East European countries for joining the single EU internal market, and the aid to these countries within the PHARE programme.

The Czech Republic submitted an official application for membership of the EU together with the explanatory memorandum on 23 January 1996. In December 1997 the European Council decided, at its session in Luxembourg, to launch negotiations with the Czech Republic within a group of six countries (the Czech Republic, Poland, Hungary, Estonia, Slovenia and Cyprus) which comply most closely with the Copenhagen criteria.

As part of the pre-accession strategy, the European Commission has prepared the *Accession Partnership*, a document that is to unite all forms of support provided by the EU to individual candidate countries into one framework and simultaneously to accommodate the support to each candidate country.

The Czech Republic has prepared a mirror document to the *Accession Partnership*, the NP (*The National Programme for the Preparation of the Czech Republic for Membership of the EU*). The NP has been drawn up more comprehensively and has also outlined some other priority areas from the Czech viewpoint within the preparations for the Czech membership of the EU (e.g. statistics, communication strategy, education of state administration in European matters, arranging official translations of EC legislation into Czech). The preparation of these *National Programmes* was based on the European Commission's opinions as well as our own needs proposed by the Czechs. In preparing the *National Programmes*, all branches of the state administration took part. On 31 May 2000 the Czech government approved an enlarged version of the *NP*. This plan sees its priority in completing adaptation to EU directives. The Czech Republic successfully negotiated all the chapters of the Accession Treaty by April 2003 and signed the Accession Treaty on 16 May 2003 in Athens. The attitude of the Czech Republic towards the European Union is generally positive. The majority of the political representation has taken the accession process as the only vital and possible consequence of the break down of the communist regime. Despite differences in positive or negative evaluation – either relating to the accession process or the functioning of the European Union and its future development - neither any of the political parties nor any major opinion leaders have expressed a total denial of the enlargement process.

5. Concluding Remarks

The view of the Czech Republic towards the EU countries, similarly as in the case of other countries from the Soviet block, was determined by the global relationship between East and West. The major breakthrough for advancing the relationship from the previous inter-trade level to a process of EU enlargement was the break-up of the Soviet block and the totalitarian systems in Central and Eastern Europe in 1989. The specificity of the Czech development constitutes mainly the break-up of Czechoslovakia, which as a consequence revived the debate about Czech nationality and national identity (which, on the other hand, did not reach the intensity of the national feelings in Slovakia).

In connection with the domestic changes from 1989 to 2002, the debates about the Czechs belonging to Europe intensified. The election slogans such as 'Back to Europe!' meant clearly the disconnection with the communist past and manifested themselves in negotiations over joining the unified Europe. The victory of the liberal conservative parties also influenced the public debate about 'our accession to Europe' by bringing skeptical views towards Europe. In contrast to etatistic and 'socialist' Europe, the emphasis was put on the need for NATO membership. The Czech right wing policy was inspired by the conservative approach to the EU common in British neo-conservative circles (Thatcher). In this approach, there is no doubt about the Czech Republic belonging to Europe; however, the question of EU membership is mostly associated with the economic advantages of this process. The elements of European identity do not predominate over the 'national interests': arguments in the discussions about the economic advantages regarding the unified market take precedence over any other integration aspects. Such discussions influenced the attitude of the public towards the EU. It reflected a more cautious approach toward the EU and resulted in the lowest level of public support of the Czech Republic for EU accession among the central and eastern countries. It was caused mainly by the previous negative assessment expressed by the European Commission regarding the readiness of the Czech Republic to join the EU. That assessment did not correspond with the public opinion about the economic status of the Czech Republic within the Central European region. Later it was also the reluctance of the neighbouring EU countries to open their labour markets to the new members. The above-mentioned aspects intensified the conviction as to the inadequacy of the membership and suspicion (having also the support in the national discourse) towards the Western European countries (e.g., anxieties such as 'others want to benefit from us').

Nevertheless, the intensity of the negotiations grew stronger after 1997 as the social-democratic party gained a majority in the Parliament and formed the government. The public endorsed the improvement of the legal system, which appeared as a consequence of harmonization with the EU (the accessing countries were required to adopt the entire EU legislature). The cross-border cooperation brought another positive moment within the so-called Euroregion. In these areas formerly situated next to the 'iron curtain' the cooperation with neighbouring EU members brought significant social and economic improvements and reversed the trend within the former Czechoslovakia towards becoming the inner periphery. The experience of shared projects and true cooperation resulted in substantial change in the relationship with German-speaking countries. It showed that mutual collaboration is capable of transforming the former historical aversion and changing it into a productive mode of joint existence.

Despite the conflicting views on EU accession, the referendum held in June 2003 resulted in a positive outcome, with 77 per cent of participating voters in favour of the Czech Republic's accession to the EU. Fifty five per cent of eligible voters took part in the referendum.

As of May 2004, the Czech Republic became a regular member of the European Union. The public attitude towards a unified Europe might change significantly as citizens learn to exercise their rights and responsibilities in the family of European nations.

References

Barša, Pavel (1999), *Politická teorie multikulturalismu*, Brno: CDK.

Barša, Pavel and Strmisk, Maxmilián (1999), *Národní stát a etnický konflikt*, Brno: CDK.

Bednář, Miloslav (1996), *České myšlení*, Praha: Filosofia.

Bock, Ivo (1994), 'Die Wiedergeburt regionaler kultureller Traditionen in Mähren', in Forschungsstelle Osteuropa an der Universität Bremen (ed.), *Kollektive Identitäten in Ostmitteleuropa: Polen und die Tschechoslowakei*, Bremen: Edition Temmen, pp. 134–184.

Čornej, Petr and Prahl, Roman (eds) (1993), *Čechy a Evropa v kultuře 19. století*, Praha: Národní galerie v Praze.

EU Accession Opinion Survey (July 2001). Sofres factum, Projects: European Union Project http://www.tnsofres.cz/.

Gabal, Ivan (1995), 'Czechoslovakia: The Two Successors', in *In Pursuit of Europe: Transformation of Postcommunist States. 1989-1994*, Warsaw: Instytut studiów politicznych PAN.

Havelka, Miloš (ed.) (1995), *Spor o smysl českých dějin 1895-1938*, Praha: Torst.

Holy, Ladislav (1996), *Little Czech and the Great Czech Nation. National Identity and the Post-communist Social Transformation*, Cambridge: Cambridge University Press.

Hroch, Miroslav (1986), *Evropská národní hnutí v 19. století*, Praha: Svoboda.

Hroch, Miroslav (1995), 'Tschechen und Slowaken im Vergleich: Geschichtsbilder aus politischer und etnischer Perspektive', in Kaschuba (ed.) *Kulturen – Identitäten – Diskurse*, Berlin: Akademie Verlag.

Hroch, Miroslav (1996), *V národním zájmu*, Praha: Filozofická fakulta UK.

Hroch, Miroslav (1999), *Na prahu národní existence: Touha a skutečnost*, Praha: Mladá fronta.

Hroch, Miroslav (2000), *In the national interest: demands and goals of European national movements of the nineteenth century: A comparative study*, Prague: Faculty of Arts, Charles University.

Hroch, Miroslav (2000), *Social preconditions of national revival in Europe: a comparative analysis of the social composition of patriotic groups among the smaller European nations*, New York: Columbia University Press.

Kaschuba, Wolfgang (ed.) (1995), *Kulturen – Identitäten – Diskurse*, Berlin: Akademie Verlag.

Kilas, Jarosław (2000), *Narodowość jako problem naukowy: Naród w socjologii czeskiej okresu międzywojennego*, Warszawa: Scholar.

Kořalka, Jiří (1996), *Češi v habsburské říši a v Evropě 1815-1914: Sociálněhistorické souvislosti vytváření novodobého národa a národnostní otázky v českých zemích*, Praha: Argo (Originally as *Tschechen im Habsburgerreich 1815-1914: Sozialgeschichtliche Zusammenhänge der neuzeitlichen Natinsbildung und der Nationalitätenfrage in der böhmischen Ländern*, Wien - München: Verlag für Geschichte und Politik & Oldenbourg 1991).

Kostelecký, Tomáš and Nedomová, Alena (1996), *Národní identita*, Working papers. Praha: Sociologický ústav AV ČR.

Krejčí, Jaroslav and Machonin, Pavel (1996), *Czechoslovakia, 1918-92. A Laboratory of Social Change*, London: Macmillan.

Křen, Jan (1992), *Historické proměny češství*, Praha: Karolinum.

Macura, Vladimír (1983), *Znamení zrodu: České obrození jako kulturní typ*, Praha: Československý spisovatel.

Macura, Vladimír (1997), 'Sémiotika Evropy', in *Evropa očima Čechů*, Praha: Nakladatelství Franze Kafky.

Machonin, Pavel (1994), 'K sociologické komparaci české a slovenské společnosti', *Sociológia*, 26: 333-346.

Machionin, Pavel (1997), Sociální *transformace a modernizace*, Praha: SLON.

Machionin, Pavel (1998), *Results of a Czech-Slovak Comparison: Actors of Social Transformation and Modernisation,* GATNAR, Lumír, BÚZIK, B., *Attitudes of Individuals and Institutions to Social Transformation*, Working papers, Praha: Sociologický ústav AV ČR.

Musil, Jiří and Suda, Zdeněk (1998), 'Czech-German Relations: A Sociological View', *Sociological Review*, 6.

Nečas, Ctibor (1995), *Romové v* České *republice včera a dnes*, Olomouc: Vydavatelství Univerzity Palackého.

Perceptions of the European Union – a qualitative study of the public's attitudes to and expectations of the European Union in the 15 member states and the 9 candidate countries. Summary of the Results, (June 2001), OPTEM, web pages of the European Commission europa.eu.int/comm/governance/areas/studies/optem-summary_en.pdf.

Pernes, Jiří (1996), *Pod moravskou orlicí aneb Dějiny moravanství*, Brno: Barrister & Principal.

Pfaff, Ivan (1996), *Česká přináležitost k Západu v letech 1815-1878: K historii českého evropanství mezi vídeňským a berlínským kongresem*, Brno: Doplněk.

Pynsent, Robert B.(1996), *Pátrání po identitě*, Praha: H & H (Originally as *Questions of Identity: Czech and Slovak Ideas of Nationality and Identity*, Budapest: Central European University Press 1994).

Rádl, Emanuel (1928), Der *Kampf zwischen Tschechen und Deutschen*, Reichenberg: Gebrüder Stiepel.

Rak, Jiří (1994), *Bývali Čechové:* České *historické mýty a stereotypy*, Jinočany: H & H.

Růžičková, Karolína (2000), *Česká národní identita aneb Cesta České Republiky do Evropy očima veřejnosti*, Dipl. Práce. Praha: FF UK.

Seibt, Ferdinand (*1996*), *Německo a Češi. Dějiny jednoho sousedství uprostřed Evropy*, Praha: Academia.

Siwek, Tadeusz (1996), *Česko-polská etnická hranice*, Ostrava: Ostravská univerzita.

Suda, Zdeněk (1997), *Slovakia in Czech National Consciousness*, in Jiří Musil (ed.). *The End of Czechoslovakia*, Budapest: Central European University Press.

Šmahel, František (2000), *Idea národa v husitských Čechách*, Praha: Argo.

Třeštík, Dušan (1999), *Mysliti dějiny*, Praha - Litomyšl: Paseka.

Tuček, Milan; Rendlová, Eliška; Rezková, Miluše; Glasová, Alice and Čermý, Jiří (1999), *Odraz společenských změn ve veřejném mínění 1990 - 1998 (analýza dat IVVM)*, Working papers, Praha: Sociologický ústav AV ČR.

VSTUP *ČR do Evropské Unie* (květen 2001), STEM, Tiskové informace (web pages of the Stemmark www.stemmark.cz).

Weiss, Hilde and Reinprecht, Christoph (1998), *Demokratischer Patriotismus oder ethnischer Nationalismus in Ost-*Mitteleuropa? *Empirische Analysen zur nationalen Identität in Ungarn,. Tschechien, Slowakei und Polen*, Wien, Köln, Weimar: Böhlau.

Z AKTUÁLNÍHO výzkumu CVVM (2001), (http://www.soc.cas.cz/cvvm/) *Postoj české a polské veřejnosti k přechodnému období pro volný pohyb pracovních sil a pro prodej půdy cizincům.* (25. 7. 2001); *K názorům na vstup ČR do Evropské unie* (27. 7. 2001).

Zich, František (1999), *Nositelé přeshraniční spolupráce na česko-německé hranici,* Working Papers, Praha: Sociologický ústav AV ČR.

Internet resources on integration of the Czech Republic to the EU:
http://europa.eu.int/comm/tfan
http://europa.eu.int/comm/enlargement/index.htm
http://europa.eu.int/comm/tfan/index_cs.html in Czech
http://www.euroskop.cz
http://www.evropska-unie.cz
http://www.integrace.cz
http://www.eu.cz

Chapter 9

Europe and the Formation of the Polish State, Nation, and National Identity

Krystyna Romaniszyn

Introduction

The very fact that Poland is situated in the geopolitical centre of Europe has exposed it to both Eastern and Western influences. While on some occasions Poles have been given the historical opportunity to choose the path they would like to follow, as at the beginning of the Polish state (in the year 966) it was determined to be rooted in Roman Christianity and Latin culture (rather than in the Byzantine East), on other occasions the country was subject to imposition of foreign control and way of life, as in the case of the Partitions (in the nineteenth century), and the Yalta and Potsdam Conference Agreements (in 1945). Thus, the Polish state, nation, and national identity have been developing, during the thousand years of their history, at the crossroads of the European West and the European East. This chapter outlines the milestones of this history.

Europe and the Polish State, Nation, and National Identity Formation

The history of the Polish state and nation constitutes a part of European history. The milestones for the formation of the Polish state and its civic-territorial model of the nation[1] have been the Jagiellonian dynasty, and the Royal or the First Republic; the decisive period for the formation of the other, ethnic-genealogical model of the nation has been that of the Partitions. The formation of modern Poland at the beginning of the twentieth century witnessed the clash of two understandings of the state and the nation. The following discussion is focused on these specific issues.

---

[1] For a definition of the models of the nation, see Smith (2000).

The Formation of the Polish State and Civic-Territorial Model of the Nation

The Polish Crown With the baptism of Prince Mieszko the First in the year 966, the Duchy of Polonia became a part of Roman Christianity and of Latin civilization, determining the alphabet and court language. The construction of the Polish realm – recognized as such by the Pope and the European powers of that time – had begun. From the very beginning, the development of the state was accompanied and strengthened by the establishment of church structures. In 999 the first capital, Gniezno, was elevated by the Pope to the level of an Archbishopric, and new bishoprics at Wrocław, Kołobrzeg, and Kraków were created. With Gniezno as capital of both the state and church, the developing Polish state structure acquired full recognition and legitimization in Roman Christendom. Under the first Polish dynasty, the Piasts (966-1386), the first parliament met in 1331; under the second, the Jagiellonian dynasty (1386-1572), Poland became a powerful state in Europe, and, with its 990,000 square kilometres after unification with Lithuania (1569-1776), it became the largest European country.

The Commonwealth of Poland-Lithuania The Royal Republic of Poland-Lithuania (*Serenissima Republica Poloniae*) came into being on 1 July 1569 through the Union of Lublin, in which the Kingdom of Poland and the Grand Duchy of Lithuania recognized each other as equal partners. From its outset, the Republic was a multiethnic state. Its population of ten million included 40 per cent of the Poles, and the peasantry comprised Polish, Ruthene, Lithuanian ethnic groups. The cities were also ethnically heterogeneous, and almost every town had its Jewish community (Zamoyski 1994).The Commonwealth was pluralistic in the religious sphere too. Besides different Christian denominations and the Jews, there were the Muslim Tartars who had settled in the fifteenth century. Ethnic and religious pluralism necessitated a specific rule and this was legal, religious freedom, and toleration of ethnic diversity. Both these Commonwealth rules and virtues have been seen by subsequent generations as a key legacy.

A distinctive feature of this political edifice was the coexistence of the monarchy with republicanism, which borrowed the style, symbolism, and concepts of the Roman Republic. The political vocabulary dealt with such terms as 'liberty,' 'equality', 'nation', 'citizen', and 'republic' (Zamoyski 1994: 98). This was, however, a democracy of the gentry (*szlachta*) – the independent magistrates over their own land – which reserved the dominant position for itself. Noticeably, superiority was offered to gentry of *any* ethnic origin. In the Commonwealth, any ethnic group's elite, but also the state, its institutions, and the legal system together created and incorporated a political nation that was not based upon ethnic or religious affinities; its members (the gentry) were equal before the law.[2]

---

[2] Belonging to the nation meant to be a subject of the Commonwealth, thus 'A baptized Jew from Volhynia would sign himself "gente Ruthenus, Natione Polonus, origine Judeaus"' (Zamoyski 1994: 178).

This was definitely not '"the nation of design" ... [of] Central and Eastern Europe' but the product of an unplanned process that some scholars reserve for 'the "old, continuous" nations of Western Europe' (Smith 2000: 717).[3] The Commonwealth's political nation is to be interpreted with reference to the 'rational', 'voluntaristic', civic-territorial model of nation formation, and certainly not with reference to the 'organic', 'mystical in character', ethnic-genealogical one. In the course of time, however, during the era of subjugation to autocratic foreign powers (1795-1918), the political nation of the Commonwealth eroded.

The Partitions and the Development of the Ethnic-Genealogical Model of Nation

The *spiritus movens* of the partitioning of Poland were Russia, expanding to the west, and Prussia, expanding to the east; the Habsburg Empress finally took her share, though objecting to this sin, as she put it. The three powers seized an opportunity during the Commonwealth decline, but they sped up and finalized the process precisely when it had begun to modernize.

The causes of the decline were economic, political, and moral. The economy had suffered from the twenty years of war in the middle of the seventeenth century. The wars with Sweden and the Swedish invasion (1617-1629) left the country – the towns in particular – ruined: the urban population declined by up to 70 per cent (Zamoyski 1994: 176), which fixed the unfavourable pattern of the Commonwealth's economy.[4] The overall standard of living of the entire population was decreased drastically between 1600 and 1700. Additionally, Poland's elected (since 1510) monarchs tended to regard the Commonwealth as a sinecure; the *Sejm* had lost most of its executive power. Along with this, old virtues faded away: religious freedom and toleration of ethnic diversity receded, and the ideal of political freedom evolved into the acceptance of anarchy. This was seized as an opportunity by its autocratic neighbours pursuing their goals; they disrupted the country's recovery fired by the spirit of the European Enlightenment.

The modernization pertained to school reform, the economy (capitalist activity), and society, and it resulted in the emergence of a new class: the intelligentsia – a reincarnation of the former political nation united by a common educational background (not social origin), and political vision (Zamoyski 1994: 237). The Commonwealth's greatest achievement, the Constitution – the first written in Europe, and second internationally to the American – became law on 3 May 1791. But a compromise between republicanism and monarchism was never implemented, due to the Partitions the Constitution directly triggered off. Still, its premises confirm the thesis of a civic-territorial route towards the nation building in Poland. The Constitution aimed at the full integration of peasants and town dwellers into the political nation. Catholicism was enshrined as the religion of the

---

[3] This is how the ideological concepts of 'Western' and 'Eastern' Europe continuously shape scholarly thinking.
[4] As Wallerstein (1974: 304-307) points out: 'Poland is by the sixteenth century integrated into the European world-economy', occupying, however, the margins of the system.

state, although every citizen was free to practice another faith. The *Sejm* became the chief legislative and executive power (Zamoyski 1994: 248).

The Constitution's proclamation was hailed in Western Europe: political clubs in Paris voted to make the Commonwealth King, Stanisław August Poniatowski, an honorary member, while Condorcet, Thomas Paine, and Edmund Burke acclaimed the Constitution as a breakthrough (Zamoyski 1994: 249). But among the east-central European emperors in Petersburg, Vienna, and Potsdam, the Constitution evoked fear as being too revolutionary. Closer co-operation ensued which resulted in subdivision of the Commonwealth: partial seizure in 1772 was followed by the Partitions of 1792 and 1794. At the time when Western Europe began developing the ideas of liberal democracy, the Commonwealth was annihilated by autocracies and feudalism: 'The three Partitions ... were carried out by gangsterish methods ... where the victims were forced to condone their own mutilation ... Many historians have accepted the view that the Poles brought disaster on themselves. It took a Burke, a Michelet, or a Macaulay to call a crime a crime' (Davies 1997: 661).

The Partitions meant colonization[5] and, with few exceptions, economic stagnation. The Austrians saw their share as a pool of manpower for the army; attempts to develop the area economically were discouraged; the taxation rate (as percentage of average earnings) was 20, while in Great Britain it was 10, and in France 12.5 (Szczepański 1887). Prussian rule meant the systematic cultural and economic repression of the Poles perceived as 'a nation of lesser cultural content'. In 1874 the use of Polish textbooks was forbidden by law, in 1876 German became the exclusive administrative language, and in 1887 the study of Polish as a second language was abolished. In 1898 a series of laws turned the Poles into second-class citizens: it became illegal for them to buy land, and a 1904 a law forbade them to build houses on their own land. At the same time the German Colonization Commission bought up land for its colonists. In Russia, Poles grasped an opportunity to speed up economic development, most spectacularly in the textile industry. Agriculture, perceived by the Russians as an economic base for the gentry, remained underdeveloped. Severe political and economic repression introduced after each of the uprisings – in 1794, 1830, and 1863 – led to the economic ruin of thousands of gentry families, and after 1863 uprising 80,000 of their members were sent to Siberia.

All Partitioning powers took measures against the church hierarchy since it, replacing the state, helped maintain Polish national identity through a religious component. In 1918 the church hierarchy supported the re-established Polish state spiritually and substantially, and this pattern of support for the nation – with or without a state – would repeat itself during the dual (German and Soviet) occupation of World War II, and the decades of the Polish Peoples Republic (PRL).

---

[5] During the last partition, 'The Prussians took Mazovia ... and called it "New South Prussia". The Austrians took another huge slice and called it "new Galicia". The Russians contented themselves with a slice the size of England' (Davies 1997: 722).

The Partitions were perceived as a catastrophe not only by the gentry. The Warsaw 'Jewish community formed up and equipped a special regiment of its own ... the first Jewish military formation since Biblical times' (Zamoyski 1994: 256) to join the uprising of 1794, along with peasant volunteers. This and the following uprisings ended in military collapse and persecutions. Though revealing the firm determination of the gentry to restore the state, the uprisings were met by the no-less-firm determination of the Partitioning powers to keep the land they had seized.

The uprisings kept European intellectuals aware of the 'Polish Question' and its relation to Europe. An example of these concerns is a speech by Karl Marx in 1867: 'There exist only two alternatives for Europe. Either Asiatic barbarism under the leadership of Moscow will fall on Europe like an avalanche – or else Europe will rebuild Poland, cutting itself off thereby from Asia with a wall of twenty million heroes' (Zamoyski 1994: 287). For Marx, Poland's resurgence was a matter of preserving European identity against non-European influences and actions. At the same time, Metternich honestly stated that the Polish cause 'does not declare war on the monarchies which possess Polish territory, it declares war on all existing institutions and proclaims the destruction of all the common foundations which form the basis of society' (Zamoyski 1994: 299).

The European system of that time was accepted by the Holy Alliance that, ironically enough, arrogated for itself the right and duty to defend European civilization. To make things more grotesque, it was about that time that an image of 'Eastern Europe' (including Russia) was developed, portraying this part of the continent as the hub of ethnic intolerance and xenophobia – an idea still haunting the collective identity of western societies (Romaniszyn 2001: 283).[6] In line with these, Polish aspirations for state resurgence came to be perceived by fellow Europeans as 'fanatic' and 'extremist' – in strong contrast to the positive connotations of German or Italian nationalists, campaigning against their regimes, as progressive and far-sighted (Davies 1991: 37). This view was rational, as supporting the Polish question would mean war. Besides, the European powers ruling their colonies saw nothing wrong with Russian or German rule of Poland. Indeed, a double standard strategy in politics has a long tradition. The background of and changing reaction to 'the Polish Question' also reveal the meanings in the development of Western European concern with the issue of political freedom.

Along with the Partitions, the Polish nation became an idea not merely persisting, but constantly developing in people's minds. The loss of the state and the possibility of following its own distinct path of nation development within the context of a 'national state' (Smith 1997: 718) resulted in a separation of the nation from the political community. Under the imposed political circumstances, the Polish political nation dissolved, and the search for a Polish national identity began in opposition to alien rule, focusing on the 'sameness' of the Poles. In the Commonwealth, to be Polish meant being the subject of the republic and loyal to the king; during the Partitions, these same people – forced to be Russian, Austrian or Prussian subjects – refused to identify themselves as Russians, Prussians or

---

[6] The idea exemplifying the 'camouflaged' cultural racism that concerns whole societies, has outlived the Iron Curtain, because of its long tradition (Romaniszyn 2001: 283).

Austrians. Such circumstances necessitated a search for other criteria of national distinction than the civic one. This would be basically the language and the literature written in that language;[7] religion; and the way of life. With this, a new chapter in the process of the nation and its identity's development had begun.

Colonization, along with the three uprisings, decisively influenced the development (and for some, discovery) of Polish national identity in the nineteenth century. In effect it was more broadly distributed among the social strata at the beginning of the twentieth century than at the end of the Commonwealth, but its 'content' varied from one social group to another. The core of the national identity drew upon the gentry's ethos and its values: individualism, liberty, courtesy, and chivalry. These values attracted members of the other social strata, who gradually accepted the core and supplemented it with religious augmentations. In the case of the peasants (regardless of ethnicity), religious identity came to equal national identity: for them, Catholic became a synonym for a Pole, Orthodox for a Russian, etc. Prior to the Partitions, the ethnically Polish urban population expressed its national identity in loyalty to the Commonwealth, confirmed by support of the uprisings during the Partitions. National identity of the labourers was largely shaped by the ethnic and social background of a given person, although they were increasingly driven by the working class political movement. A striving for state restoration, which materialized after World War I, served as a test of national identity for all.

Along with the evolutions of national identity, the concept of the 'nation' also evolved into two main discourses: the Romantic and the Positivist. The former was influenced by German philosophy of the era; the formative works by Józef Gołuchowski, a student of Schelling, and August Cieszkowski, a Hegelian, were written in German. Developed by philosophers, the messianic visions of nations were further expanded by poets. The most popular one was Adam Mickiewicz's image of Poland crucified for the cause of righteousness; Poland would expiate the political sins – ours, those of the Partitioning powers, and those of the European powers who accepted the crime of the Partitions – and lead to resurrection. Faith in Poland's sacrifices endowed reality with sense, gave hope, offered healing, and saved from despair. The Romantic idea of the nation was underpinned by an assumption that it would be possible in the future to combine a nation-state with a multiethnic society. This rested upon the perception of the Polish nation as composed of the ethnic groups which had formerly constituted the Commonwealth.

This perception of the nation became the subject of critique when the French concept of nation and state – presupposing the unifying role of the state in nation-building, and viewing the nation-state as an ethnically homogeneous unit – permeated Polish political discourse. Moreover, in the last decades of the nineteenth century, a new philosophical current arose – Positivism. It drew upon the works of August Comte, John S. Mill, and Charles Darwin, contradicted the Romantic concept of the nation as a spirit, and replaced it with the concept of the

---

[7] In the Commonwealth, the *lingua franca* of the elites was Latin. During the Partitions the Polish language undertook the Latin role, and became a medium unifying Poles across all social strata.

nation as an organism.[8] The prescription for progress was work in the economic
and social spheres, aimed at strengthening economic and cultural resources, and at
curbing all political demands beyond local autonomy. This work resulted in
improvement of everyday life, education, and the economy. The shortcomings of
the Positivists' perception of the nation and its future was its inability to provide
the people with the hope and courage needed for the restoration of the state.

Modern Poland – Between the Civic and Ethnic Perceptions of Nation

Poland's restoration after WWI was not welcomed with much enthusiasm by the
European powers of the time. Key European figures expressed feelings far from
enthusiastic: for Molotov the Polish state was the horrible bastard of the Treaty of
Versailles; for Keynes its existence was economically impossible; Lewis Namier
viewed it as 'pathological'; for Carr it was a 'farce'; Lloyd George perceived it as a
'defect of history'; and for Adolf Hitler, Poland was a 'so-called state, lacking any
national, historic, cultural or moral foundations' (Davies 1991: 494).

The reappearance of the Polish state after over a century of its non-
existence in Europe was neither accidental nor the effect of the political decision or
vision of European powers. Its recreation was the result of the deliberate action of,
and maximum effort – political and military – exerted by all the nation's social
strata. Thus the state's resurgence can be viewed, not metaphorically, as the
success of the nation's determination. This nation, however, differed from the
political one of the Commonwealth; this time, due to the lack of a state, it was
precisely the outcome of a politicization and mass mobilization of the demotic
ethnie through the intelligentsia (Smith 1997: 718).

The Second Polish Republic (1918-1939), created out of the peripheries of
the Partitioning states and devastated by war, needed to unite different currencies,
fiscal and administrative systems, railway networks, legal codes, etc. The twenty
years of independence did bring achievements: illiteracy was halved;
industrialization was encouraged;[9] and land reform was launched.[10] The Republic
was about half the size of the Commonwealth of 1772, but still multiethnic. The
ethnic mosaic comprised Ukrainians, Jews, Belarussians, Germans, plus smaller
numbers of Lithuanians, Russians, Slovaks, Czechs, Tartars, Roma, and folk
populations identifying themselves as 'indigenous'.

The status of the minorities (around one-third of the population) was
regulated by the constitution of 1921. This did not eradicate the tensions that had
built up between the minority and dominant groups, which fuelled by the economic
hardships of the 1930s depression when ethnic conflicts intensified in Poland as in
other parts of Europe. To stop xenophobic or racist attitudes and actions, the
Parliament adopted a law (in 1932) that penalized religious, linguistic and national

---

[8] Henry Buckle's *History of Civilization in England* (1861) was translated into Polish and
published one year later.
[9] In the 1930s, Poland was the eighth largest steel producer in the world, and ninth of iron;
the merchant and navy marines had been built 'from scratch'.
[10] This was vital since 64 per cent of the population lived off the land.

discrimination, and aimed at a political alliance of all the state's nationalities. Its proponents advocated the revival of the Commonwealth political nation. The attempt, however, was aborted by right-wing national extremism of various national provenance: 'the Ukrainian OUN indulged in common terrorism and provoked brutal pacification of the peasants'; 'Zionism made rapid headway in the Jewish community'; 'A Nazi Fifth Column was organized among the German minority', while Roman Dmowski's nationalists hailed a 'Poland for the Poles'. All these 'fuelled the fires of mutual hatred' (Davies 1997: 978).

On the eve of the Polish state restoration, political life in the Partitions had been polarized by two basic national movements: the National Democratic movement of Roman Dmowski, and the Polish independence movement of Józef Piłsudski. The common aim and platform for both movements was the resurgence of the state, but they differed with respect to their understanding of 'nation'. The national movement interpreted it as an ethnic community having an inalienable and exclusive right to territory inherited from its ancestors – from which followed the idea of minority assimilation. Regarding state resurgence, the nationalists assumed an alliance with Russia against Germany. The independence movement, in contrast, perceived Russia as the greatest enemy, and saw the nation as a community based upon a common perception of history and culture – united, but not unified (in the French style) by the state in one political community. As a direct continuation of the gentry democracy model, this stance differed substantially from the French understanding of the state as an ethnically homogenizing political edifice. In the interpretation underpinned by the Commonwealth tradition, the state embraces all ethnic groups living in a territory dominated by one of them, whereby all become citizens of a state while keeping their national distinctiveness. Paradoxically, the national movement was labelled as 'realistic' for its readiness to compromise with the Partitioning powers, while the independent one was called 'romantic' for its determination to fight for independence. Soon, history proved these labels completely false.

The course of these two modern understandings of the nation reveals that they had neither been initiated 'from the top' by the actual state, nor had they been sponsored by the establishment of the concept of 'citizenship'. This was objectively impossible because of the Partitions; the opportunity of building the modern nation by civic or state nationalism had not been offered to Poles dominated by the empires of that time. Under these circumstances, the modern Polish nation and its identity could only develop at the 'grassroots' level. However, one of these 'roots' had been fed by the constantly living memory of the Commonwealth political nation. The described pattern does not fit Anthony Smith's two types of nation-building in Europe: the ethnic-genealogical type, allegedly characteristic of eastern Europe, and the civic-territorial, allegedly specific to the western parts of Europe. In fact, a clear-cut, bipolar model when applied literally rather oversimplifies and distorts the facts it is to explain. If we situate Poland in eastern Europe, we need to exclude – in order to validate the model – one substantive and living part of the country's history and political tradition (the Commonwealth). In order to recount Poland's history and validate the model, we need to say that both routes to nation formation pertain to the case.

Obviously they have not been followed simultaneously, but each in its time. Phrasing this distinct pattern of the state and nation development in a sentence, one could say that it runs from the state to the nation, and from the nation to the state, with the Partitions as the turning point.

In Polish history, the spontaneous formation of the Royal (First) Republic constitutes the first stage of nation development. This was interrupted by the Partitions, but this historical period was never forgotten nor abandoned by the people identifying themselves as Poles. Due to this memory, the nationalist interpretation of the nation that developed in the nineteenth century has constantly been contradicted by the civic and territorial interpretation, sometimes referred to as the Jagiellonian. These two models were tested in the relatively short period of the Second Polish Republic (1918-1939) with the ethnic-genealogical interpretation prevailing in the 1930s. In contemporary Poland the civic-territorial continuously dominates the political discourse.

The Trauma of WWII and the Challenge of the Post-war Communist Period

In the face of German resentment and Russian reluctance to be pushed back eastwards, Poland expended maximum diplomatic efforts to make itself secure. In 1932, a non-aggression pact was signed with the Soviet Union; in 1934 a ten-year non-aggression pact was signed with Hitler.[11] In April 1939 a full military alliance was signed by Britain, France and Poland. Despite these efforts, on 1 September 1939 the Wehrmacht invaded Poland from the west, north, and south; on 17 September the Red Army invaded Poland from the east. A new Partitioning of Poland had been accomplished.[12] The trauma of the War and its aftermath reshaped the state and the nation.

Both aggressors, Nazi Germany and Soviet Russia, deliberately attempted to enact a final solution to the 'Polish Problem' by annihilating the state and its elite, and enslaving the rest of the nation. Following the 1 and 17 September 1939,[13] the policy of planned extermination had been introduced. Hidden from the outside world, the occupying powers conducted their plan, an effect of which was that 'a third of the educated elite were "liquidated" and, in all, six million Poles lost their lives, half of them Jews slaughtered in concentration camps' (Webster's 1992: 891f). The prime target for extinction was the elite. If not slain immediately, they were transported – in cattle trucks – to forced labour in the Third Reich, to German concentration and death camps, to Soviet Gulag camps and Asiatic republics like Kazakhstan. With these mass shifts of Poles, the mass forced transportations of civilians, and a sad history of expulsion and expellees had begun.

---

[11] According to Davies (1997: 977) when in 1934 'Marshal Pilsudski took soundings in Paris about a preventive war against Nazi Germany, he elicited no response'.

[12] In August 1939, Ribbentrop and Molotov had signed a non-aggression pact to which was appended a secret protocol between Germany and the Soviet Union pre-establishing new borders precisely across the Polish Republic.

[13] Poland was fighting alone: France launched no offensive, and Great Britain limited its assistance to dropping leaflets over Berlin (Davies 1997: 1001).

In the German zone, 'In an act of cold-blooded genocide, the so-called AB-Aktion, some 15,000 Polish intellectuals, officials, politicians, and clergy were selected for shooting or for consignment to concentration camps' (Davies 1997: 1002). From 1939 until 1944, about 1.3 million Poles were taken from the 'General-Gouvernment' and shipped to the Reich as slave labour; some 750,000 Germans were brought in to colonize the Polish territories attached to the Reich; and some 2 million Poles were moved out of the Reich into the 'General-Gouvernment'[14] (Zamoyski 1994: 358). Among the places of mass extinction of the Polish intelligentsia were Dachau (Germany) and Mauthausen (Austria)[15] concentration camps, while the Auschwitz Nazi concentration camp[16] – located on Polish territory made part of the III Reich – had become the burial ground for almost all Polish and most of European Jewry, and thus a symbol of the Shoah (Holocaust).[17]

In the Soviet zone, 'By the summer of 1941 between 1 and 2 million individuals had been transported either to the Arctic camps or to forced exile in Central Asia' (Davis 1997: 1003). Besides, in 1940 'some 26,000 Polish prisoners of war – mainly reserve officers, and hence intellectuals, officials, politicians, and clergy – were taken from their camps and shot in a series of massacres known under the collective name of Katyń' (Davis 1997: 1003). Significantly, until 1990, the Russians tried to place the Katyń Forest massacres on the list of German war crimes while the Western allies kept silent. The successful partnership in dealing with 'the Polish Problem' compelled the Soviet newspaper *Pravda* to announce in 1941: 'German-Soviet friendship is now established forever' (Davis 1997: 1003).

The War ended in 1945; however, the Yalta agreements that shaped the post-war Europe located Poland within the Soviet Union domain, and the Red Army that marched into the country in 1944 stayed continuously until 1993.[18] The Polish eastern frontier was established along the Curzon Line. The country lost 181,350 sq km in the east to the USSR, and gained 101,000 sq km in the west from Germany. The westward shift of the country had been welcomed as a return to the cradle of the Polish state, settled there by the first dynasty, the Piasts. Nevertheless these shifts caused the mass deportations of the population. About 3.5 million Germans either fled or were removed, their place taken by Poles – 2.2 million persons returning from slave labour and concentration camps in Germany, and 1.5

---

[14] The Germans incorporated some of the conquered territory into the Reich, while the remainder was designated as the General-Gouvernement.

[15] Mauthausen (near Linz) had 58 branches; in one of them, Gusen, some 123,000 people lost their lives. Other German concentration camps in which Poles died were Buchenwald, Gross-Rosen, Ravensbruck, Stutthof, Sachsenhausen-Oranienburg.

[16] In fact, 'Auschwitz I had been established as the Nazis' instrument to subjugate the Poles into serfdom – an enslavement the Poles rightly interpreted as the initial step to a "Final Solution" to a Polish problem' (Dwork and van Pelt 1994: 241).

[17] The irony was that it would be economically facile for Germany to establish its ghettos and death camps on the land where an estimated 3.5 million Jews comprised the largest Jewish community in Europe.

[18] 'On 17 January 1945 the Red Army marched into the ruins of Warsaw and within a couple of months the whole of Poland was in Soviet hands' (Zamoyski 1994: 369).

million persons ousted from the eastern territories taken over by the Soviet Union (Zamoyski 1994: 370). All together, the War deportations and migrations involved over 25 million people on the Polish territory. These mass population and border shifts have resulted in a persistent syndrome of loss on the part of both Poles and Germans.

Poland re-appeared with: 6 million people (or 22 per cent of population) murdered, its borders shifted, its socio-political system guarded by the Red Army bases, and 40 per cent of its national wealth destroyed.[19] The human and material devastation was augmented by the moral damage caused by the War trauma and paid by Polish society. This, among other things, led to a negative attitude towards Germans, and a feeling of resentment towards the Western allies. The latter have been perceived by subsequent generations as those who betrayed Poland – in 1939 at the war's outbreak, and in 1945 in Yalta and Potsdam – despite the country's contribution to the defeat of Nazi Germany.[20]

The War aftermath was another milestone for the Polish state and nation. The introduction of the new order in 1945 under the Soviet auspices was supported by the military presence of the Red Army and of the Soviet secret police (NKVD) that helped to establish its Polish counterpart. Forced imposition of a communist government[21] triggered military resistance, answered by combat and deportations to the USSR. Tens of thousands of Home Army members, landowners, political activists, and soldiers who had served in Polish forces abroad and returned were jailed, tortured and/or murdered.[22] This, along with the extermination policy and political emigration, deprived the country of an excessive number of its elites and most creative citizens. As a rule, after 1945 political leaders no longer arose from the intelligentsia or upper class, but out of the lower classes.

The Polish Peoples Republic was proclaimed formally in 1952 after the civil war (1944-1947) had been put to an end. The 'peoples democracy' became a legally confirmed hoax. Nominally, the Parliament was the superior representative power; until 1989 the real power was enjoyed by the Polish United Workers Party (PZPR). Despite forced registration, in some areas, it numbered some[23] 3 million

---

[19] The reconstruction of the ruined country mobilized the nation, specifically the rebuilding of Warsaw (90 per cent levelled during and immediately after the Warsaw Uprising of August-September 1944, in which 250,000 civilians were slaughtered, by a German *Vernichtungskommando* that methodologically blew up building after building).

[20] Between 1939 and 1945, 600,000 Polish soldiers of the Government in-Exile who had fled to the West fought together with the Allied forces. In occupied Poland, the underground Home Army directly subordinated to the government – which by 1944 numbered nearly 400,000 fighters and was the largest resistance movement in Europe – was engaging substantive German forces.

[21] The Polish Communist Party, banned in 1938, had never been a significant force on the interwar political scene; 'its exiled leadership, largely Jewish, was liquidated en masse during Stalin's purges' (Davies 1997: 978). Those who survived inside Polish jails formed the country's political leadership after 1945.

[22] Up to 16,000 people are thought to have died in this way (Zamoyski 1994: 370).

[23] A disproportionate number of Party members were Polish Jews who owed their lives to the USSR, where they escaped running from the German occupation.

people, never reaching even half the approximately 10 million which Solidarity would win during its 16-month official existence in 1980-1981.[24]

The decades of the communist state, introduced and safeguarded by a foreign power, constituted another foreign input into the country's history and were perceived as such. Thus, in order to capture the people's minds and to rule effectively, the authority deliberately attempted to negate and annihilate Polish history. Distortion of history would mean not only that 3 May Constitution Day and 11 November Independence Day were struck from the calendar of official commemoration and banned, but that the October Revolution, May Day, and 22 July 1944 would be annually and gloriously celebrated as the breakthrough dates for 'our state'.[25] The only real social force able to, and actually opposing the indoctrination, was the Roman Catholic Church, which became a subject of permanent persecution by the regime. Nevertheless, the church significantly contributed to the downfall of communism basically by providing a free zone for independent thinking, and asylum for all the opposition elite included especially during and after martial law (1981-83).

Communist's propaganda, hypocrisy, lack of freedom, and subjugation to the state had had their devastating moral consequences. Firstly, the state, only nominally sovereign, had come to be perceived – and ignored – as alien and oppressive, as 'theirs' not 'ours'. Secondly, and despite ignoring the state, a new mentality of being a 'client' to 'the socialist welfare-state' had developed which still haunts many. Thirdly, an inability to accept the country's defeat during the War, and its following subservience to a foreign power, has led some Poles to a highly critical attitude towards themselves and fellow countrymen.

The Revival

The two correlated factors that triggered off a moral and then sovereign state revival were the election of Pope John Paul II (1978), and the emergence of the Solidarity Independent Trade Union (1980). The first papal visit to Poland (1979), spontaneously attended by the masses, was the first post-war experience of freedom of such magnitude. Pushed by this groundbreaking impetus, mass resistance arose the following year. The establishment of Solidarity was the culmination of earlier social upheavals in 1956, 1968, 1970, and 1976. This time, however, co-operation between the workers and intellectuals, co-ordinated nationwide, resulted in a victory of the people over the regime. Martial law (1981) temporarily put an end to this victory, but was unable to reverse the current of political change.

---

[24] In PRL history, the following phases were distinguished: the establishment of communist rule (1944-1948); the Stalinist terror (1948-1956); and hegemony of indigenous apparatus (1956-1989) (Davies 1991: 687).
[25] 22 July 1944 marks the beginning of the post-war political order imposition on the territories already 'liberated' by the Red Army. Thus 1980s propaganda would proclaim that 'Our state is now 40 years old'.

The Round Table talks of 1989 initiated the overall peaceful political reconstruction of this entire European region. The immediate result was the introduction of a semi-democratic[26] parliamentary election in Poland in June 1989. This led to a crushing defeat of the communist party, paving the way for the establishment of the first, post-1945, sovereign Polish cabinet. This was a signal for other central European nations. Shortly thereafter, Hungarians dissolved their communist party, beginning a series of reforms and declaring independence; the Czechs were next to put an end to communist party rule. Ultimately, this movement brought the Berlin Wall down. Six months after the June 1989 elections in Poland, the post-war Yalta order was dismantled. This is how the peaceful revolutions in central Europe changed Europe as a whole.

The reborn *Res Publica*, proclaimed in January 1990, put an end to the PRL and the eagle stripped of its royal crown. The transition undertaken after 1989 refers directly to the tradition of the Commonwealth culminated in the 3 May Constitution. Relations with neighbours were henceforth shaped by the will to promote the aspirations of Ukraine and Lithuania to (re)create their states; to co-operate with the Vysehrad Group; to open a new chapter in Polish-German relations based on the Treaty on Friendly Co-operation and Recognition of Borders; and to redefine Polish-Russian relations after the departure of Russian troops.

The Significant 'Others'

Polish national identity, like any national identity, has developed vis-à-vis significant 'Others'. In this case, it has generally been the Jews, Germans, Russians, and Ukrainians who have always, or nearly always, been present in Polish life and consciousness despite WWII, the Shoah, the mass deportations, and the shift of frontiers that had changed the country's ethnic structure from multi, to almost mono-ethnic one.

The Polish-Polish Jewish relationship began at a time when the Jewish nation had been persecuted and expelled all over Europe. During the First Republic, the Jews fit well into the political, economic and cultural framework. This age-old symbiosis decomposed after the break-up of the Commonwealth, 'the only large state to have provided a safe haven in preceding centuries' for the Jews (Davies 1997: 842). During the Partitions, Polish Jews found themselves in direct economic competition with the impoverished gentry, peasants, and urban dwellers; this new pattern of coexistence continued into the Second Polish Republic, still worsened by the economic hardships of the 1930s when numerous Jews were caught in a poverty trap. Still, a considerable Jewish elite – in 1931, 46 per cent of all lawyers and nearly 50 per cent of all doctors were Jews (Zamoyski 1994: 346) – fuelled the envy of the upwardly mobile. The resentment expressed by the latter was utilized by the National Democrats who reinvented themselves around anti-

---

[26] The majority of seats in the lower house were guaranteed to the PZPR members.

Semitism. In the years after Marshal Piłsudski's death in 1935, 'Various forms of petty harassment ... were on the rise, but these were nothing to compare with the rampages of the Nazis ... To say, as is sometimes done, that Polish Jewry was "on the edge of destruction" is true enough; but it is to read history backwards' (Davies 1997: 978).

WWII marks the turning point in this relationship. The Shoah reduced the number of Polish Jews from some 10 per cent to a fraction of a percentage. Concurrently, Western accusations of an alleged Polish responsibility for the Shoah had been made and, on occasion, fuelled. In fact, under the Nazi German occupation, the Home Army set up a unit which saved the lives of at least 10,000 Jews, provided with false papers; the Army also supplied the Jewish resistance with arms before and during the uprising in the Warsaw ghetto (Zamoyski 1994: 361).[27] Additionally, executions were carried out of those Poles who betrayed Jews to the Germans.

This stand and policy was not enough, however, to eliminate wartime crimes committed by ethnic Poles against Jews, including the massacre committed in the town of Jedwabne where up to 250 Jews were burned in a barn by local Poles.[28] In other barns in occupied Poland, however, Jews were rescued by Poles,[29] despite the fact that only in Poland was there a German death penalty imposed for all involved in lending assistance to a Jew (this meant execution of whole families). Nevertheless, some 6,000 Poles – more than any other nationals – are recognised by Yad Vashem as Righteous Among the Nations of the World. Also the Roman Catholic Church organized rescue for Jews: many convents and parishes hid Jewish children under threat of death for all involved. These facts have too often been ignored in, actually political, libellous Western references to 'Polish' – as if they were not German – death camps, and to 'Polish anti-Semitism' as the reason for the Shoah. However, 'Antisemitism in the sense of "Jew-hatred" had been endemic throughout European history ... What could not have been easily predicted was that antisemitism ... would assume its most virulent form in Germany and Austria, where Jews were relatively few' Davies (1997: 847). A contemporary study identifies two kinds of anti-Semitism in Poland: the disappearing traditional, religious anti-Judaic, confined mostly to the elderly and under-educated rural population and manifested in declared attitudes rather than in overt behaviour (as opposed to France and Germany); and the modern, socio-political known worldwide – envisioning a Jewish conspiracy of economic and political power – that has supplanted the traditional one, at levels comparable to others in Europe.

The most candid interpretation of the Polish-German relationship would be that it has always been driven by a self-declared mission on the part of the

---

[27] At the same time, Western Jews, including the American Jews, despite being precisely informed by the Home Army couriers about the systematic mass murder of their compatriots by Germans in occupied Poland, did not offer any help (Karski 1944).

[28] Those accused of this massacre were tried and sentenced immediately after the war ended.

[29] This remark was made by the Israeli Ambassador in Warsaw who himself, along with his family, survived the Nazi German occupation in a Polish barn.

Germans. The first 'missionaries' were the Teutonic Knights, finally defeated at Grunwald in 1410. Then, after centuries of peaceful coexistence, Prussia, and later the Third Reich, took up colonization and occupation of Poland in the name of a 'cultural mission' or *Kulturkampf*. The 'missionary' attitude has rested upon a conviction that the Poles form 'a nation of lesser cultural content'– openly expressed during the Partitions, recently echoed in more subtle allusions to a cultural asymmetry between the two nations (Spohn 2003: 136). The persistence, despite all the experiences of the last two centuries, of this of German cultural superiority idea – however phrased – illustrates an apparent inability to avoid viewing the Polish neighbour through the prism of a constructed hierarchy; this type of comparison can lead, although unintentionally, to cultural racism. Nevertheless, during the centuries of German settlement on Polish territories, very many Germans, despite 'the cultural asymmetry', were attracted to Polish culture and successfully Polonized.

As mentioned, WWII had a devastating effect on Polish-German relations; for decades after the war, in public opinion studies Germans were in first place among nationalities that Polish respondents disliked and distrusted. This negative attitude towards Germans began to slowly but steadily decrease in the second half of the 1980s, and recently has been on the verge of transforming into a slightly positive one. On the political level, the Polish Roman Catholic bishops' plea – 'we forgive, and ask for forgiveness' – addressed to the German episcopate in the 1960s, paved the way for reconciliation between the two nations. This was augmented by Willy Brandt's politics. These positive changes in still very fragile Polish-German relations have recently been challenged by the German expellee organization initiative to commemorate their trauma – though completely and deliberately taken out of its historical and factual context – by building a centre in Berlin in close proximity to a Holocaust memorial.

For the Polish-Ukrainian (Ruthenian) relationship, the seventeenth century was the turning point – in the wrong direction, however. The Dnieper Cossack war (1648-54) led by Chmielnicki brought an army of Cossacks and Tartars right up to the Vistula river and 'left a swathe of butchered Catholics and Jews across the Ukraine' (Davies 1997: 555). Eventually, Poland and Muscovy divided the Ukraine among themselves (1667) along the Dnieper River. Until the mid-nineteenth century, the level of Ukrainian national identity, 'an overwhelmingly peasant people...was necessarily low... their political awakening gathered pace in later decades' (Davies 1997: 831). By the time of these awakenings, the Ukrainians' homeland was long settled by Poles, Jews, and other less numerous nationalities. Driven by the will to establish their own nation-state, the Ukrainians found themselves in direct conflict with Poles defending the land they had inhabited for centuries. At the end of WWI this led to an inevitable clash; the Ukrainians were defeated and the entire interwar period was marked by tensions between Poles and Ukrainians, whose activists began to look to Germany for help and got it (Davies 1997: 833). In 1930, a sabotage campaign funded by Germany and carried out by Ukrainian national organizations drew a military response by Polish authorities; within ten weeks peace was returned, until 1939 when followers of the movement re-emerged as a German fifth-column (Zamoyski 1994: 344), later forming Ukrainian units under German command, such as the SS-Galizien.

The War additionally worsened Polish-Ukrainian relations, as the Ukrainian Insurrection Army (UPA) began its fight for an independent state. This battle included ethnic cleansing in southeastern, pre-war, Poland. In 1943-1944, in Volhynia alone, between 50,000-60,000 Polish victims of this cleansing – men, women, and children – were murdered. In self-defence actions undertaken by the Home Army in the region, and after the war in Poland, between 15,000-20,000 Ukrainians were killed in the years 1943-1947. Additionally, to stop the cleansing and deprive the UPA of a local supply base, the post-war Polish government commanded the mass deportation of ethnic Ukrainians from southeastern Poland, and their resettlement in northern and western Poland. The decade-long 'hibernation' of these bitter events – during the era of the official socialist states friendship – further poisoned the relationship. This has been mirrored in public opinion studies showing that Ukrainians are constantly placed among nationalities that Polish respondents dislike and distrust. A step towards reconciliation may be the official commemoration of the Volhynia ethnic cleansing on 11 July 2003 in the village of Pavlivka.[30] The relationship between the two states – after the establishment of the Ukrainian state (1991), which Poland was the first to officially recognize – contrasts the lack of trust revealed in personal contacts.

The Polish-Russian relationship is no less complex than the others discussed heretofore. The 'view of Russians and Poles as hating each other is a cliché which ignores facts' (Zamoyski 1994: 308). Still, throughout their common history, contacts between political entities – the Commonwealth or the Second Polish Republic vis-à-vis Muscovy or the USSR – 'were beset by mutual suspicion'. At the same time, 'contacts between Poles and Russians were a different matter; even during the Partitions there was considerable cordiality between Poles and Russians whenever hostilities ceased' (Zamoyski 1994: 308). However, 'This love was never allowed to develop. Whenever Russian troops marched in, the Poles would veer towards the attitude that the Russians were hopeless primitives incapable of grasping the concept of civilization and too brutish to allow others to enjoy it' (Zamoyski 1994: 308). And the Russians would retreat into their traditional view of the Poles as arrogant rogues, idlers, drunkards and cowards. 'The Russians never understood the Polish occupation with civil liberty and constitutional legality. They tended to view a constitution as a totem to be admired rather than as a mechanism to be used' (Zamoyski 1994: 308-309). The pattern of sudden shifts from love to hatred between the two nations has been repeating itself until the present, and explains the swings in attitudes towards the Russians shown in public opinion studies. The Russians (not the Soviet authority) were among nations whom Poles liked most in the 1970s, this changed in the 1980s – precisely when martial law was introduced – when sympathy towards Russians significantly decreased. In accordance with these shifts, the notion of 'Russians' acquires or loses its negative connotation in everyday Polish language.

---

[30] Its dwellers, a few hundred local Polish peasants, were murdered in one night 60 years earlier.

The relationships between Poles and significant 'Others' have been built on tensions and co-operations, frequently marked by negative stereotypes rather than positive connotations on either side. Such uneasy and highly ambivalent relationships must have influenced the national identity of Poles, and of the members of the involved nations. However, in order to avoid the error of hypostasising, these effects need to be analyzed solely at the personal level. Apart from qualitative research focused on this issue, another way of affording some insight into the way in which mutual relationships shape the national identity of the nations involved are public opinion surveys.

On the Eve of the Accession

Poland's accession to the European Union has been marked by a motif, constantly reappearing in public debate, of whether 'Europe is returning to us' or we are 're-joining Europe'. This question mirrors the two different stances. The first is represented by those who themselves or whose relatives experienced a feeling of abandonment after Yalta and have preserved this memory. An illustration of this conviction is an opinion that 'Europe is returning to us from Yalta'. The second attitude is represented by those whose historical memory is much more brief and free of Yalta connotations. The proponents of the former stance believe that the country has never ceased being an integral part of Europe; proponents of the latter emphasize the 'civilizational' setback resulting from the forced isolation of the country from Europe (1939-1989).

The accession makes the European frame of reference for the reconstruction of Polish national identity a topical issue. The data show that the Polish self-portrait against the profile of an imagined European is humble. And Polish self-criticism, which discounts the accusation of Polish megalomania, is supplemented by the conviction that some Western Europeans do not treat Poles as equal partners. Still, the research shows that the national and the European identities are mutually inclusive, and being a Pole means being a European.

Throughout the 1990s the surveys showed two basic attitudes towards the accession: 'the Euroenthusiastic', and 'the Eurosceptic'. The 'Euroenthusiasts', while viewing accession as an objective necessity in the era of globalization, focused on the need to fulfil Solidarity's goal to anchor the country for good in the realm of European civilization, and on necessary economic modernization. The 'Eurosceptics' saw the integration as, unfortunately, the only guarantee of a more advantageous position of Poland in the global division of labour, an alternative to which would be marginalization or economic crisis. For the 'Euroenthusiasts', the EU constitutes an arena of partnership of civil societies that would give new impetus to the socio-economic transformation, safeguard the country's political security, enrich its culture, and strengthen the rule of law. For the 'Eurosceptics', the EU is a forum of rivalry between nation-states, and the accession would mean an economic subjugation to Brussels, the limitation of national sovereignty, and a cosmopolitan impact on Polish national identity.

At the time of the signing of the Association Agreement (1991) the accession was supported by the majority of the population. At that time, however, knowledge about the EU and integration conditions has been limited, and substituted by idealist imaginations. With the passage of time and more knowledge, this perception has changed along with support. This correlates with the net balance after perceived, mostly economic, advantages and disadvantages of the integration are taken into account. The preoccupation with economic issues matches the same concern of EU partners. This sober perception of the accession, or just pragmatism, contrasts with the euphoria of the year 1989 in the Polish society.

Conclusion

During its thousand-year history Poland – located between the European East and West – has (on some occasions) been pushed towards, while (on others) it has chosen one of two directions. Nevertheless Poland has always been anchored in the mainstream European discourses, and has always perceived itself as being an integral part of Europe. This conviction, however, has not been an opinion so obvious and shared in Europe, especially whenever the 'Polish Question' or 'Problem' has arisen in European history.

References

Davies, N. (1991), *Boże Igrzysko. Historia Polski*, Kraków: Znak.
_____ (1997), *Europe: A History*, London: Pimlico.
Dwork, D. and van Pelt R. (1994), 'Reclaiming Auschwitz', in G. Hartman (ed.), *Holocaust Remembrance: The Shapes of Memory*, Oxford: Basil Blackwell.
Karski, J. (1944), *Story of a Secret State*, Boston: Riberside Press.
Romaniszyn, K. (2001), 'European Racism: Origins and Contemporary Development', in J. Dacyl (ed.), *Challenges of Cultural Diversity in Europe*, Stockholm: CEIFO, pp. 271-292.
Smith, A. (2000), 'The politics of culture: ethnicity and nationalism', in T. Ingold (ed.), *Companion Encyclopedia of Anthropology, Humanity, Culture, and Social Life*, London: Routledge, pp. 706-733.
Spohn, W. (2003), 'European East-West integration, nation-building and national identities: the reconstruction of German-Polish relations', in W. Spohn and A. Triandafyllidou (eds) *Europeanisation, National Identity and Migration*, London: Routledge, pp. 123-143.
Szczepański, S. (1887), *Nędza Galicji*, Warsaw: Lwów.
Wallerstein, J. (1974), *The Modern World-System: Capitalism, Agriculture of the Origins of the European World-Economy in the Sixteenth Century*, New York: Academic Press.
Webster's New World Encyclopedia (1992), New York-London: Prentice Hall.
Zamoyski, A. (1994), *The Polish Way. A Thousand-Year History of the Poles and their Culture*, New York: Hippocrene Books.

Index